GENERAL EDITOR'S INTRODUCTION TO THE SERIES

AUTHORS' INTRODUCTION TO FOOD PRODUCTION (iv)

1 WE ARE WHAT WE EAT 1

2 PLANT GROWTH 6

3 CROP PRODUCTION 15

4 PLANTS FOR FOOD 34

5 CATTLE 53

6 CHICKENS 71

7 FISH 85

8 BEES - A SPECIAL CASE STUDY 94

9 POSTHARVEST BIOLOGY 101

10 FOOD PRODUCTION - SOME PERSPECTIVES 109

INDEX 122

CONTENTS

General Editor's Introduction to the Series

Biology - Advanced Studies is a series of modular textbooks which are intended for students following advanced courses in biological subjects. The series offers the flexibility essential for working on modern syllabuses which often have core material and option topics. In particular, the books should be very useful for the new modular science courses which are emerging at A Level.

In most of the titles in the series, one of the authors is a very experienced teacher (often also an examiner) and is sympathetic to the problems of learning at this level. The second author usually has research experience and is familiar with the subject at a higher level. In addition, several members of the writing team have been closely involved in the development of the latest syllabuses.

As with all textbooks, the reader may expect not to read from cover to cover but to study one topic at a time, or dip in for information as needed. Where questions are asked, an attempt should be made at an answer because this type of active reading is the best way to develop an understanding of what is read.

We have referred throughout to *Biological nomenclature - Recommendations on terms, units and symbols*, Institute of Biology, London, 1989. We are delighted to be able to thank the many friends and colleagues who have helped with original ideas, the reading of drafts and the supply of illustrations.

Alan Cadogan
General Editor

Authors' Introduction to Food Production

The theme of this book is *what* is produced for food and how it is done. A limited number of examples of plants and animals have been selected to illustrate the biological principles involved and to help trace the story of food production from the earliest forms of agriculture in settled human communities through to modern times. It is essentially a story of exploitation and of evolution in certain biological species. Since cultivation began, the crop plants and domesticated animals used for food have changed in their characteristics and there have also been changes in techniques of farming. There has been a gradual shift to dependence on mechanisation at the expense of labour and, particularly in the last fifty years, an increasing application of scientific principles to farming as a means of maximising productivity. The farmer (or grower) involved in food production is concerned primarily with aspects of nutrition and reproduction. Enhanced understanding of biological systems has resulted in enormous increases in yields: this has been achieved by altering methods of cultivation or feeding regimes, by manipulating life cycles or applying precision in selection of genetic stock. It has become possible to control the environment artificially, with respect to light, temperature, nutrient supply or water availability, often linked to highly intensive systems of cultivation and production. The farmer can avoid losses associated with competition or disease and is able to maintain continuity of supply of many foods on a worldwide basis, regardless of the season. Out of necessity, the modern farmer has become a manager, requiring both technological and scientific knowledge as well as experience to achieve success.

Inevitably there is a price to pay: the demands on natural resources are considerable and the consequences of increasing productivity are not confined to a single farm or a single country, but become global issues. There is interaction with the environment, with economics and with politics and of course with people, their culture and their lives. You will have to think about the issues of poverty, subsistence, hunger and disease, or of affluence and indulgence and the associated health related diseases. Throughout the book, discussion focuses mainly on the production of raw or fresh foods from plants and animals, with only limited reference to the events and effects of processing of food.

We hope this book gives you a better knowledge of the biology of food production so that you can understand the principles that are applied in commercial agriculture and horticulture as well as in small scale backyard or garden activities. Remember that throughout history food has been necessary for the nutrition and health of people of the world and has also played a very important part in our social culture. We hope we can continue to enjoy food as an essential part of our lives.

"Earth provides enough to satisfy every man's need, but not every man's greed."
Mohandas Karamchand GANDHI (1869-1948)

Erica Larkcom and Ruth Miller

FOOD PRODUCTION

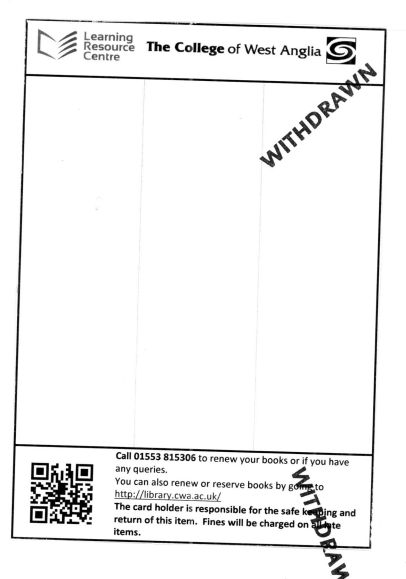

Erica Larkcom

B.A., M.A., C. Biol., M.I. Biol.,
Subject Officer for A Level
Biology for a major Examining
Board, Formerly Head of
Biology, Great Cornard Upper
School, Suffolk

&

Ruth Miller

B. Sc., C. Biol., M. I. Biol.,
Chief Examiner for AS and
A Level Biology, Formerly
Head of Biology, Sir William
Perkins's School, Chertsey

Nelson

Thomas Nelson & Sons Ltd
Nelson House Mayfield Road
Walton-on-Thames Surrey
KT12 5PL UK

Nelson Blackie
Wester Cleddens Road
Bishopbriggs
Glasgow
G64 2NZ UK

Thomas Nelson (Hong Kong) Ltd
Toppan Building 10/F
22a Westlands Road
Quarry Bay Hong Kong

Thomas Nelson Australia
102 Dodds Street
South Melbourne
Victoria 3205 Australia

Nelson Canada
1120 Birchmount Road
Scarborough Ontario
MIK 5G4 Canada

© Erica Larkcom and Ruth Miller 1994

First published by Thomas Nelson and Sons Ltd 1994

ISBN 0-17-448228-0
NPN 9 8 7 6 5 4 3 2 1

Printed in China

ACKNOWLEDGEMENTS

The authors extend their warm thanks to many friends, colleagues and teachers who have contributed, perhaps unknowingly, with their ideas and questions, but in particular to the following for help and encouragement during the preparation of the text:

Richard Bampton (and colleagues at Hadlow College), Alan Doherty, Derrick Guy, David Hartley, Joe Johnston, Joy Larkcom, Dean Madden, National Centre for Biology Education, J Sainsbury plc (Bury St Edmunds), John Schollar, Mike Walker, World Wide Fund for Nature.

Photographic material:
Erica Larkcom 1, 4, 8 (bottom), 15, 22, 34, 39, 54 (bottom), 71, 72 (bottom), 73, 89 (left), 91, 93, 99, 101, 102, 111, 116, 118 and 119; Rothampstead Research Centre 8 (top); John Howard/Science Photo Library 16; Joy Larkcom 19 and 110; The Royal Horticultural Society/Jacqui Hurst 20; J. Hutchings/Frank Lane Picture Agency 24; Robert Brook/Environmental Picture Agency 26; Ruth Miller 32, 89 (right) and 92; Philip Perry/Frank Lane Picture Agency 43; Rod Salm/Planet Earth Pictures 53 (left); Anne Stephens 53 (top) and 54 (top); Alan Dunkley 53 (bottom); Richard Bampton 65; Peter Dean/Frank Lane Picture Agency 68; J. C. Allen/Frank Lane Picture Agency 72 (top) and 82; S. Solomon 75 (from the book *Egg and Eggshell Quality*); ADAS Nottingham 83; ADAS Gleadthorpe 84 (left); Fibropower 84 (right); Harvey Pincis/Science Photo Library 94; Horticulture Research International 104 (bottom); The Farmers' Dairy Co. Ltd 114; David Border/Hensby Biotech Ltd 120.

The Soil Association symbol on page 114 is reproduced with the permission of the Soil Association Organic Marketing Company Ltd.

Cover photograph by Erica Larkcom.

(M)630 L

CHAPTER 1

WE ARE WHAT WE EAT

Human beings are heterotrophic and so depend on a variety of plants and animals for nutrition. In common with all other living organisms, we need to obtain enough energy and body building materials from our food to grow and reproduce, and to repair and replace tissues. In addition, vitamins and minerals are needed for the healthy functioning of the body systems. Energy is obtained from foods containing carbohydrates and fats, whereas body building materials are supplied mainly from proteins. These major components of the diet are essential and should be available in sufficient quantity, and in the correct proportions, depending on the age and occupation of the individual.

Being *heterotrophic* consumers means that we depend directly or indirectly on the producers, the green plants, found in the first trophic level of any food chain or food web. If we eat plants, then we are primary consumers, feeding at the second trophic level, like the *herbivores*. However, if we eat animals or animal products, such as beef or milk, then we become secondary consumers, feeding at the third trophic level, like *carnivores*. As we can eat both plant and animal food, we are also known as *omnivores*. Food chains involving humans do not usually consist of more than three trophic levels (as we rarely consume carnivores), although if we include certain types of fish in our diets, there may be more trophic levels (see *Biology Advanced Studies - Environment and Ecology*).

Grass → Cow → Human (milk, meat)

Grass → Chicken → Human (eggs, meat)

Wheat → Human (flour)

Plant plankton → Animal plankton →
$\qquad\qquad\qquad$ Herring → Human

Fig.1.1 Food chains

Through history, producing food and eating food have become essential parts of the culture of a nation

The energy that the producers need for the synthesis of organic compounds comes from the sun, and when the herbivores and carnivores eat other organisms, food containing energy is transferred from one trophic level to the next. Not all the materials and energy contained in this food is available to the next trophic level, as some of it passes through the organism without being digested and there are losses of energy due to respiration and excretion. As a result, the energy transfer between trophic levels is only between 5% and 20% efficient. Herbivores make less efficient use of their food than carnivores, and on average only 10% of the energy available to them gets passed on to the next level, whereas it can be as much as 20% from carnivore to carnivore.

The implications to humans of this loss of energy have become clear. It would be more efficient to eat at a lower trophic level (as vegans) in order to extract the maximum amount of energy from the system, than to feed livestock and eat the meat or animal products. This might sound a simple solution to the food problems of the world, but there are other factors to be taken into consideration. Not all plant proteins contain the essential amino acids we need in our diet, and we would have to ensure that some pulses (legumes) were included in the diet to remedy this. In addition, in some areas of the world, it would be difficult to grow enough plant crops to sustain the population, due to the nature of the land. Apart from these considerations, a mixture of plant and animal products provides variety, although most Western diets would benefit from the inclusion of more fibre from plant food and smaller amounts of saturated animal fats, to avoid the risk of heart disease and other ailments.

■ EARLY MAN

It is probable that human beings evolved from tree-dwelling apes, who lived on a diet of fruit and seeds. At some time, between 10 and 4 million years ago, due to a change in climate which altered the all-year-round availability of such foods, the apes came down to the ground and began to supplement their diet with bark, young shoots, edible roots and small animals, such as ants, termites, insect grubs, lizards and frogs. Thus the mainly herbivorous diet changed to an omnivorous one.

Fig.1.2 Prehistoric man

Other features evolved, associated with a diet containing fruits and small mammals, including:
• sharp eyes to find fruit and small creatures;
• manual dexterity to pluck the fruit and pick up the small insects;
• taste to sample the food;
• the ability to digest protein.

There is archaeological evidence to show that the size of the teeth reduced as the transition from man-like apes to ape-like men occurred. This reduction in teeth, and also jaw size, proceeded rapidly after the discovery of cooking (and it is still taking place today, providing work for orthodontists).

Gradually, the diet changed as our ancestors learned to kill larger animals by throwing stones at them. A more upright stance and the ability to throw, whilst moving on two legs rather than four, were clear advantages for this type of food-gathering. The next major step forwards in evolution was the ability to manufacture tools, which could be used to kill larger prey more effectively. There is evidence that Peking Man, one of our distant hominid ancestors, believed to have been living about 500 000 years ago, was a cave dweller known to have used fire and whose diet consisted mainly of venison.

Most apes show some co-operation in collecting or sharing food, but we know that our primitive ancestors lived in small groups, where the tasks were shared. In the hunting-fishing-gathering groups, the strongest and most active members of the community, the young men, were the hunters and the women were the gatherers.

Estimates have been made as to how much food would be needed to feed a small group of primitive people in a cold climate, and it was suggested that each adult would require about 1 kg of boneless meat per day to stay alive. An average-sized bull would provide enough food for 20 adults for a week. Bigger prey, such as mammoth, would last longer, but would be more difficult to kill and also too heavy to drag back to the caves where the groups lived. It is likely that the carcasses were cut up at the killing sites and then portions taken back to the group. In the colder climates, meat left out in the open would probably keep for quite a long time, becoming more acceptable as it matured. It is quite possible that use was also made of icy conditions for preservation. Killing large animals required efficient weapons, such as flint-tipped spears, together with improved co-ordination between hand and eye.

Fish would have been available to these hunter-gatherers and fish hooks appeared to be in use from around 25 000 BC. The most likely method of catching fish from rivers and streams would have been by trapping or spearing them, but the larger fish could be lured by baited hooks and eventually killed by harpoon-like implements. Fishing around the coasts or in the deeper waters

2

of lakes did not start until about 8000 BC when dug-out canoes and rafts first made their appearance.

Women, whose activities were restricted because of children, were the gatherers, collecting small animals and picking berries, nuts and edible roots. Further changes in the climate, together with the effects of hunting, resulted in changes in the fauna and the gathering of plant food became more important. Gradually, a more settled existence evolved, as the hunters found that they could entice the animals to come to them by providing food, and the gatherers began to stay near their sources of plant food, ready for the harvest, instead of going back to their caves or shelters. It was a slow process and occurred at different times in different parts of the world, but by about 9000 BC there were many small settlements where the inhabitants existed by hunting and intensive gathering (see *Biology Advanced Studies - Human and Social Biology*).

In order to make hunting easier, the vegetation was deliberately burnt down to encourage the wild animals to graze nearer human settlements, and this signalled the beginning of the destruction of natural ecosystems in attempts to provide food. The gatherers discovered that they could guarantee some of the same food, particularly cereal grains, the following year if they left some of the grains on the plants. This led to the clearing and cultivation of an area, followed by the sowing of some of the grain saved from the previous year's harvest. In Neolithic times, about 5000 BC, widespread forest clearance took place to provide land for cultivation. The land was farmed until the soil was depleted of its minerals and yields became poor, at which point the groups moved to a new area and the whole process of burning, clearing and cultivation was repeated. This shifting cultivation is still practised in some parts of the world today.

In the Iron and Bronze Ages, more agricultural communities developed and the population began to increase, which in turn increased the need for more food. The world population in 10 000 BC was estimated to have been about 3 million, but by 3000 BC this had increased to around a 100 million, due to improved living conditions and better nutrition. Better tools could be made and these were used to work the land more effectively, improving the yields from plant crops. The domestication of plants took place before that of animals, and as animals became important to humans, they were provided with food and

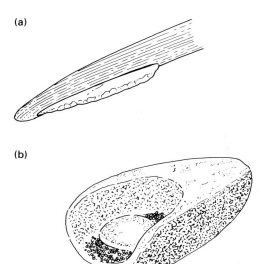

Fig.1.3 Prehistoric tools of man: (a) a small sickle for cutting corn and (b) a grindstone for corn

enclosures built to protect them from their predators.

■ Domestication of animals

The first animals to be domesticated were dogs. Packs of wild dogs would follow hunters and feed on the scraps left after the carcasses had been cut up. Our ancestors realised that these dogs could supplement their hunting skills and make them more efficient, as well as warning and protecting them against other animals. So dogs became exploited for hunting and retrieving, herding other domesticated animals and hauling loads, in return for food. Grazing animals, such as sheep and goats, were seen to pose a threat to the yield of the grain crops, but they provided a source of meat when larger prey were scarce, so it must have been a logical step to provide them with pasture and kill them when needed. The domestication of pigs came later, as they did not compete with humans for the crops, but could be fed on the scraps and surplus food.

Last of all to be domesticated were the cattle, as only the most docile could be caught and contained. It is important to realise that these animals did not just provide primitive man with food, but they were useful in a number of other ways. The goats provided milk and skins, which could be made into water-tight containers; wool and fat came from the sheep; bristles, lard and skin were obtained from the pigs; and the cattle provided hide and dung for fuel.

Using cattle to plough the land in Yunnan, SW China

Many of the animals were used to tread in seeds, to thresh grain and eventually to pull ploughs and other implements. By choosing the best animals for breeding, favourable characteristics were selected for, resulting in the range of domesticated animals from which our present strains have been derived. These animals occupy ecological niches which have been created and maintained by humans, but they would revert to the wild if they were deprived of this continuous protection and intervention. Similarly, with plant crops, the clearing of the land removed the competitors and resulted in improving yields. Seeds saved from the best plants could be sown the following season, ensuring a crop with a good chance of producing a similar yield. Selective breeding began thousands of years ago, providing the basis for modern breeding programmes still centred on producing more food to feed an increasing population.

Domestication has provided us with a wide range of species, breeds of animals and varieties of plants, which produce food, and in order to improve production, it has been necessary to replace the arbitrary selection made by our ancestors with precise, conscious selection. We have a greater knowledge of the life cycles and requirements of the plants and animals used for food, together with a knowledge of their genetics, and it is possible to make predictions of the demand for food in the future. With an increasing world population, the emphasis is still on improving yields, as well as improving the quality.

An increase in both plant yield and quality can be achieved by providing good growing conditions such as fertile soil, with a plentiful supply of mineral ions, and adequate moisture. It is also beneficial to remove competing weed species and to guard against the spread of disease. Animals need to be provided with a suitable diet, containing all the relevant minerals and vitamins. The food supplied should be suited to the species: it would be wasteful to provide non-ruminants with a diet high in plant fibre which they cannot digest. It is also important for domesticated animals to have a balanced diet. Like humans, pigs and chickens will thrive if their diet contains the correct proportions of the essential amino acids. Feeding animals to achieve maximum productivity depends on a good knowledge of the needs of the animal plus sensible use of the available foodstuffs.

■ Recent advances
A knowledge of the reproductive processes and genetics of crop plants and domesticated animals has enabled us to make further progress in improving the quality of food. We understand that self-fertilisation in plants leads to inbred lines, which can perpetuate favourable characteristics, while cross-fertilisation leads to outbreeding and variation amongst the offspring. Many food plants are propagated vegetatively, thus ensuring that any favourable characteristics are retained and the product is exactly the same year after year. Artificial propagation techniques, such as grafting and, more recently, micropropagation by means of tissue culture (see Fig. 4.17), are now available to the plant breeder, and have played a significant role in the development of new varieties. In animal rearing the superior offspring are retained for breeding and the inferior used for food.

Examples of the application of scientific knowledge to breeding programmes include:
· genetic selection in pigs to reduce the amount of fat, producing leaner carcasses;
· broiler chickens selected for their rapid growth;
· selection for increased egg production in laying hens;
· progeny testing in the selection of bulls for the breeding of dairy herds;
· development of short-stemmed varieties of wheat, rice and barley leading to an increase in the harvest index;
· an increase in the lysine content of maize; and
· different types of oilseed rape for industrial and edible use.

Breeding for disease resistance is also important and has been carried out for the majority of crop plants.

Traditionally in most cultures, food production was carried out by small groups of people, growing a variety of crops and supplying the needs of the immediate neighbourhood, and this way of life is still to be found in some parts of the world. With the improved techniques and conditions in the developed world, food production has intensified and changed so that resources are now concentrated into the production of large amounts of one crop in one area. In Britain, it is now rare to find mixed farms, with a mixture of arable crops and grazing for cattle and sheep. Instead, most farmers have found that it is more economical to concentrate on the production of one or two crops, so that maximum use can be made of expensive and specialised machinery.

Monoculture has its advantages, but it has resulted in a loss of hedgerows, as bigger and better machines make small fields impractical. There is also a major problem associated with the rearing of large numbers of animals in a small area - it is very difficult to get rid of their excrement.

It is possible to improve yields and maintain quality by controlling the environment in which the crop is produced. Intensive systems for rearing animals have precisely controlled temperature, lighting and feeding arrangements, carefully calculated to give a guaranteed end product. The regime for producing broiler chickens or veal is different from that employed for egg production. With the production of plants, it is possible to control the carbon dioxide content of the atmosphere, the temperature and the light intensity in a glasshouse, in order to maximise photosynthesis. Precise control of the mineral nutrients can also be achieved.

In many glasshouses, crops are grown without soil, using a *hydroponic* method called NFT, the *nutrient film technique*. A solution of mineral ions is slowly circulated around troughs containing the roots of the plants, eliminating the need for soil and avoiding wastage of excess ions. Soil-borne diseases are avoided, the yield is increased and the harvested plants are cleaner. These systems are more expensive to install, maintain and operate, but this is offset by the increased yield of high-quality produce.

In the developed world, food production is highly mechanised and the emphasis now appears to be on the production of better quality produce, which is available all the year round, so that there is choice and variety for the consumer. This has been achieved by better production techniques, including the use of genetically engineered varieties that will grow outside their natural range, and also by improved transport and postharvest handling of the products.

In many developing countries, the emphasis is on making the land more productive so that more food can be grown to feed an ever-increasing population. The donation of surplus food from the developed world is only a short-term solution to the problem, and progress will only come through helping the developing countries to improve their agricultural techniques.

2 PLANT GROWTH

■ PHOTOSYNTHESIS

Since basic food production begins in plants, we need to examine the process in some detail. Green plants are *autotrophic* organisms, i.e. organisms capable of building up complex organic molecules from inorganic raw materials, using energy from light. This process, known as *photosynthesis*, requires, in addition to light, a supply of carbon dioxide, water and mineral ions (Fig.2.1). In the presence of the green pigment *chlorophyll*, found in chloroplasts in the leaves and green stems of the plants, the inorganic raw materials are converted to carbohydrates, fats and proteins, which supply the plant with a source of energy for metabolic activities and also with the materials from which new cells are made, resulting in growth.

$$6CO_2 + 12H_2O \xrightarrow[\text{Chlorophyll}]{\text{Light}} C_6H_{12}O_6 + 6O_2 + 6H_2O$$

Carbon + Water $\longrightarrow$ Glucose + Oxygen + Water
dioxide (carbohydrate)

Fig.2.1 Summary equation for the process of photosynthesis

The rate at which energy is stored by plants in the form of organic compounds which can be used as food is known as the *primary productivity*. In the first instance, primary productivity depends on the amount of solar radiation intercepted by the plants and this in turn depends on a number of different factors such as latitude, aspect and light quality. In the UK, roughly 1% of the total solar radiation is intercepted by plants, averaging about 1×10^6 kJ m^{-2} yr^{-1}, but not all of it is used. Between 95% and 99% is immediately reflected, radiated or lost as heat of evaporation, which leaves between 1% and 5% to be absorbed by the chlorophyll

molecules. The rate at which chemical energy is stored is known as the *gross primary productivity (GPP)*, but not all this energy is available to the next trophic level because a significant amount, as much as 50% of the GPP, is lost due to respiration and other factors. What remains is known as the *net primary productivity (NPP)*. This can be measured as the increase in dry mass of a crop over a period of time. Productivity is calculated on a yearly basis, so it takes into account any variations due to seasonal changes. In the UK, we would expect GPP, and hence NPP, to be greater during the spring and summer than during the winter. As solar radiation energy differs in different parts of the world, so GPP and NPP will vary. The primary productivity potential of tropical regions is almost double that of the UK.

In addition to light, two other major environmental factors control the rate of photosynthesis: *carbon dioxide* concentration and *temperature*. The carbon dioxide concentration in the atmosphere is more or less constant at about 0.03 - 0.04% of the total composition, but there are wide fluctuations in the temperature due to latitude and seasonal variations. Temperature is important in the light-independent reactions of the photosynthetic process, which are enzyme controlled. As a general rule, an increase in temperature, up to about 40°C, will increase the rate of photosynthesis if no other factors are limiting, so the rate will be higher on a bright, warm day than on a cool, dull one.

There is a maximum temperature beyond which plants will be killed, but this will vary from species to species, as some are more tolerant of high temperatures than others. If the environmental temperature increases, then the rate at which evaporation, and hence transpiration, occurs will increase, bringing risks of water shortage and desiccation. High temperatures associated with direct sunlight may damage fruit crops by scorching them and high soil surface temperatures can reduce seed germination rates.

■ Assimilation of carbon dioxide

Green plants have different mechanisms for incorporating carbon dioxide into organic compounds. In one group of plants, known as C3 plants (e.g. wheat, barley, rice and soya bean), the carbon dioxide combines with ribulose bisphosphate (RuBP), catalysed by the enzyme *ribulose bisphosphate carboxylase*, to form an unstable six-carbon compound which immediately breaks down to glycerate-3-phosphate (GP), the first product of photosynthesis. The GP is then reduced to glyceraldehyde-3-phosphate (triose phosphate or TP) and converted into sugars or used to regenerate ribulose bisphosphate, the *acceptor molecule*. This pathway was worked out by Calvin and his associates in the 1950s using radioactively labelled carbon dioxide and the unicellular alga *Chlorella*, and it thus became known as the *Calvin cycle* (Fig.2.2). (For more details see *Biology Advanced Studies - Biochemistry*.)

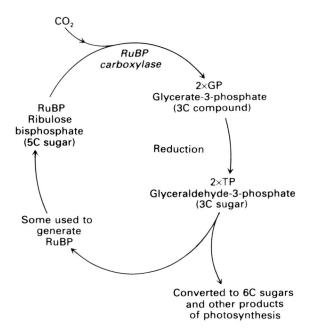

Fig.2.2 Summary of the events of the Calvin cycle

In another group of plants, known as C4 plants (e.g. maize and sugar cane), the carbon dioxide first combines with phosphoenolpyruvate (PEP) to form oxaloacetate (OAA), the enzyme involved being *phosphoenolpyruvate carboxylase*. The oxaloacetate is then converted to malate and later reactions involve the release of carbon dioxide, which then combines with ribulose bisphosphate in the same way as it does in the C3 plants. This is known as the *Hatch-Slack pathway*, named after the two people who worked it out in the 1960s (Fig.2.3). The terms C3 and C4 were used to distinguish the two groups of plants by referring to the first organic compounds formed in photosynthesis: GP having three carbon atoms, and OAA having four carbon atoms.

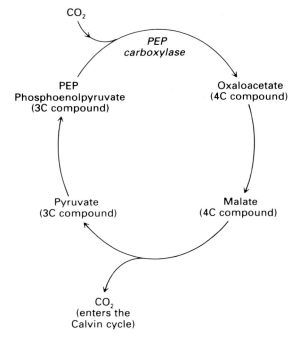

Fig.2.3 Summary of the stages of the Hatch-Slack pathway in which carbon dioxide is fixed in C4 plants

The efficiency of photosynthesis is greater in C4 plants because the enzyme *PEP carboxylase* is better at catalysing the reaction between carbon dioxide and phospho enol pyruvate when carbon dioxide levels are low and the light intensity is high. In C3 plants under these conditions, a process called *photorespiration* occurs and carbon dioxide is actually produced by the plants. Photorespiration, so called as it involves the uptake of oxygen and the release of carbon dioxide in the presence of light, occurs because the enzyme RuBP carboxylase can accept both carbon dioxide and oxygen as substrates. The two gases compete for the active site of the enzyme, so, as the concentration of carbon dioxide decreases, more oxygen molecules combine with the enzyme and the efficiency of the photosynthetic process is reduced. Some GP is made in this process but energy is used up in converting other products of the pathway. Photorespiration is considered to be responsible for the big difference between GPP and NPP in C3 plants.

When photosynthesis evolved, it was probable that the Earth's atmosphere had a higher carbon dioxide concentration and a lower oxygen concentration than it does today. Under those conditions, RuBP carboxylase would accept carbon dioxide in preference to oxygen and there would not be any photorespiration. Over millions of years, this situation has changed and the higher concentrations of oxygen present in the atmosphere now favour photorespiration. In C4 plants, when carbon dioxide is released from malate and combines with RuBP, the concentration of carbon dioxide is relatively high and no photorespiration occurs. It is likely that the C4 pathway evolved as an adaptation to the increased concentration of oxygen in the atmosphere and at a much later date than the C3 pathway. C4 plants are found in tropical climates, where there are high temperatures, whereas C3 plants are typical of temperate regions (see *Biology Advanced Studies - Biochemistry*).

Many comparisons have been made between the two groups, in attempts to establish whether photorespiration can be eliminated or reduced, thereby improving the productivity of C3 crop plants, but the plants have very different anatomies and both are suited to the climate of their natural habitats. C3 plants do better than C4 plants at lower temperatures and lower light intensities, because photorespiration is not favoured. The C4 pathway requires about 15% more energy to fix carbon dioxide, so at lower light intensities C3 plants may have an advantage. C4 plants grow faster in conditions of high light intensity where carbon dioxide concentrations are low; they are also more tolerant of dry conditions.

Research has been centred on finding ways of inhibiting photorespiration and some chemical compounds have been discovered which have this effect. They need to be sprayed on to the plants, and it has been shown that if they are used, then the net productivity of the crop can be doubled. Such compounds have not been investigated thoroughly as they would be difficult, and probably expensive, to use on a large scale. Where crops such as

C3 plant - wheat

C4 plant - maize in Kenya

tomatoes and flowers are grown in glasshouses, it is possible to control the atmosphere, maintaining higher levels of carbon dioxide so that photorespiration is prevented. Attempts are being made to extend the range of C4 plants by breeding new varieties, and it may be possible to introduce the genes which are responsible for promoting the C4 pathway into C3 plants by genetic engineering techniques.

■ Water

Water is essential to green plants for the maintenance of turgidity in cells, for the transport of soluble materials around the plant and as the medium in which all the metabolic reactions take place. It is also the raw material in the manufacture of organic compounds, as it provides a source of electrons and hydrogen ions for the reactions of the light-independent stages of photosynthesis.

Water is continually being lost as water vapour from the aerial parts of the plant during daytime (*transpiration*), and this must be replaced by the uptake of water from the soil if growth is to continue. The transpiration rate increases as the temperature rises, with increase in air movements and in conditions of low humidity, when the air is dry. If water loss through transpiration exceeds water uptake by the roots, then the plants will *wilt*. Recovery from wilting can occur if the rate of transpiration decreases or if more water is made available to the plants. A prolonged period of wilting results in the death of the plant.

Wilting causes the stomata on the leaves and green stems to close, thus reducing the uptake of carbon dioxide for photosynthesis and so the growth of the plant is affected. The amount of water a crop requires varies with species, and with the time of year or season in which it is grown. Water availability in different parts of the world determines which crops will grow satisfactorily, and a number of agroclimatic zones have been defined based on temperature and rainfall.

■ MINERAL NUTRITION

Green plants require a supply of *mineral ions* for the synthesis of proteins, nucleic acids and other organic compounds. *Nitrates, phosphates* and *sulphates* are essential for the synthesis of amino acids, the building blocks of proteins. Other ions, such as *sodium* and *potassium*, are involved in osmotic and anion/cation balance. *Magnesium, iron* and *molybdenum* are components of pigments or co-factors of enzymes. Deficiency of these mineral ions may result in stunted growth of the plants, often accompanied by yellowing of the leaves, known as chlorosis. Crop plants obtain their mineral ions from the soil. They are absorbed through the roots from the soil solution by a process of active uptake, requiring energy derived from respiration. Different crop plants need different amounts of mineral nutrients for optimum growth.

The most important mineral element needed by plants is *nitrogen*, which most plants obtain in the form of nitrate ions from the soil. Once inside the plant, the nitrate ions are reduced to nitrites, and then to ammonium ions before combining with an organic acid, a product of photosynthesis, to form an amino acid (Fig.2.4). This process involves reduction reactions and takes place mostly in the chloroplasts present in the palisade and mesophyll cells of the leaves, using energy and hydrogen ions from the light-dependent stage of photosynthesis. The amino acids formed can then be used to build the specific proteins required by the plant.

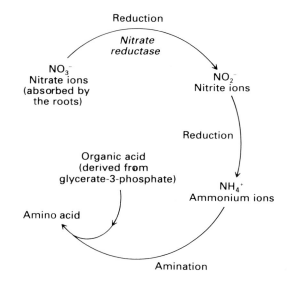

Fig.2.4 Summary of reactions involved in amino acid synthesis in plants

The nitrate ions present in the soil are derived from the decay of organic matter and excreta from plants and animals. Saprotrophic bacteria and fungi, the decomposers, feed on the organic matter, releasing ammonium compounds into the soil. These compounds are oxidised by chemosynthetic bacteria, such as *Nitrosomonas* and *Nitrobacter*, forming first nitrites and then nitrates, which can be taken up by green plants. The chemosynthetic bacteria are called *nitrifying bacteria* and obtain energy for their own metabolism from these reactions.

Leguminous crops, such as clover, soya beans and pulses, have a *symbiotic*, or *mutualistic*, association with the nitrogen-fixing bacterium *Rhizobium*, which can use atmospheric nitrogen gas to build up amino acids and proteins. The bacteria enter the roots of the plants through the root hairs, get into the cells of the cortex, which then multiply to form the characteristic *root nodules*. The bacteria obtain carbohydrates from the photosynthetic activities of the plants, and the plants benefit from the fixed nitrogen, in the form of ammonium ions, which can be used to build up amino acids and proteins. The nitrogenase enzyme involved in the fixation of the nitrogen is inhibited by oxygen gas and the plants produce a special compound, *leghaemoglobin*, which enables the bacteria to obtain oxygen for respiration in anaerobic conditions. Leghaemoglobin is similar in structure to haemoglobin found in vertebrate red blood cells and it makes the interior of the nodules pink. This association between the legumes and *Rhizobium* can benefit us in two ways: the leguminous crops can be grown for food for ourselves and as fodder for cattle, and the plants can be used to improve soil fertility prior to growing different crops, either by *green manuring*, where they are ploughed back into the soil, or as part of a *crop rotation*. Legumes are able to grow in nitrogen-deficient soils, an advantage over other crops which would need a supply of nitrate fertiliser or manure, or some system of crop rotation.

■ SOIL

Soil is a thin layer covering a large part of the land surface of the Earth. It consists of rock or mineral particles (46-60%), organic material called humus (~10%), water (25-35%), air (15-25%) and living organisms (variable). It provides anchorage and support for the growth of the green plants which provide us with food crops, pastures for grazing animals and materials to make clothes, construct buildings and use as fuel. For many centuries, humans have been aware of the need to conserve this valuable asset. In several parts of the world, terracing has been in use to prevent soil from being washed away, and it has been realised that leaving land fallow, or unused, for a period of time could improve soil fertility. Although the nature of the soil in a particular region will determine which crops can be grown, the use of fertilisers, modern machinery and irrigation, together with the development of new varieties of plants, can help make unsuitable land productive.

The *mineral particles* are derived from the breaking up, or *weathering*, of rocks by physical and chemical processes over a long period of time. These processes include alternate expansion and contraction of rocks due to temperature changes, cracking caused by ice formation and the action of water and carbon dioxide on the chemical components of the rocks. Disintegration occurs and results in a range of differently sized rock particles, the smallest being less than 0.002 mm in diameter forming the clay fraction and those greater than 2 mm being referred to as gravel.

Type of particle	Diameter/mm
Gravel	> 2.0
Coarse sand	0.2-2.0
Fine sand	0.02-0.2
Silt	0.002-0.02
Clay	< 0.002

Table 2.1 Mineral particle sizes in soils

Good agricultural soils are usually described as *loams*, containing mixtures of differently sized particles and can be classified according to the relative proportions of these particles present. Thus a sandy loam will have a higher proportion of sand particles than a silty or clay loam. Clay particles carry a negative charge and form colloidal suspensions in water. Clay has a great effect on the mineral content of soil as positively charged ions are attracted and held in the soil instead of being leached out.

The texture of a soil can be determined by its 'feel', when it is rolled between the thumb and forefinger, and by a simple analysis of particle size, which can be done by shaking up some soil in water and allowing the particles to settle.

The mineral particles are held together by the organic matter, forming a crumb structure which is important in determining the amount of air and water present in the soil. Water will drain more easily through a soil with large particles or crumbs, than through one which consists of finer particles, although the latter will retain more water, held by the capillary action in the small pores. As both air and water are important, the ideal soil is one which drains fairly readily, but which contains enough smaller particles to retain sufficient water for plant growth. Soils are often referred to as being 'heavy' or 'light'. Heavy soils contain a large proportion of clay particles and so do not drain rapidly, making them sticky and difficult to work. When these soils dry out on the surface, the soil becomes compacted and thick clods can form which are difficult to break up. These soils do not warm up quickly in the spring as the lighter soils do. Light soils drain more easily as they contain a higher proportion of sand particles, although this does result in valuable nutrients being lost through leaching. Soils with a high proportion of particles over 2 mm in diameter (gravel and small stones) can cause damage to agricultural machinery.

The *organic matter* in the soil consists of the dead remains of whole organisms, parts of organisms such as leaves, animal faeces and excretory products. The undecomposed organic material is referred to as *litter* and forms the food of detritivores, such as earthworms, and decomposers, the bacteria and fungi. During the process of breakdown, organic compounds undergo *mineralisation*, releasing ammonium, phosphate and sulphate ions into the soil, and carbon dioxide is given off as a result of the respiratory activities of the decomposers and detritivores. The term *humus* is used to describe the organic chemical complex which remains, and it is a mixture of brown and dark brown colloidal substances, important in cementing mineral particles together to form soil crumbs. Because it is colloidal, it can stick to the clay particles to form a clay-humus complex and, like clay, it has a large surface area and is negatively charged, so it contributes to the ability of the soil to retain positively charged ions and water. In order for humus formation to occur, the soil needs to be well aerated otherwise, in anaerobic or waterlogged conditions, the activity of the decomposers will be restricted.

Soil porosity, the number and size of the pores present, determines the amount of water and air a soil contains and also the rate at which drainage occurs. Porosity will increase with larger sizes of particles or soil crumbs, so we would expect a sandy loam to have a greater porosity than a clay or silt loam. The amount of air in the soil will depend on the amount of water present, and if one increases, the other will decrease. After heavy rain, much of the pore space will be occupied by water, but as this drains or evaporates from the surface layers, air is drawn in to replace it. The larger the pores, as in sandy soils, the more quickly the water drains and is replaced by air, whereas clay soils with their smaller pores tend to retain water much longer.

The *air* in the soil differs from atmospheric air in that there is slightly less oxygen and more carbon dioxide, due to the respiratory activities of the soil organisms. Soil oxygen is important to these organisms and also for the growth of the roots of the green plants.

Immediately after heavy rain, all the pore spaces in the soil fill with water and the soil is said to be *saturated*. Water then begins to drain out of the soil, first and most quickly from the larger pores. This water, known as *gravitational water*, is available to plants only for a short time. After the gravitational water has drained away, films of water, known as *capillary water*, are left around the soil particles and in the very small pores. The soil is then said to be at its *field capacity*. The capillary water is available to the plant roots.

Most soils support large populations of *living organisms*. Apart from the roots of green plants, there are enormous numbers of microorganisms, together with nematodes, arthropods and earthworms. The micro-organisms include bacteria, algae, actinomycetes, fungi and protozoa. Most of the bacteria, the protozoa and the actinomycetes will be found in the films of water surrounding the soil particles. The photosynthetic bacteria and the algae will be restricted to the surface layers where they can obtain light, and the fungi will be present as spores or as mycelia growing between the soil particles.

Most of the microorganisms are *saprotrophic* (feeding by secreting digestive enzymes on to the organic matter in the soil and then absorbing the soluble products that result). Bacteria and fungi are particularly abundant around the roots of plants, in an area known as the *rhizosphere*, where they benefit from sugars and other organic compounds exuded from the roots. They can also break down any dead cells or worn-out root hairs from the plants. *Nematodes* are worm-like and occur in vast numbers in the soil. Some can enter the roots of plants and cause damage to crops (for example 'eelworm' of potatoes). Damage to crop plants can also be caused by many of the insect larvae which are present in soil.

Earthworms are found in all but the most acid and dry soils. Their varied activities have been considered beneficial to soil fertility, but their presence has not yet been shown to improve crop yields.

 List the ways in which earthworms may improve the soil.

■ Soil acidification
The *acidity* or *alkalinity* of a soil, its *pH*, is a useful guide to its suitability for crop growth. In the UK, most soils are slightly acid, with pH values around 6.5. Chalky soils, with a high calcium carbonate content, have a pH of about 8.0, and in the sandy soils associated with heath and moorland, the pH can be as low as 3.0 or 4.0. Most crop plants can tolerate some acidity, but grow best in soils with a neutral pH, pH 7.0.

Crop	pH range
Oats, rye	5.5-7.5
Maize, wheat	6.0-7.5
Barley	6.5-7.5
Lucerne (alfalfa)	7.0-8.0

Table 2.2 pH and crop tolerance

Soils undergo a natural process of acidification brought about by:
• the leaching action of rainwater;
• the process of nitrification (nitrate ions);
• production of organic acids by microorganisms;
• increase in organic matter.

If the rainwater contains high levels of pollutants such as nitrates and sulphates from the burning of fossil fuels, then the process of acidification is speeded up. As the soils become acid, calcium and magnesium ions become more soluble and are leached out in the drainage water, which means they are not available for plant growth, but they may be replaced by the natural weathering of mineral particles. Increased acidity also causes aluminium ions to become more soluble, and these, together with others such as manganese, can accumulate and may reach toxic levels.

Harvesting crops can result in the soil becoming more acid, because mineral ions such as calcium and magnesium which have been removed by the plants are not returned by the natural process of decay. Addition of excess fertiliser can make the situation worse as it will increase the concentration of nitrate ions, and fertilisers containing ammonium salts or urea will stimulate nitrification.

Other consequences of acidification are:
• reduced uptake of phosphate ions;
• inhibition of the nitrification processes; and
• nitrogen fixation by legumes is inhibited unless *Rhizobium* is acid tolerant.

In temperate regions, the usual agricultural practice is to keep soil pH about 6.0 to 6.5 by adding lime as calcium carbonate, calcium hydroxide or calcium oxide. The selection and breeding of varieties of crop plants less sensitive to acid conditions will mean less need to add lime.

■ MEASURING PLANT GROWTH

Before considering the factors involved in successful crop production, we need to consider the overall efficiency of plant growth and how it can be measured. Growth has been defined as an irreversible increase in dry mass: not an easy measurement to make and one which involves destruction of the living organism, but it is possible to sample populations of organisms and by measuring growth in a relatively small number of individuals, it is possible to make judgements about the whole population (by extrapolation).

If measurements of a plant's mass, volume or height are made and plotted against time, then a *growth curve* is produced, often showing a characteristic S-shape (Fig.2.5). Growth is slow at first, then enters an exponential phase, eventually slowing down as the plant reaches maturity.

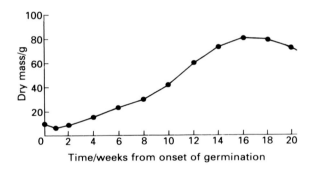

Fig.2.5 Normal growth curve for a bean

Absolute growth rate, which is the average increase in plant biomass (which could be measured as dry mass) per unit time, can be measured by taking samples of plants from a population at timed intervals, and drying to constant mass. The same number of plants would need to be taken at each sampling, and an average dry mass per plant calculated.

The difference in mass at each time interval could then be used to calculate the increase in dry mass per unit time:

x_1 g = average dry mass of plant from first sample taken at t_1 days
x_2 g = average dry mass of plant from second sample taken at t_2 days

$$\text{Growth rate (G)} = \frac{x_2 - x_1}{t_2 - t_1} \, g \, \text{day}^{-1}$$

An absolute growth rate curve (Fig.2.6) can be produced by plotting the changes in growth rate against time. This curve is usually bell-shaped and shows the period when growth is most rapid.

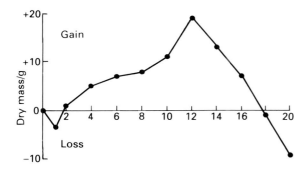

Fig.2.6 Absolute growth curve for a bean

This measurement is of limited value as it does not enable comparisons of the growth of different crop plants to be made. *Relative growth rate*, measured as increase in mass per unit mass per unit time, is a much better indicator, enabling comparisons between differently sized plants as well as comparisons at different stages of development, or under different conditions and in different environments. It could be used to compare the effects of varying light intensity or carbon dioxide concentration on a crop grown in a glasshouse, or the effects of different fertiliser treatments on a wheat crop. If a series of measurements is taken and the values are plotted, a relative growth rate curve (Fig.2.7) is produced, which can then be used to compare plants grown under different conditions or subjected to different treatments. It should then be possible to determine the most favourable conditions for growth.

Usually only certain parts of the plant, such as grains from a cereal, stem tubers of potatoes or leaves of lettuce, are of use and economic value to the crop producer, rather than the total biomass. The amount of dry matter capable of being harvested is known as the *harvestable dry matter*. If hay or silage for feeding cattle is being made,

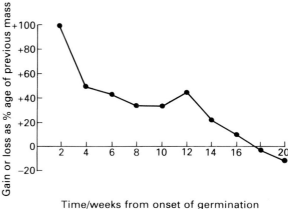

Fig.2.7 Relative growth curve for a bean

then all the plant biomass which is harvested (the biological yield) is used in the product (the economic yield). In the case of a cereal crop such as maize or a crop of garden peas, only the grains of maize and the seeds of the peas are used, the rest of the plant having no commercial value. In this case the economic yield is only a proportion of the biological yield. This proportion is called the *harvest index*.

Quantity, in terms of high yields, may be important, but so is quality, especially if the crop is produced for a specific purpose. Wheat grown for bread-making or for animal feed should have the right amount of protein (*harvestable protein*) and *digestible energy*, which is that proportion of the energy content that can be digested or absorbed. It is therefore necessary for the producer to monitor the quality of the crop and, if possible, adjust the factors involved, particularly those related to soil fertility, to ensure that the product reaches the required standard.

■ OTHER GROWTH MEASURES

In an attempt to overcome some of the limitations of basing comparisons only on the growth of whole plants, it is possible to relate increase in biomass to the growth of a particular plant organ. The *net assimilation rate* (*NAR*) or *unit leaf rate* (*ULR*) gives a measurement of net increase in plant biomass per unit leaf area per unit time, and is obtained by means of measuring those parts of the plant involved in the production of the materials needed for growth, i.e. the leaves. It is assumed that there is a direct relationship between leaf area and plant biomass.

$$\text{Net assimilation rate} = \frac{\text{increase in dry mass per unit time}}{\text{leaf area}}$$

While it is interesting and often relevant to gather information about the performance of individual plants, the crop producer is concerned with the growth rate of the whole crop, which will be affected by the NAR, i.e. the rate at which new material is synthesised, and also by the *leaf area index (LAI)*, which is a measure of the leaf area per unit of ground area at a given time. In order to calculate this index, it is necessary to cut off and measure the area of all the leaves of the crop plant in a selected ground area, say 0.5 m^2. This index will vary with the stages of growth of the crop, being small when the crop plants have just germinated and reaching a maximum when they are mature. Plants with a large LAI will be able to absorb more light than those with small LAI. It is possible to compare the times when different crops reach their maximum value for LAI and NAR. The highest values for NAR all occur in June and July, when photosynthesis is likely to be at its maximum, whereas the highest LAI values depend on when the crop was planted. Winter wheat reaches its maximum LAI value in late May, but sugar beet does not achieve its maximum until late September.

The *growth rate of a crop* is expressed as the increase in crop mass per unit area per unit time and can be calculated by multiplying the LAI by the NAR. This can provide valuable information as to the most suitable density of planting, as well as a means of comparing the effects of different treatments on the crop.

Another indicator of yield is given by the *leaf area duration (LAD)*, which is a measure of the ability of a crop to photosynthesise and produce organic material during a given period. If the leaf

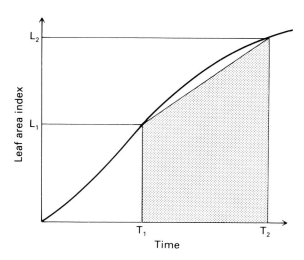

Fig.2.8 Leaf area duration (LAD) is given by the area under the curve

area index is plotted against time, then a curve is produced (Fig.2.8); the area under the curve is the leaf area duration. If the leaf area duration is multiplied by the NAR, then this will give an estimate of crop yield (Table 2.3).

Crop	Yield/ tonnes per ha	LAD/ weeks	Mean NAR/ tonnes per ha per week
Barley	7.3	17	0.43
Potatoes	7.7	21	0.36
Wheat	9.5	25	0.38
Sugar beet	12.0	33	0.36

Table 2.3 Comparison of yield, LAD and NAR in four crops

The mean NAR is obtained by dividing the yield by the LAD. As can be seen from Table 2.3, the mean NAR is fairly constant for all four crops, indicating that the LAD gives a fairly accurate prediction of the final yield.

CROP PRODUCTION

If you are hoping to get high yields of good quality produce from your garden you will have to be able to control pests - but you must also start with the right soil type and good climatic conditions. This also applies to successful crop production in a smallholding or a farm of large acreage. If crops are grown in small enclosed areas such as glasshouses, the environment can be modified to provide suitable conditions of temperature, light and carbon dioxide. Where crops are grown on large areas of land, year after year, then careful management of the soil is necessary if it is to continue to be fertile and thus productive. The two main areas of management - soil structure and soil fertility - are interlinked as many of the practices involved in maintaining soil fertility also affect soil structure.

Using a tractor to spread lime on the soil (UK)

■ SOIL STRUCTURE AND SOIL FERTILITY

■ Cultivation

Cultivation controls the physical condition of the soil so that it is suitable for plant growth. The formation of a good tilth is mainly achieved through mechanical cultivation, a practice known as *tillage*. The aims of tillage are to:
- produce good conditions for seed germination, i.e. a seed bed with the right crumb structure, where suitably sized soil crumbs or aggregates are near the soil surface, providing water and oxygen for seed germination, and allowing the establishment of the young seedlings;
- provide suitable conditions for the continued growth of the plant, enabling root penetration and development;
- improve aeration and drainage of the soil;
- bury weeds and crop remains, incorporating organic matter into the soil;
- provide for special requirements of crops, such as terraces to prevent erosion or furrows for planting crops such as potatoes.

Tillage in developed agricultural countries is achieved through ploughing, followed by harrowing, discing and rolling operations, depending on the soil and conditions. Deep ploughing is often carried out in the autumn, to give maximum time for the weathering or break up of the clods and for the incorporation of organic material.

This type of cultivation is not suitable for all soils. It may not, for example, be possible on thin 'chalky' soils or necessary on sandy or loamy soils, but it is extremely useful on clay soils and where deep-rooting crops such as potatoes and sugar beet are to be grown.

The timing of ploughing is crucial: if there has been a period of wet weather, the soil needs to dry out, as deep ploughing in wet weather can damage soil structure. Apart from the problems of severe leaching and erosion, heavy machinery tends to compact wet soil. Compression by continual ploughing can cause the formation of a *plough pan* beneath the plough layer, which inhibits root penetration. The cost of labour and fuel has to be taken into consideration when assessing the value of deep ploughing.

Because of the problems and expense associated with these conventional methods of cultivation, especially those involving deep ploughing, alternative systems have been introduced which reduce the amount of ploughing or eliminate it altogether. One alternative, called

direct drilling, involves no cultivation prior to sowing. In this system, seed, together with the fertiliser, is drilled directly into the stubble or residues of the previous crop. There are many advantages associated with this practice:
• the soil is not laid bare;
• soil structure suffers less damage;
• there is less chance of erosion;
• land does not have to be prepared too long before sowing;
• livestock can be grazed on the crop residues.

Seed drill in operation

The practice of direct drilling is not common in the UK, but it is used where soil erosion is a problem. There are other systems which involve ploughing the surface layers only, undercutting weeds and crop residues without turning the soil over. Soil disturbance reaches 6-10 cm in these systems.

With all the alternative methods of cultivation, there is still the problem of weed control, which may necessitate the use of herbicides.

 What reasons can you suggest for killing weeds in a crop?

■ LIMING

The addition of *lime* to the soil has several effects. It raises the pH, that is it makes the soil more alkaline or less acid, but it also helps in the formation of a good crumb structure and it provides a source of calcium and magnesium ions for plant nutrition. The most suitable pH for the majority of crop plants is about 6.5. At this pH, there is greater availability and uptake of some ions than there is at lower or higher pH values. Calcium, phosphorus, magnesium and molybdenum are available, and there is a reduction in the availability

of ions such as manganese, iron and aluminium, which can reach toxic levels if the pH is very low. A pH of around 6.5 will provide suitable conditions for the activities of the soil microorganisms involved in the formation of humus, with the accompanying release of nitrates and sulphates.

The formation of a good crumb structure is particularly important in clay soils, and the addition of lime promotes the clumping together, or flocculation, of the particles. This effect of lime can be demonstrated easily by shaking up a sample of clay soil in a test tube with some water to which calcium hydroxide has been added. The clumps of soil particles formed sink to the bottom of the tube, leaving a clear solution above.

The amount of lime which should be added to the soil depends on a number of factors including:
• soil characteristics, including pH, soil type and amount of organic matter present;
• the proposed crop;
• the cost of purchase and application.

The timing of the application does not matter, and the lime is usually spread on the surface and ploughed in when convenient to the farmer. It does not necessarily need to be done every year, but it might depend on the nature of the crop that is being grown and the land. As for the cost, the finer lime is more expensive, as it has to be processed more.

■ FERTILISERS

Land that is being used to produce crops on a regular basis is continually depleted of certain nutrients which need to be replaced in order to maintain and boost yields. The development of the *Haber process* in 1908 for converting nitrogen gas into ammonia has resulted in the production of large quantities of nitrogen-containing fertilisers and this in turn has contributed to the widespread use of inorganic fertilisers in preference to organic ones such as farmyard manure.

 What are the possible environmental consequences of this development?

The most common essential mineral nutrients which need to be supplied to crops are nitrogen, phosphorus and potassium. Other essential elements, such as calcium and magnesium can be supplied by liming the soil; sulphur is rarely deficient as sulphates are present in rain water. The simplest way of replenishing nitrogen, phosphorus and potassium is to use inorganic fertilisers which can either be supplied separately or as a combination, the so-called NPK fertilisers, in either liquid or solid form. When supplied as pellets or granules, they can be spread over large areas quickly by machinery.

■ Nitrogen

Nitrate fertilisers (e.g. sodium nitrate) supply nitrogen as nitrate ions which are soluble and can be readily absorbed by plants. Ammonium phosphate, anhydrous ammonia and aqua ammonia release ammonium ions which are also soluble. These ions can be absorbed by some plants but they can also be oxidised to nitrate ions by bacteria. The nitrogen-containing compounds in organic fertilisers such as farmyard manure and compost are insoluble and the material has to be decomposed by microorganisms before there is any benefit to crop plants.

Because nitrate and ammonium ions stay in solution in the soil water and are not held around the soil particles by adsorption, they are easily leached from the surface layers of the soil and can drain off agricultural land into lakes and reservoirs. Particular concern has been shown about the levels of nitrate ions in our drinking water. The European Commission guidelines set a limit of less than 50 mg dm^{-3} but this can be exceeded in parts of eastern Britain where levels of over 100 mg dm^{-3} have been recorded, necessitating dilution with water of low nitrate content before distribution. High nitrate levels have been linked to the formation of possible cancer-causing compounds in the human gut, but the evidence suggests that this is not a problem in well-nourished adults. Bottle-fed babies under the age of six months may develop a condition known as methaemoglobaemia, in which the oxygen-carrying capacity of the blood is lowered, if their intake of nitrogen is too high.

Q You may read that high levels of nitrate in lakes can cause eutrophication. What does this mean? (See *Biology Advanced Studies - Environment and Ecology.*)

■ Phosphate

The concentration of phosphate ions in the soil water is usually low because, although soluble, they readily form complexes with iron and aluminium ions and are then absorbed on to the surface of the clay particles, where they are held or 'fixed' and are unavailable to plant roots. The presence of high levels of calcium ions, as in chalky soils or soils that have been limed, will also decrease the availability of phosphate. This emphasises the complexity of the balance of ions and the way in which they interact with each other.

Phosphate fertilisers usually consist of superphosphates, made by treating rock phosphate with sulphuric acid, or ammonium phosphate, both of which are soluble in water. These fertilisers are described according to the amount of phosphorus pentoxide (P_2O_5) they contain; superphosphate having about 20% P_2O_5. Ammonium phosphate can also supply nitrogen in the form of ammonium ions and is a component of mixed or compound fertilisers.

■ Potassium

Fruity and leafy crops remove large amounts of potassium from soils, so in order to maintain yields potassium sulphate or potassium chloride is commonly applied as a fertiliser, the amount of available potassium being expressed as the amount of potash (K_2O). Potassium chloride is cheaper than potassium sulphate, but the latter is preferred by horticulturalists as it is considered to give a better quality product.

■ Mineral nutrients

Different crops require different amounts of mineral nutrients, so the farmer or grower should be able to tailor the amount to the particular crop being grown. NPK fertilisers can have different ratios of constituents: a fertiliser described as 10:10:10: will have 10% nitrogen, 10% phosphate (in the form of P_2O_5) and 10% potassium (in the form of potash). For a crop such as clover or beans, a 0:30:30 fertiliser could be used. In this case, extra nitrogen does not need to be supplied as there are nitrogen-fixing bacteria (*Rhizobium*) present in the root nodules of the plants.

It is important to make the fertiliser available to the crop when the uptake of mineral nutrients by the plants is at its greatest, so that maximum benefit is derived. This is usually during the early growth of the plants, but a number of other factors need to be taken into consideration. In the UK, wheat sown in spring (spring wheat) is fertilised at the time of sowing or beforehand. However, with winter wheat, none is applied before the following spring as there is minimal growth during the period of low temperature and the nutrients could be washed away in the rain. If fertilisers are applied too early in the spring, then there could again be loss due to leaching, cancelling out any benefit to be gained from taking advantage of warmer temperatures. Most fertilisers are applied to cereal crops in late April or early May.

■ Inorganic fertilisers

Although inorganic fertilisers are expensive as they have to be processed, their wise use can be beneficial in maintaining crop yields and soil fertility. Disadvantages of their use include the risk of *eutrophication* if excess is applied, their contribution to the acidification of soils and the possibility of 'burning' or 'scorch' damage to roots.

Alternatives to the use of inorganic fertilisers are:
• farmyard manure (FYM);
• animal slurries;
• sewage sludge;
• compost;
• green manuring.

Each of these alternatives adds organic material to the soil but the essential mineral nutrients will not become available for the plant uptake until after decomposition has taken place. All the alternatives also have a lot of carbon and little nitrogen, i.e. a high C/N ratio. The soil microorganisms feed on the organic matter and the carbon-containing compounds are used to provide energy, with the carbon being released as carbon dioxide as a result of respiration. Other nutrients, including the nitrogen-containing compounds, are needed by the microorganisms for their nutrition and subsequent growth, so amino acids and ammonium ions are taken up rapidly as the populations of microorganisms increase, resulting in a shortage of these in the soil. When the microorganisms die, the mineral nutrients are released into the soil, but the process is a slow one.

Farmyard manure consists of urine and faeces from cattle, pigs and horses, and bedding material such as straw. When spread on the land and ploughed in, it adds organic matter and nutrients to the soil, and can improve aeration and drainage. Table 3.1 compares farmyard manure with inorganic fertilisers, and it can be seen that there are advantages and disadvantages associated with the use of both types of fertiliser. Ideally, farmyard manure should be well-rotted before it is used, and should contain plenty of straw. Fresh manure releases ammonia which could damage plants.

Animal slurries are semi-liquid forms of faeces and urine from the same sources as the farmyard manure, but because of their liquid nature, they can be sprayed on to grassland or on to soil before planting.

Sewage sludge is a byproduct from sewage treatment works. It is cheap and plentiful, but it may contain high concentrations of heavy metal ions such as zinc, copper and nickel which could be toxic to plants and get into the food chains. As with all manure-based fertilisers, there are drawbacks, not the least being the associated smells! However, new techniques developed by enterprises such as Wessex Water yield an odourless product.

For your garden you may make use of *compost* which recycles household and garden waste. Compost usually consists of vegetable and animal wastes, and is a readily available source of organic matter to the gardener. The best type, aerobic compost, can be made from any organic matter in about two to six months. It needs to be kept in a large container with access to the air, and the end product is blackish-brown in colour, and crumbly with a uniform texture. Anaerobic compost can be

Inorganic fertilisers	Farmyard manure
High mineral nutrient content	Low mineral nutrient content
Exact composition known	Variable composition
All mineral nutrients can be supplied	Low in phosphates; need to be given as supplement
Mineral nutrients available to crop straight away	Slow release of mineral nutrients; may take years for decomposition to occur
No weed seeds or spores of pathogens	May contain weed seeds and spores of pathogens
Easy to handle	Bulky and heavy
Can be applied evenly to crop or soil	Difficult to apply evenly
Light machinery needed when applying so less danger of compaction of soil or damage to crop	Needs heavy machinery when applying so risk of soil compaction
Not smelly	Smelly

Table 3.1 Comparison of inorganic fertilisers with farmyard manure

made by piling up organic wastes, covering it with polythene sheeting and leaving it for about a year. Air is excluded, so the process of decomposition is slowed down. Spent mushroom compost is often used on gardens.

Green manuring is the general term used for a number of practices including:
- the ploughing in of a crop (the whole plant breaks down in the soil);
- the ploughing in of crop residues such as stubble;
- crop left on soil surface, subsequent crop planted through it by direct drilling.

Crops which are suitable as green manures include clovers and field beans, with root nodules containing nitrogen-fixing bacteria, or quick-growing leafy plants such as mustard or rape.

Organic matter is added to the soil, with all the consequent benefits, but decay is slow. Where a crop is left in the ground, it can act as a cover crop, preventing soil erosion and helping to control weeds and retaining mineral nutrients by reducing losses due to leaching.

 What evidence would be used by 'organic food' enthusiasts to support their case?

■ IRRIGATION

In order to grow crops without irrigation, a rainfall of at least 50 cm a year is required. This means that about half of the total land mass available for cultivation would need to be irrigated if it were all to be productive. At the present time, 15% of all arable land in use is irrigated, and this is increasing as more arid areas are being cultivated and more irrigation schemes are put into action. It is important to have a good knowledge of the climate of an area, so that suitable crops can be grown and harvested at appropriate times of the year, taking full advantage of seasonal variations.

A knowledge of the requirements of the crop at different stages of growth can enable the farmer to irrigate only when needed, thus saving water and cutting down on expense. Irrigation can be beneficial to crops grown in temperate regions, where rainfall exceeds 50 cm, especially as the rainy season does not always coincide with the requirements of the crop. All crops need water for germination and some crops, such as tomatoes and cucumbers, make heavy demands for water at the fruit development stage, while lettuces and other leafy crops benefit from watering during vegetative growth.

Irrigation pipes in a market garden (Santa Cruz, USA)

Three main methods of irrigation in use are:
- sprinklers or overhead irrigation;
- surface irrigation;
- sub-surface irrigation.
The method chosen depends on a number of factors, including the cost of installation, the nature of the crop and the nature of the land.

The practice of *mulching* can be used to reduce the amount of evaporation from the soil surface, and thus avoid the need for extra water or irrigation. This involves the spreading of peat, bark, straw, manure or even black plastic sheeting on the soil surface around the crop plants. Whilst this is very effective, with the added advantage of reducing competition from weeds, it is not practical for large areas of field crops, but it is being used increasingly in horticulture. The use of peat is being discouraged due to pressure from environmentalists because of the rapid loss of unique peatlands habitats.

Lettuces mulched with black polythene to keep down weeds and conserve moisture

The quality of the water used for irrigation is important. Water containing large amounts of dissolved salts, as in salt or sea water, could upset the balance of ions in the soil and alter the availability of some ions needed for plant growth. In addition, sodium ions are known to make the soil less permeable, and when evaporation occurs, sodium chloride crystals are left behind on the surface, causing a reduction in growth of the crop. Continual irrigation can bring about the leaching of valuable mineral ions as well as the possibility of causing the soil to become waterlogged. It is extremely difficult to ensure that the crop gets sufficient water for good growth without supplying water in excess, so good drainage is necessary on irrigated land.

Too much water in the soil can be as much of a problem as too little water. Wet soils are cold soils and waterlogged soils have a low oxygen content, creating anaerobic conditions in which denitrification occurs and nitrates are converted to nitrogen gas by bacteria, thus plant growth is inhibited. Wet soils are heavy to work and there is the problem of compaction if heavy machinery is used when ploughing and preparing the land for planting. Chalky and sandy soils drain readily, but clay soils, the peaty soils, found in areas such as Lancashire and East Anglia, retain water and need to be drained if they are to be productive.

Surface drains are the cheapest to install and can carry large amounts of water away. They consist of open ditches, which work best if they are dug across the direction of cultivation or across a slope. The main disadvantages are that they are expensive to maintain, they interfere with cultivation and they use up productive land, and may damage the ecology of the environment.

Underground drainage systems are more expensive to install but more efficient than either surface or mole drains (formed by dragging a special tool through the soil). Once installed, the only maintenance needed is to keep them free from obstructions. The most common types are tile drains or perforated plastic pipes. Tile drains consist of clay pipes, which are laid at the bottom of an open ditch, then surrounded by straw or gravel and finally the ditches are filled in with soil.

■ SOWING THE SEED

Having prepared a good seed bed and considered the mineral content, moisture and drainage of the soil, it is important to obtain and sow good seed. The seed should come from a reliable source, be true to type, free from weed seeds and have a good percentage germination rate. Seeds sold in the UK have to conform to certain standards of cleanliness and viability (see *Biology Advanced Studies - Plant Science*). Seed viability refers to the ability of the seed to germinate. The most reliable way of testing this is to provide the appropriate conditions and see what happens. It is unlikely that there will be 100% germination, but the rate needs to be high enough to establish a crop at a suitable density. Sometimes seeds are treated with fungicide to protect them against soil-borne diseases. Where large areas are under cultivation, the seeds are sown mechanically, but for the gardener there are several different ways in which seeds are packaged to make sowing easier.

Seeds may be pelleted, which involves coating individual seeds with a protective material. This makes the seeds easier to handle as they can be planted exactly where they are required and there is no need to thin out the seedlings once germination has occurred. Seeds can be incorporated into tapes or sheets, which are laid on the seed bed, watered and then covered with soil. The material forming the tape or sheet dissolves, leaving the seeds suitably spaced out.

Sowing seeds

For seed germination to occur, there needs to be sufficient moisture available in the soil, oxygen and a suitable temperature. Each crop species will have a minimum, optimum and maximum temperature for germination, as well as for growth, and these temperatures need to be taken into consideration when determining the time of sowing. It is important to choose crops that are compatible with the environment. Winter wheat varieties will not flower unless they have been exposed to a period of cold temperatures or if planted in tropical regions; the plants need a cold shock, called a vernalisation requirement. This can be overcome by soaking the seeds and then keeping them at a temperature of 2 °C for a period of six weeks. This procedure is not feasible for the production of a field crop, but is useful for experimental purposes, such as cross-breeding a winter wheat variety with a spring wheat, as they can then be made to flower at the same time.

The rate and depth of sowing depends on the species. Nowadays machinery is used to plant most seeds and the rate and depth can be controlled. Large-seeded crops, such as soya beans, are usually planted 2-5 cm below the surface, but those with smaller seeds 6-12 mm deep. In general, the larger the seeds, the deeper they can be planted.

The density of seeding is significant for some crops. If the plants are too close together, then they may compete with each other for available nutrients (intra-specific competition), thus reducing the overall yield of the crop. In the case of cereal crops, less dense seeding could encourage the growth of side shoots (tillering), which will compensate for the low density of plants. For a crop that is to be used for animal forage dense seeding results in plants with fine stems which are more palatable.

In gardens and smallholdings, seeds are often planted quite densely and then thinned out by hand once the seedlings have grown. In order to make the best possible use of the space available, two different crops can be sown together, one slow-growing such as parsnips with one fast-growing such as radishes or lettuces. The radishes or lettuces will be ready for harvesting before the parsnips need the space, and so there is no competition between the two crops. This practice is known as intercropping and other forms of it include growing young and mature plants together, using the space between rows as a seedbed for other vegetables and growing low crops such as salads beneath taller ones such as sweet corn or winter brassicas (a technique known as undercropping). Apart from the obvious advantage of using all the space available, it does provide the gardener with the opportunity to grow a greater variety of crops and, for the smalholding, it can be a further source of income. The rows might need to be spaced a little further apart than they would be if only one crop was being grown, but it does provide a means of controlling weeds.

■ WEEDS

Growth of weeds amongst the crop plants is a form of inter-specific competition. A *weed* can be defined as any plant which grows where it is not wanted, though this definition has been modified to include plants not deliberately cultivated by human beings, but able to grow in situations disturbed by them. Such plants are found in many flowering plant families, though one study carried out in the USA showed that 60% of the species recognised as weeds came from only seven families, and most of those belonged to the daisy family or Compositae.

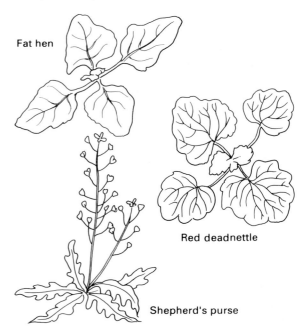

Fig.3.1 Some common weeds

Control of weeds is important to crop producers, whatever the scale of the crop production because weeds compete for the available resources, such as light, water and mineral nutrients, causing a potential loss in yield. Most weeds compete with the crop plant while it is growing and it has been estimated that they contribute to a 10% loss in yield on average, but this figure depends on the nature of the crop and the situation. Such losses can be reduced or eliminated by their removal.

We can trace the history of weeds in the UK. Much of it is linked with the development of agriculture, although species we recognise as weeds were in existence long before human beings were around. The remains of some weed species such as knotgrass (*Polygonum aviculare*) and chickweed (*Stellaria media*) have been found preserved in peat deposits dating back 600 000 years. Nomadic people did not cultivate the land, but they probably left rubbish heaps which would have provided ideal conditions for the growth of some of these species. Once settlements were established and land was cleared of trees for cultivation, weed species flourished in the conditions provided. As well as native species, many weeds have been introduced from other countries, notable contributions from the Roman invasion being the red deadnettle (*Lamium purpureum*) and the corn marigold (*Chrysanthemum segetum*).

■ Competition

The main effects of weeds are that they occupy space which might be used by crop plants and that they use up water and nutrients for their growth. With respect to competition for space, the more successful weeds bear a morphological resemblance to the crop they are competing with. The greater the similarity in growth form, the more successful the competing weed is likely to be: the effects are the same as intra-specific competition where the crop plants are competing with each other. A good example of this is seen with the wild oat (*Avena fatua*), a frequent contaminant of the planted cereal crop.

It is difficult to separate out the effect of competition by weeds for water, light and mineral nutrients, but there is little doubt that the crop yield will suffer if there is a heavy weed infestation. If the weed population grows faster than the crop, then the crop could be deprived of water in the early stages as the weed cover may prevent rain from penetrating through into the soil. Development of root systems is important in both crop and weeds. Weed species have been shown to develop just as extensive root systems as crop plants, although some weed species may benefit from being shallower or deeper rooting than the crop. Some weed species are known to be particularly effective in taking up specific nutrients, for example fat hen (*Chenopodium album*) takes up potassium ions readily. Experiments with common couch-grass (*Agropyron repens*) as a weed amongst maize showed that couch-grass took up most of its

A strip ploughed around the edge of a crop can prevent invasion by weeds

nitrogen, phosphorus and potassium requirements early in its growth so that the maize, which starts its major period of growth later in the second half of June, suffered from the reduced nutrient availability of the soil.

Broad-leaved weeds, such as daisies, plantains and docks, compete very effectively in pasture as they have large leaves which spread out and absorb light. Fat hen and chickweed compete by being tall or scrambling over other plants, but the effect is complicated by competition for other factors.

The greatest effect of competition from weeds occurs during their early stages of growth, the critical period being the first four to six weeks. It is thus very important to keep the crop weed-free for this period. This will allow the crop plants to become established and increase the chance of a good yield.

With some crops it makes a difference whether the weeds are in amongst the plants or whether they are in between the rows. It has been shown that plants, such as beet, compete more successfully if the weed species are in the rows amongst the crop plants rather than in the area between the rows.

Many investigations have been made into the interactions between one crop plant and one weed, but in one complex study, intra-specific competition amongst the weed and crop species was studied as well as inter-specific competition. Both barley and white mustard showed their greatest competitive ability against themselves, i.e. intra-specific competition was stronger than inter-specific competition (see Fig.3.2).

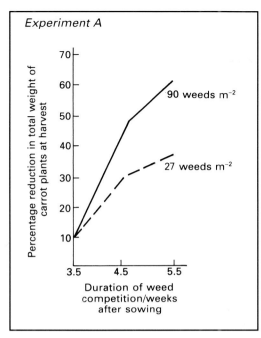

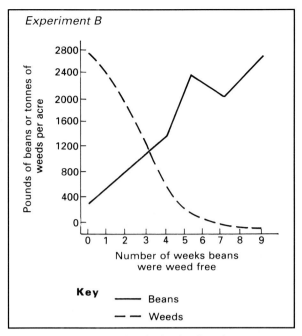

Fig.3.2 Results of experiments on interference caused by weeds. Experiment A results show that the density of weeds in a carrot crop will affect the yield at harvest. Experiment B results show that the length of the weed-free period affects the yield of beans. Keeping the crop free of weeds for up to five weeks after sowing has the greatest effect on the yield.

■ The action of weeds

Some weed species are thought to produce chemical substances from their roots or leaves which will inhibit the growth of other plants nearby, but it is very difficult to devise experiments which will test this hypothesis satisfactorily.

Apart from causing a loss in yield of a crop, weeds may have other effects on crop production and farming practices. They may, for example:
- be parasitic on the crop plants - this is not a problem in the UK but affects maize in the USA and Africa;
- be hosts for the diseases and pests of the crop plants, e.g. fat hen and other leguminous weeds can be hosts for the black bean aphid (*Aphis fabae*), a pest of field beans, and wild members of the Cruciferae can host *Plasmodiophora brassicae*, the organism which causes club roots in cabbages;
- be poisonous to grazing animals and contaminate hay and silage;
- have spines or thorns which could cause injury to grazing animals;
- be unpalatable to animals, or nutritionally poor, tainting animal products, e.g. wild onion flavours milk and meat;
- interfere with farm machinery especially during harvesting, e.g. knotgrass;

- block drainage channels and irrigation ditches, e.g. water hyacinth (*Eichornia crassipes*);
- contaminate seed crops with their seeds; a particular problem is contamination of the pea crop, used for canning and freezing, with the fruits of black nightshade (*Solanum nigrum*);
- affect land, such as road verges and railway embankments, which can be expensive to keep clear; these areas then provide a reservoir of seeds which can colonise agricultural land when the opportunity arises.

Most weed species owe their success to some of the following characteristic features of their life cycle:
- the life cycle may be a short one (these plants are known as *ephemerals*);
- a high output of seeds when growing conditions are favourable;
- ability to produce some seeds even in poor growing conditions;
- seed production in some species may be spread over a long period of time;
- seed production can start after a short period of vegetative growth;
- seeds can remain viable in the soil for long periods;
- rapid growth of seedlings.

23

■ Seed production

For all plant species, the production of seeds is important for survival, but for weed species it is a particular advantage to produce abundant seeds. Some common weed species produce very large numbers of fruits or seeds. For example, groundsel (*Senecio vulgaris*) produces between 1000 and 2000 fruits per plant, shepherd's purse (*Capsella bursa-pastoris*) produces about 3500-4000 seeds per plant and the common poppy (*Papaver rhoeas*) produces up to 19 500 seeds per plant. Usually the seeds are small and light, but this is not always an advantage as such seeds would not contain as much stored food. For perennial weed species, there is less advantage in producing large quantities of seed, but many do.

Poppy (*Papaver rhoeas*) flowers and seed-heads

Even in poor conditions, when the plants may be small, most weed species produce some seeds. Often weed species are self-compatible, eliminating the need for cross-pollination.

■ Dormancy

Variable seed dormancy is a characteristic which is vital to the success of weed species and contrasts with most crop plants which have been selected for their rapid, uniform germination. Seeds show three main types of dormancy: innate, induced and enforced. *Innate dormancy* is genetically determined, and the seeds will not germinate for a period after they are shed from the plant. *Induced dormancy* is caused by the presence of a specific condition, the removal of which will permit germination to occur. In some plants, dormancy is caused by high concentrations of

carbon dioxide, so seeds that are buried will not germinate. When the seeds are brought to the surface by cultivation, the excess carbon dioxide can diffuse away, allowing germination to proceed. *Enforced dormancy* occurs when the environmental conditions are unsuitable. Some seeds require light and remain dormant if buried.

Although a large number of weeds show innate seed dormancy, there are plenty which show the other types of dormancy so that they germinate when conditions are suitable, especially if brought to the surface of the soil by cultivation techniques. Most crop seeds do not survive long if buried in the soil, but weed seeds do, and experiments have shown that many weed species showed high percentages of germination after being buried for long periods of time. For example, the seeds of shepherd's purse (*Capsella bursa-pastoris*) showed 47% germination after 16 years.

It has been estimated that arable land contains large numbers of weed seeds per square metre, most of them being in the upper 10 cm of the soil. If only a small proportion of those weed seeds is exposed and germinate each year, then a significant number of plants would be produced, adding to the crop producer's problems. There is much truth in the old saying 'One year seeding, seven years' weeding'.

 Devise an investigation on the germination of seeds buried at different depths in the soil.

■ Weed germination

Generalisations about the environmental germination requirements of weed seeds can be misleading, as there are many variations. Obviously, if the germination were to be linked to the cultivation procedures, then the weed species is more likely to be successful. For example, digging or ploughing brings seeds to the surface and germination follows, but this is linked more with dormancy than with the environmental conditions. Winter wild oats are insignificant as a weed in spring cereals, whereas spring wild oats need a period of dormancy followed by a cold period before they will germinate in the spring. They then compete successfully with spring sown cereals.

Some weeds show rapid and synchronous germination, similar to crop plants, while others show germination over a longer period and there are some which show intermittent germination. All these strategies have their advantages and, within the same genus, the conditions needed for germination can vary. Non-weed species of the genus *Chenopodium* have a much narrower range of conditions for germination than the weed species, fat hen.

In general, weed species show more tolerance of variations in the physical environment, such as extremes of temperature, high evaporation rates and often high nutrient levels for a short time, than their non-weed relatives.

Weed species are adapted for long and short distance dispersal, but human activities are often the major agents of dispersal. They possess similar dispersal mechanisms to the other members of the genus or family to which they belong, but they often show good powers of vegetative propagation and the ability to regenerate when divided into fragments. Couch-grass (*Agropyron repens*), field bindweed (*Convolvulus arvensis*) and ground elder (*Aegopodium podagraria*) all show vigorous powers of spread and reproduction by vegetative means, and intense methods of cultivation are required to get rid of them. All the fragments of the plants must be removed or killed if the land is to be clear of these weeds. An interesting comparison can be made between the common couch-grass and ground elder, both perennials with shallow rhizomes. In ground elder, seed production is insignificant, and once the ground has been cleared of the rhizomes, this species is not a serious weed in agriculture, but it is common in gardens. The common couch-grass produces lots of seed, so it is more difficult to get rid of, and remains a serious pest to both gardeners and farmers.

There are obvious advantages for *perennial* plants (i.e. those which continue growth from year to year). Food reserves allow vigorous growth at the start of the season, enabling successful competition with the growing crop. The perennial weed will have a larger food store than the crop and this will enable the weed to sustain its growth. The disadvantages are that the perennial weed often produces less seed and there is genetic uniformity. Perennial weeds are more of a problem to the gardener and smallholder than to the farmer, because land cultivated for arable crops on a large scale will be subject to deeper ploughing and preparation which will destroy the underground perennating organs. In pastures, perennial weeds such as dandelions (*Taraxacum officinale*), plantains (*Plantago* spp.) and ragwort (*Senecio jacobea*), can become a problem in the contamination of hay and may harm grazing animals.

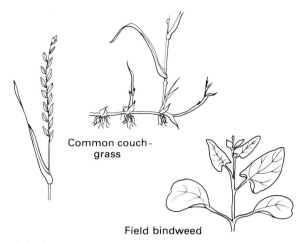

Common couch-grass

Field bindweed

Fig.3.3 Some perennial weeds

Weeds are considered to possess competitive ability, which means that when growing amongst other plants, particularly crop plants, they show some of the following qualities:
- efficient ion uptake;
- rapid root growth;
- ability to climb up other plants (bindweed);
- ability to scramble over competitors (chickweed);
- rosette habit (daisy, dandelion, plantain);
- ability to grow larger and more vigorous (charlock).

Most of these qualities are linked with the ability to obtain the fundamental requirements for growth such as light, water and mineral nutrients, at the expense of their competitors, that is to grow to maturity faster and to reproduce, taking advantage of the available resources.

As has already been indicated, humans are responsible for the spread of weed species over wide geographical areas. Weed seeds do not often cross mountain ranges or oceans, but they can be carried by human transport. Weed seeds often contaminate crop seed, hay, silage, animal food and packaging material. They can be present on wool, on hooves and in the alimentary tracts of animals that are being moved from one location to another. Another source of weed species is from botanic gardens and 'garden escapes'. A plant that is introduced as an exotic garden plant can escape into the wild, where it will have no pests or diseases in the new area. A good example of the problems that can arise is shown by the spread of the giant hogweed, introduced into Britain as an exotic garden plant, and the prickly pear (*Opuntia*) in Australia, where only the introduction of the appropriate pest enabled control of a serious weed to be achieved.

■ WEED CONTROL

■ Herbicides

Where crops are grown on a large scale, weeds are usually controlled by the use of chemicals called herbicides. There are three major types of herbicide: contact, soil-acting and selective. The choice of which one to use must depend on the nature of the crop and the weed species.

Spraying herbicide

Contact herbicides, such as paraquat and diquat, act only on the regions of the plant with which they come into contact, which is usually the leaves. They act by interfering with the mechanism of photosynthesis, destroying the thylakoid membranes of the chloroplasts. They are good for general weed control and they act rapidly and breakdown quickly into harmless products. They are often used to treat an area prior to the sowing of seed, because there is no need to plough the area, thus avoiding the chances of soil erosion.

Soil-acting herbicides, such as simazine, are chemicals applied directly to the soil and remain in the top 2 cm, killing off germinating seeds. They act by inhibiting the light reactions of photosynthesis in the weed seedlings as they emerge. This type of herbicide is selective in that the deeper-rooted species are not affected.

Selective herbicides are growth regulators such as 2,4-D (2,4-dichlorophenoxyacetic acid), which is absorbed by the leaves and promotes abnormal growth. Cell division and elongation in the roots is inhibited, and cell respiration, together with the synthesis of fats and proteins, is disrupted. They act on the broad-leaved dicotyledonous plants, leaving the narrow-leaved monocotyledonous plants unaffected, so they are particularly useful in protecting cereal crops and keeping lawns free from weeds. These chemicals are very similar to naturally-occurring growth substances in plants such as IAA (indole acetic acid)

Selective herbicides like 2,4-D must be taken in by the plant and transported internally to the site of action. Foliar sprays are often used. In the plant 2,4-D takes the same path as sugars and moves in the cytoplasm, entering the phloem transport system. Herbicides such as simazine travel in the apoplast system, through the cell walls into the xylem and then to the leaf. Much interest has been shown in the herbicide glyphosate, which is based on the amino acid glycine. It is readily translocated through the plant, and is broken down to harmless end products in the soil by microorganisms. It has a low toxicity to mammals and it is effective against all types of plant.

■ Other control measures

Weeds can be controlled without using chemicals, but the procedures are more time-consuming and not always as effective. *Cultivation*, or *secondary tillage*, which involves hoeing, discing and harrowing, will kill off weed species, especially the perennial kinds. Inter-row cultivators and hoes can be used for keeping weeds down between the rows of crops such as potatoes and maize.

Flame-weeders, which involve exposing the weeds to temperatures in excess of 100 °C for one tenth of a second, are used for weed control within rows. The technique does not burn up the weeds but dehydrates the tissues and coagulates the proteins. The cost of the propane fuel is high, but there is a saving on hand-weeding costs. The best time to apply this technique is when the leaves are dry and most weeds can be killed at the two-leaf stage.

It is also important to sow good, *certified seed*, which is guaranteed to be free from weed seeds. Often crop producers will save some seed from a crop to plant the following year, but care needs to be taken to ensure that the seed is free from weed contaminants. This is time-consuming, unless the weed seeds are a different size from the crop, in which case simple sieving will suffice.

Weeds can be reduced by careful management of the land, such as *crop rotation*. If different crop plants are grown each year, then the weed species do not have a chance to build up. Methods of cultivation are different for root crops and cereals, the ground being more deeply ploughed or dug for the former, and this will help to eradicate weeds. If pasture is included in the rotation, then grasses compete quite successfully with most broad-leaved weeds, and if the pasture is grazed, this will also have an effect as the weed species could be eaten before the plants can produce flowers and seeds.

Where crop production is on a smaller scale, in gardens and smallholdings, weeds can be removed manually, and some of the practices already mentioned, such as intercropping and mulching, do cut down on the incidence of weeds.

Biological control of weeds involves the introduction of organisms which feed on the weed species but not on the crop. This type of control has been effective in Australia, where the insect *Cactoblastis* was introduced, so that its larvae could feed on the prickly pear.

■ PLANT DISEASES

Plant diseases result in loss of yield because of their effect on the metabolism of the plant, slowing down growth, as well as affecting the appearance of the crop. In extreme cases the whole crop may not be fit for human consumption. Diseases can affect the whole plant, or part of the plant and affect the life cycle at any point. They are classified as infectious or non-infectious. The infectious diseases are caused by other living organisms and can be transferred from plant to plant (see *Biology Advanced Studies - Microbiology and Biotechnology*), whereas the non-infectious diseases do not involve other living organisms and are not transferable.

Infectious diseases can be caused by:
• fungi (rusts and smuts of cereals, late blight of potatoes);
• bacteria (potato scab, wilts, club root of brassicas);
• viruses (stunting and mosaic diseases, leaf roll).

Fungi are the most numerous of the plant pathogens and can be transmitted through the soil or through the air. Viruses are transmitted by aphids when feeding on the plants and the diseases get into the whole plant.

Most pathogenic, that is disease-causing, organisms have a specific host range, many affecting only one or a few species, e.g. *Botrytis cinerea* is a grey mould which affects strawberries, grapes, lettuces and tobacco.

Non-infectious diseases can be due to:
• mineral deficiencies (yellowing of the leaves indicating lack of chlorophyll is caused by a deficiency of iron or magnesium);
• improper use of irrigation - too much or too little water;
• excessive exposure to direct sunlight;
• chemicals such as insecticides.

■ DISEASE CONTROL

The best way to control crop diseases is to prevent the pathogens infecting the plants, and so the emphasis must be on protection and elimination of the sources of infection. It is extremely difficult to eliminate a disease completely unless the crop is grown in an enclosed area such as a glasshouse, and the sources of the pathogens of most field crops are very widespread. There are several ways in which diseases can be avoided or controlled in addition to the chemical sprays of pesticides, and these are summarised in the Table 3.2.

Disease-resistant varieties of crop plants can be produced and grown. These are specially selected because they are immune or resistant to specific diseases. Virus-free vegetatively propagated plants, such as potatoes, can be produced by heat treatment followed by *micropropagation* (see p.50) involving meristem tip culture. This results in the establishment of virus-free stocks. Certification schemes, which ensure that a particular variety is virus free, exist for potatoes and for many soft fruits, with rigorous testing and regular inspection of the crop. They are expensive to produce, but will result in a disease-free crop, which will mean an increased profit for the producer.

Legislation exists in many countries, designed to prevent or restrict the spread of certain diseases, and in the UK outbreaks of diseases such as fireblight of apples and potato wart have to be reported to the Ministry of Agriculture, Fisheries and Food. Disease-free crops result in produce which is more acceptable to the consumer as no chemicals have been used to control pests. If the pathogens change, then the disease-resistance of a variety may be lost. Plant breeders are continually searching for varieties which combine resistance to specific diseases with the desirable qualities of the crop.

Method	Notes
Soil sterilisation	Destroys pathogens in the soil; can be carried out using liquid or steam. Useful in glasshouses and small areas, but not practicable for large areas
Destruction of crop residues	Pathogens are often present in crop residues, e.g. cereal stubble. Residues can be removed by deep ploughing, treatment with chemicals or by burning; the latter must be controlled
Crop rotation - a different crop on the land each year in a cycle, e.g. legumes - potatoes - roots - fallow.	Many pathogens are host-specific, i.e. will only attack one or a few related species, so with rotation the number of pathogens for any crop in the rotation is reduced
Use of disease-free seed	Use of certified seed recommended. Seed can be treated before planting, e.g. wheat seed is dusted with fungicide to kill smut spores
Control of vectors	Spraying with insecticide to control aphid populations will reduce infection by viruses; also spray to reduce loss in yield due to other insect pests
Use of correct irrigation procedures	Overhead irrigation makes leaf surfaces wet and encourages growth of fungal spores. If soil is too wet, growth of soil-borne fungal pathogens encouraged.
Farm cleanliness	Machinery, tools and equipment should be kept clean to avoid the spread of spores (and also weed seeds) from one crop to another.

Table 3.2 Methods used to control the spread of plant diseases

■ Fungicides

If disease-resistant varieties of crops are not available, then crops have to be protected by the use of chemicals which are toxic to the pathogen but not to the plant. Fungicides are used to protect against and destroy fungal pathogens. They can be protectant or systemic in the way in which they work. Protectant fungicides act as poisons and disrupt enzyme function and protein structure generally. Systemic fungicides affect specific biochemical and metabolic functions.

Protectant fungicides are applied to seeds, tubers or foliage of infected plants to kill off the fungal spores and mycelium on the outside of the plant. Protectants containing copper compounds have been in use for over a hundred years for the control of diseases such as potato blight, caused by the fungus *Phytophthora infestans* (see *Biology Advanced Studies - Microbiology and Biotechnology*), downy mildews and damping-off diseases, caused by *Pythium spp*.

Bordeaux mixture, containing copper sulphate and calcium hydroxide in water, was first used to control downy mildew on vines in France, and it has been effective against many fungal pathogens, but its use has declined over the past thirty years. Although it kills off the fungi, it is tedious to make up and has been shown to damage the leaves of plants. Other less toxic copper compounds are now in use, together with fungicides based on tin, mercury and sulphur. Organosulphur compounds, such as thiram, ferbam and mancozeb (which also contains zinc and manganese) are extensively used.

Other protectants, particularly effective in controlling apple scab and diseases caused by *Pythium*, are the phthalimides and dicarboximides, such as captan. Elvaron is successful against the grey mould *Botrytis cinerea*, and ronilan and rovral control diseases of oilseed rape. All these compounds can be used as seed dressings or sprayed on to the foliage of the crop plants. Their effectiveness depends on the activity of the compound, the rate of application, the persistence of the compound and the timing of application. Spraying of large areas of crops is usually only carried out after warnings of the incidence of the disease, and has to take weather conditions into consideration.

Systemic fungicides are taken up and translocated around the crop plant and the whole plant can become resistant to the infection. As well as giving protection, many of the systemic fungicides will also kill off the fungus if it is already in the plant. These fungicides work by interfering with the growth of the mycelium. There is a large number of different compounds available, all of which interfere with some aspect of the fungal metabolism, but which are non-toxic to the crop plant.

Ethirimol is used to control cereal smut diseases and powdery mildews by killing the mycelium in the seedlings. It is often used as a component of seed dressings, so that it is taken up by the seedlings soon after germination. Benomyl is a systemic fungicide found to be effective against several fungal diseases. It has proved effective against *Botrytis cinerea* and in controlling stem canker fungus of oilseed rape. Benomyl is known to interfere with microtubule formation in dividing cells, so disrupting the process of mitosis and inhibiting growth.

Fungi can become resistant to the fungicide, though this is more common with systemic fungicides than with protectants. Resistance develops most quickly with fungi that produce vast numbers of spores, with a greater capacity for variability. With this in mind, crop producers are recommended to use fungicides sparingly and rotate their use, so that they do not use the same one year after year. With such a large number on the market, this should not be difficult. Mixtures of different fungicides have been tried out, and this does seem to avoid the establishment of resistant strains, as well as providing protection against a number of different fungal diseases.

Other methods of control include growing the crop when the pathogen is not around. Crops can be planted early, so that they can become established before the pathogen can have too great an effect (e.g. early potatoes).

■ ANIMAL PESTS OF CROP PLANTS

A pest is an organism that causes harm or damage to crops, and for agricultural purposes it is defined as causing a loss in yield of more than 5-10%. There are many animal pests of crops, some causing considerable damage to plants as well as transmitting diseases (Table 3.3).

Animal group	Damage caused	Remedy
Mammals: Rabbits	Burrowing, eating foliage	Mesh wire fencing: 1 m high, 15 cm below ground
Deer	Strip bark, eat crops	High/electric fencing
Moles	Burrowing, tunnelling	Humane traps
Mice	Eat seeds, seedlings	Mouse traps
Birds: Pigeons, pheasants	Strip brassicas and peas	Bird scarers, humming tape, cages for crop
Sparrows	Eat seedlings	Black cotton across rows
Slugs and snails	Eat plants, leave holes in leaves, spoil appearance of the crop	Metaldehyde pellets; aluminium sulphate at seedling stage; pick off by hand and kill at night
Nematodes (eelworms)	Can cause disease in roots, stems and bulbs, causes stunted growth	Infested plants need to be removed and destroyed; 3 or 4 year crop rotation to prevent buildup

Table 3.3 Non-arthropod pests of crop plants

Arthropods, and particularly insects, cause considerable damage to crops. There are two types of damage: direct, where plant structures are affected; and indirect, which might involve a disease (Table 3.4).

It is important for the grower to assess the potential damage that can be done to a crop by a particular pest, so that preventive measures can be taken to minimise losses. The *economic injury level* is the lowest population density of a pest that will cause economic damage to a crop. This value will vary according to the crop, the season of the year and the area. By the time this level in pest numbers is reached, much damage will have already have been done to the crop and pest numbers will be rising rapidly. If action is to be taken against the pest, then control measures must be taken earlier and the *economic damage threshold* is defined as the point at which these preventive measures should be started in order to prevent the economic injury level being reached.

Type of insect	Direct damage	Example	Indirect damage	Example
Chewers	Reduction in leaf tissue, resulting in reduction of photosynthesis	Cabbage White caterpillars; locusts (can consume own mass in vegetation per day)	Stem borers cause plant distortion so plants more difficult to harvest	'Dead heart' of cereals caused by larvae of fruit fly; causes tillering so plants have more spreading growth habit
	Boring into stems damaging phloem, affecting flow of sap	Wheat stem sawfly	Reduction in crop quality during storage	Grain weevils in stored cereals; carrot fly larvae in carrots
	Destruction of buds on fruit trees	Fruit bud weevils		
	Premature fruit fall	Codling moth		
	Destruction of roots, reducing water and mineral uptake	Leather jackets, wire worms		
Piercers/ suckers	Reduction in plant vigour due to removal of sap; cause wilting and distortion of leaves	Aphids, particularly on peaches and potatoes	Transmission of pathogens	Aphids as vectors of virus diseases
	Damage to flowers so seed production reduced	Capsid bugs		

Table 3.4 Insect damage to crop plants

■ Insect pest control

Insect pests can be controlled in three ways:
- chemical control involving the use of chemicals called insecticides;
- biological control; or
- integrated pest management.

There are many types of insecticide available to the crop producer, all of them involving some hazards. Table 3.5 summaries the effects and uses of some of the major groups of compounds.

Insect growth regulators have been used with some success as they are highly specific and do not affect other groups of animals such as vertebrates, although they do affect the useful insects as well as the pests. These compounds (e.g. diflubenzron, methoprene) mimic the action of the insect hormones which affect development. They can either prevent the larval stage of the insect from developing into an adult, by interfering with the formation of the adult type of cuticle, or they can prevent the new cuticle from forming after moulting.

Type of insecticide	Mode of action	Problems
Organochlorines (chlorinated hydrocarbons), e.g. DDT, aldrin, dieldrin, lindande, metoxychlor, chlordane	Insoluble in water, so used as powders, seed dressings, emulsions; absorbed directly by insects; act by interfering with nerve transmission	Persistent; kill wide range of insects; accumulate in food chains
Organophosphates, e.g. malathion, parathion, diazinon	More soluble in water and less persistent than organochlorines; can be incorporated into a granule and placed in soil; can be used systematically in plants so effective against aphids; acts by inhibiting cholinesterase at nerve synapses	More poisonous than organochlorines; poisonous to humans
Carbamates, e.g. carbaryl, primicarb	Similar to organophosphates; carbaryl used against caterpillars and other surface feeders; primicarb developed as a systemic to kill off aphids; selective as will kill aphids but not ladybirds; less toxic to mammals than organophosphates	Highly toxic to bees and parasitic wasps that are the natural predators of insect pests; less persistent than organochlorines, but more so than organophosphates
Pyrethroids, e.g. rotenone extracted from derris plants, nicotine from tobacco, natural extracts from flowers of *Pyrethrum*; synthetic pyrethroids include cypermethrin, deltamethrin.	Powerful contact and stomach poisons; cause paralysis by interfering with nerve impulse transmission; penetrate through cuticle or ingested; shortlived, breakdown rapid so useful for small areas. Commercially produced synthetic pyrethroids more stable than naturally occurring compounds.	Highly toxic to bees and fish

Table 3.5 Different types of insecticides

The problems with the use of insecticides are very similar to those already mentioned in connection with fungicides. Any chemical substance used to control pests will affect the environment in some way and it is difficult to ensure that only the pest organism is affected, leaving the crop and soil uncontaminated. Many of the chemicals used have to be sprayed on to the crops, with the added risk of contaminating plants and animals in the adjacent area. To ensure that the chemical is present in sufficiently high amounts to kill or control the pest, there is the danger that excess is applied and that some will contaminate water supplies and get into food chains, as has been the case with DDT. Long-term use of an insecticide can result in the insects becoming immune or resistant and it will take increasing amounts of the chemical to kill off or control the infestation. Because more insecticide has to be used, the additional cost will reduce the producer's profits to such an extent that it becomes uneconomical to treat the crop.

Pesticide resistance will have a genetic basis, but it should be pointed out that the alleles conferring resistance are present in the pest population before it is exposed to the pesticide. The pesticide does not cause the mutations. When pesticide is applied to a crop, those members of the pest population that possess the alleles for resistance will survive, reproduce and pass on their resistant alleles to their offspring, while the rest of the population will perish. The frequency of the resistant alleles in the population will increase unless the pesticide is changed or a combination of several chemicals is used.

■ Other control measures

As we have become more aware of the dangers of pesticides polluting the environment and our food, alternative methods of protecting our crops from pests have been investigated. It is possible to reduce the incidence of some pests by effective farming practices, such as good tillage which will bury insect larvae. Suitable rotation of crops will reduce or control the numbers of some insects, and the planting of crops can be timed to avoid certain stages in the pest's life cycle. For example, the seeding of winter wheat can be delayed until after the Hessian fly has laid its eggs. For this type of control to be successful, a good knowledge of both the crop and the habits and life cycle of the insect pest is required.

Biological control involves a knowledge of the natural predators and parasites of the pest

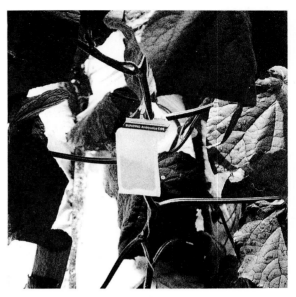

Predatory mites used to control red spider mite as part of a biological control programme in cucumber cultivation in glasshouses

organism, and if properly applied can be used to control or eliminate a pest population without the need for chemicals. In just the same way that chemicals need to be thoroughly investigated before they are used, we need to be sure that the natural predator will only attack the pest organism and will not create other problems in the environment. The predator should be able to grow well and reproduce in the same conditions that favour the pest, so that the control is maintained from season to season. As well as using the natural predators of pests (for example ladybirds and hoverfly larvae eat aphids, and *Cactoblastis* larvae eat the prickly pear weed pest), insect diseases caused by fungi, bacteria and viruses have been used to protect crops. A fungus, *Verticillium sp.*, has been used to control aphids in glasshouses, and sawfly infestations of spruce trees have been prevented by infecting the insects with a virus, the nuclear polyhedrosis virus (NPV).

There are now many examples of the successful use of biological control, but each one has to be thoroughly researched to ensure that new problems are not being introduced. Such research is time-consuming and expensive, but the long-term effects are beneficial to the environment.

Biological control is not a quick solution to the pest problem, because the populations of predators take some time to build up and the damage to the crop might exceed the economic injury level before the predator is effective. It is also an unsuitable method if the crop is susceptible to a number of different pests, since eradication of a specific pest will leave its predator with no food. If this predator dies out or moves away, the crop is left unprotected should re-infection occur at a later date. Overall, the benefits outweigh the disadvantages and eventually biological control methods should prove less costly to the crop producer and more acceptable environmentally.

Other methods of controlling insect pests, which involve a knowledge of their biology, include the sterilisation of males, and the use of attractants, repellants, pheromones and insect hormones.

Male insects can be sterilised by exposing them to X-rays, gamma rays or chemicals, and then releasing them into a population where they will mate with normal females. This will result in a reduction in population numbers, provided that large numbers of males can be reared and that the sterilisation procedure does not affect the normal sexual behaviour of the male. It works for insects where mating only takes place once, and has been successful in reducing screw worm in cattle in the southern USA.

Repellants and attractants have proved successful in specific cases. The broadcasting of bat calls in orchards has been shown to drive moths away and the use of tarry discs around cabbage plants prevents the female cabbage root flies from laying their eggs. Unlikely though it may seem, foil strips between the rows of a crop induce aphids to fly upwards instead of landing. This method is time-consuming and expensive, but has been effective in controlling aphid-borne diseases of high-value crops such as flowers.

Control methods which involve the use of chemicals, attracting large numbers of insects to one place have proved much more effective. Many insects can detect very small quantities of chemicals in the environment and it is possible, using extracts from the females, to attract large numbers of males to a location where they can be killed by a pesticide or sterilised. Some of the chemical substances used in this way are the naturally-occuring *pheromones* which insects produce and which control their behaviour. Pheromones are highly species specific and are effective in small quantities, qualities which make them ideal for use in controlling pest populations.

No one method of control is 100% effective so the modern approach is to institute a pest management scheme, where suitable techniques and control measures are combined to keep the pest population at low levels. The pest is not eradicated, but numbers are kept below the economic damage threshold. This form of pest control is called *integrated pest management (IPM)*, and involves a good understanding of the biology of both the crops and its pests, working out the economic damage thresholds for the pests concerned and a knowledge of the physical factors of the environment, such as the climate and soil in the area. This type of pest management can involve regulations governing the time of planting of the crop, the time of harvesting and regular checks in between to estimate the number of beneficial organisms as well as the number of pests. Use has been made of computers in putting all the information together and then devising programmes of management.

PLANTS FOR FOOD

CHAPTER 4

Supermarkets and shops throughout the developed world display a fascinating range of botanical specimens (imported out-of-season) and exotic fruits and vegetables. Developing countries import little expensive plant food but often markets have their own fascinating range of botanical specimens.

Food obtained from plants makes a significant contribution, directly or indirectly, to the diet of human beings. In the affluent developed countries, people have access to a wide range of both plant and animal foods, leading to a varied and potentially healthy diet. However, in the developing countries the diet is more restricted and is often based on one major food, referred to as the staple. Agriculture, in both the developed and developing countries, produces plant crops, but in the latter most of these are eaten by people, with little being fed to animals. So, diets tend to be high in carbohydrate, with little protein and fat. In the developed countries, the situation is reversed and more of the plant crops, especially cereals, are fed to domestic animals, which provide good sources of protein in dairy produce and meat.

About half of all the land available for growing crops is used to produce cereals, which are the staple foods in most human diets. Cereal grains, if stored under the right conditions, will keep for a number of years without deteriorating. There are many different species of cereals, each having a large number of varieties, so they are adapted to many habitats and have a worldwide distribution. Wheat, maize and rice account for 75% of the world grain production tonnage, the remaining 25% being made up of oats, millet and sorghum. Non-cereal staples such as potatoes, yams and legumes have a much more restricted distribution as they are not suited to all climates.

Usually only one part of the crop plant is harvested for food: it may be the leaves (cabbages and lettuce), the stem (sugar cane), the root (carrot and turnip), the fruits (apples, tomatoes) or seeds (peas and beans). The distinction between 'fruits' and 'vegetables' has no scientific basis, as many of the so-called vegetables, such as tomatoes and

Supermarket shelves

marrows, are fruits, produced as a result of fertilisation. We have to be careful with the term 'root' vegetable as well, as this has been used incorrectly to describe potatoes, which are *stem* tubers.

Most of the crop plants, with the exception of the leafy brassicas and lettuces, exploit the food stores and storage organs linked with the reproductive processes of the plants. Seeds, such as peas and beans, and the cereal grains, which are one-seeded fruits, have large stores of carbohydrates. These are produced by the photosynthetic activities of the plant for the use of the embryo during germination. Many of the soft fruits, such as raspberries, blackberries and strawberries are sweet and juicy, characteristics which evolved to attract animals to eat them and so disperse the seeds a long way from the parent plant.

The starch stored in the potato tubers is laid down in one season to provide food for the growth of the new shoots in the following season, and the food stored in the carrot roots enables rapid growth in the second year when flowering takes place prior to seed production. Humans have selected the desirable characteristics of food plants over many centuries of cultivation, and the varieties we grow today are very different from their immediate ancestors and their wild relatives. Crab apples are small and very sour compared to a Cox's Orange Pippin or a Bramley's seedling. Through selective breeding, the quality and yield of the plant product has gradually improved, though it is a pity that we do not always find a wide range of varieties available in the shops. Large-scale commercial production of food plants tends to concentrate on a few well-known varieties, but reference to seed catalogues and gardening books indicates that a much wider range of varieties is available. It is important to maintain this range in order to provide the genetic material from which new varieties can be derived to meet future economic and social needs. Should the gene pool become too small, then the whole species could become extinct if it is unable to adapt to changing conditions or develop resistance to a pest.

■ CEREALS

Cereals are the most important crop plants, with about 1800 million tonnes of grain being produced worldwide each year. The cereals and the grasses belong to the plant family Graminae. The distinction between 'cereals' and 'grasses' is that the former are grown for their grains, while the latter are grown for their leaves (or foliage), which are eaten by animals or used to make hay and silage. The Graminae are monocotyledons (i.e. they have long, narrow leaves with parallel veins and produce one-seeded fruits, the grains). The Graminae have the ability to grow quickly by producing a number of axillary (side) shoots, or tillers, in quick succession. The flowers are adapted to wind pollination, lacking scent, nectar, petals and sepals, but producing large quantities of light pollen from large anthers and possessing long, feathery stigmas. In temperate regions, flower formation is triggered off by increase in day length, although some species need a cold period first. Winter sown cereals need to be subjected to cold temperatures before increasing day lengths in order to flower, whereas the varieties which are sown in the spring do not have this requirement.

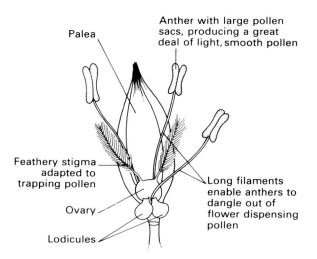

Fig.4.1 Typical grass flower showing adaptations for wind pollination

The flowers are grouped together in an *inflorescence* (see Fig.4.1). Most cereal flowers are hermaphrodite, i.e. containing both male and female reproductive structures, but maize has separate male and female flowers on the same plant (*monoecious*). The one-seeded fruit formed after fertilisation is often called a grain or a seed (botanically termed a caryopsis), in which the seed coat (testa) and the ovary wall (pericarp) have fused during development, see Fig.4.2.

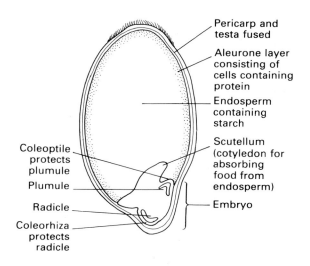

Fig.4.2 Section through a wheat grain (seed)

Harvesting the grain involves first cutting off the stalks at ground level and then separating the grain from the rest of the plant. At first, this was done in two separate operations, but modern combine harvesters can perform both operations at the same time, saving time and manpower.

The members of the Graminae which produce cereal grains are grown as annuals, completing their life cycle in one growing season. The grasses grown in pasture are grazed and persist from year to year. Grazing removes the stem apices, so that flowering is prevented, and the grasses produce many tillers. These spread and enable the plants to perennate, i.e. to persist from year to year.

■ Wheat (*Triticum spp.*)

Wheat is grown extensively in temperate climates, where there is a definite cold season, and about 500 million tonnes are produced annually. Wheat will grow at high altitudes in the tropics and thrives in areas which are either too dry or too cold for rice and maize.

Wheat requires:
• up to 750 mm annual rainfall;
• cool temperatures for germination and early growth;
• bright summers for harvest.

It does not grow well in tropical climates because it is a C3 plant and, when temperatures are high, photorespiration occurs and can exceed photosynthesis, resulting in a decrease in yield (see page 7 and *Biology Advanced Studies - Biochemistry*).

In the UK, wheat is grown mainly in the south, where there is usually less rain and more sunshine than in the north. It is an important staple food for more than a third of the world's population. Nutritionally, wheat contains a high proportion of the essential nutrients in the human diet. It has a low water content, is easy to store and transport, and it can be processed without difficulty. Production has gradually increased due to the use of fertilisers and as better varieties have been developed.

It is probable that wheat was the first plant to be grown by humans for food, and its history can be traced back some 10 000 years. It is thought to have originated in or around Iraq, its cultivation spreading to Europe and then to North America and other parts of the world. Three different groups of wheats with different chromosome numbers are now recognised by taxonomists.

Diploid wheats, with a chromosome number of 14, include wild 'einkorn' (*Triticum monococcum*) believed to be an ancestor of the modern hexaploid species. Cultivated 'einkorn' is a low-yielding species of wheat, still found growing as a crop in Turkey and parts of Europe. If *T. monococcum* is hybridised with a diploid goat grass of the genus *Aegilops*, it gives rise, after chromosome doubling, to the *tetraploid* group with a chromosome number of 28.

Tetraploid wheats, with a chromosome number of 28, include several domesticated forms, which are still grown in the Balkans, Northeast India and Ethiopia. They are referred to as 'emmer' wheats (Fig.4.4), and were important for bread and beer making. They became more common than the einkorns and spread to other regions. The wild emmer and some of the cultivated forms have covered, or hulled, grains, but the durum wheat, *Triticum turgidum* var. *durum*, has naked grains which, when threshed, are free from the bracts of the flower, or the chaff.

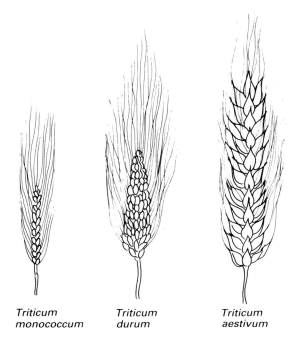

Triticum monococcum Triticum durum Triticum aestivum

Fig.4.3 Different types of wheat

Hexaploid wheats, with a chromosome number of 42, have arisen by hybridisation between emmer wheat and another goat grass, *Aegilops squarrosa*, followed by chromosome doubling (see Fig.4.4). This group includes varieties with hulled grains such as spelt, which used to be the main wheat grown in Europe, and the bread wheat, *Triticum aestivum*, which has naked grains.

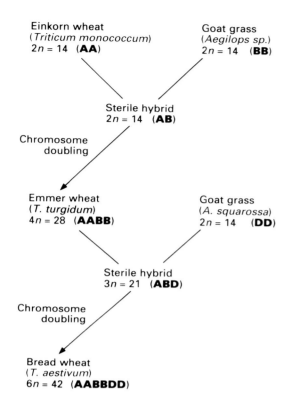

Einkorn wheat
(*Triticum monococcum*)
2n = 14 (**AA**)

Goat grass
(*Aegilops sp.*)
2n = 14 (**BB**)

Sterile hybrid
2n = 14 (**AB**)

Chromosome
doubling

Emmer wheat
(*T. turgidum*)
4n = 28 (**AABB**)

Goat grass
(*A. squarossa*)
2n = 14 (**DD**)

Sterile hybrid
3n = 21 (**ABD**)

Chromosome
doubling

Bread wheat
(*T. aestivum*)
6n = 42 (**AABBDD**)

Fig.4.4 Diagram to show the development of hexaploid wheat

■ Modern wheat

Modern wheats are hexaploid (i.e. the chromosome number is 6n) and are varieties of *Triticum aestivum* var. *aestivum* which are valued for their high gluten content. Gluten is a complex of proteins which during breadmaking produces sticky dough, so that the bubbles of carbon dioxide formed during the fermentation of the yeast are trapped and retained, allowing the dough to rise and resulting in bread with a spongy texture. Breadmaking wheats are referred to as 'hard' and 'strong', which means they produce a coarse, gritty flour with a high protein content. These two characteristics are genetically determined, but are usually found together.

The best breadmaking wheats are grown in North America and Russia, where there is limited rainfall and the summers are hot. 'Soft' wheats produce a finer flour with a lower protein content, and are used for animal feeds, biscuit making and in confectionery. Climatic conditions in the UK favour the growth of the 'soft' wheats and breadmaking wheat has to be imported (usually from Canada). Recent advances in breadmaking technology have

enabled bakers to use more flour with a lower protein content, so there is less need for imported 'strong' wheat. Plant breeders are also trying to develop more suitable varieties of bread wheat for growing in the UK. If Vitamin C (ascorbic acid) is added to the dough, the gluten in the flour becomes more elastic and this means a reduction in the time needed for the rising process.

A modern tetraploid (4n) wheat, grown in the Mediterranean region and in India, is durum wheat, *Triticum turgidum* var. *durum*. It produces flour with a low gluten content and is used to make macaroni and other types of pasta.

Nowadays, wheat is more widely used than any other cereal for breadmaking, but the early varieties were unsuitable because of their lower gluten content, and were probably used to make a sort of porridge. The grains were ground up, or milled, between large round stones, called millstones, the chaff was removed and then the resulting grist was cooked. Some was also fermented to make a kind of beer, by mixing it with wild strains of yeast.

The hexaploid wheats are more suitable for making bread, because they have a higher gluten content, thought to come from the D genome via hybridisation of the emmer wheats with the goat grass. The grains have to be milled very finely to produce flour, and modern milling processes are able to produce white flour, bran and wheatgerm, as well as wholemeal flour (Fig.4.5).

Bleach is sometimes used to whiten the flour and chemicals are often added to improve its keeping and baking properties.

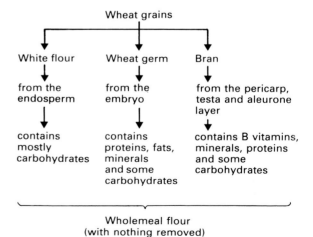

Fig.4.5 Milled products of bread wheat

Q Why is white flour a less nutritious product than wholemeal flour?

The cultivation of wheat during the last thirty years has been influenced by the introduction of shorter-stemmed, or semi-dwarf, varieties which grow well and produce higher yields of grain. In these varieties, a greater proportion of the total biomass is grain and less is straw, giving an increase in the harvest index (the ratio of grain mass to total biomass) from 0.35 to 0.50. Using these varieties, farmers can increase their yields by the application of more fertiliser, without the risk of the stems falling over, or lodging. Increases in wheat yield are also due to improved farming techniques, such as the use of combine harvesters, and to better weed control. Research has indicated that, if further increases are to occur, then there needs to be an overall increase in plant biomass, i.e. the plants need to photosynthesise more efficiently. This would result in the selection of varieties that have a higher photosynthetic rate per unit leaf area, or plants with a slightly different structure that would allow more light through to the lower leaves.

Loss in yield can be due to diseases spreading through a crop (Table 4.1). Monocultures (i.e. only one crop planted over a large area) provide ideal conditions for the rapid spread of a disease, which can cause the loss of a whole crop. Disease resistance, particularly to stem rust fungus and powdery mildews, is important when selecting varieties to grow, but there are numerous strains of the *pathogens* (disease agents), which can change through hybridisation and mutation. For some time, crop producers have been encouraged to make use of the highly specific systemic fungicides available to them, rather than depend on the production of new disease-resistant varieties. Concern for the development of strains of pathogens which are tolerant to the fungicides, together with the environmental considerations of using potentially toxic chemicals, has led to a renewed interest in breeding for disease resistance using some of the older varieties of wheat.

It has been shown experimentally that the rate of buildup of disease in a crop is much less if a mixture of varieties is sown rather than a pure stand, but this is not always very practical on a large scale. In the UK, there is legislation ensuring that seeds sold to crop producers are pure: it would be impractical to grow together varieties which are very different in height as this would make harvesting difficult.

Name of disease	Organism causing disease	Effect on wheat plants
Wheat bunt, or stinking smut disease (plants have an odour of bad fish)	Smut fungus, *Tilletia caries*	Infects seedlings; affects grains, which become filled with smut spores
Black stem rust	Rust fungus, *Puccinia graminis*	Black spore masses on stems
Yellow rust, or stripe rust	Rust fungus, *Puccinia striiformis*	Yellow pustules on mature leaves
Damping-off disease	*Fusarium avanaceum* and other *Fusarium spp.*	Affects seedlings; causes them to flop
Powdery mildew	Powdery mildew fungus *Erysiphe graminis*	Superficial mycelium and spores all over stem and leaves
Wheat streak mosaic, or yellow mosaic	Caused by a virus transmitted by the leaf curl mite, *Aceria tulipae*	Causes yellow streaks on leaves
Wheat scab	*Gibberella zeae*	Infects head and grains; spores then contaminate the seed

Table 4.1 Some diseases of wheat crops

■ Rice (*Oryza sativa*)

Rice is grown in the tropics, where consistent short day conditions initiate flowering in most varieties. Other requirements for successful growth are:
- a minimum temperature of 20 °C throughout the growing period;
- prolonged sunshine for good growth and rapid maturing;
- a constant supply of fresh water for irrigation;
- slightly acid soil conditions.

Most rice is grown at low altitudes in flooded fields, called paddy fields, under 5 to 10 cm of water, but about 10% is grown at higher altitudes, with no extra irrigation, in regions of high rainfall. The yields of crops grown at higher altitudes are lower than for those grown in the paddy fields.

Rice growing in paddy fields (Yunnan, SW China)

Rice is the second most important food crop in terms of area grown and amount of grain produced (450 million tonnes annually). It is the principal food crop in that it is the staple diet of about half of the world's population. The greatest production is in China, where one third of the world's total crop is grown. Other countries in Asia and South America produce large amounts of rice and, in fact, 95% is grown in less developed countries. Some rice is grown in Europe, around the Rhone delta in the Camargue region of France, and in the USA, where the cultivation is more highly mechanised than in Asia. Most of the rice grown in the world is consumed directly by humans. It requires very little postharvest treatment, needing only to be de-hulled and boiled before being eaten. In the humid and sub-humid tropics of Asia, rice is the primary source of human energy for over 90% of the population. It therefore comes as no surprise to discover that only 5% of the total global output enters world trade. Most rice is consumed where it is grown.

In the most favourable growing conditions in the tropics, a rice crop is ready to be harvested about five months after planting, so it is possible to grow more than one crop per year. It is a partial *hydrophyte*, growing best with its roots submerged in water. In its roots and stems, there is special tissue with large intercellular air spaces called *aerenchyma*, which enables the diffusion of oxygen and carbon dioxide between the root cells and the atmosphere (Fig.4.6).

Fig.4.6 Rice plant

Rice is an annual plant, which grows to a height of 80 to 150 cm, with an inflorescence consisting of about a hundred single-flowered spikelets. The seeds are sown in seed beds and after germination the young seedlings are transplanted into the flooded fields by hand. The flowers are self-pollinating and the grains are ready for harvesting from 20 to 40 days after pollination. Ripening can take place if the fields remain flooded during this period, but in most cases, where the water supply can be controlled, the paddy fields are drained about 10 days before harvesting.

After harvesting, the hulls or husks, which are the remains of the lemma and palea of the flower, are removed by threshing and winnowing, leaving the whole kernels known as *brown rice*. In the developing countries, most of the rice is then cooked and eaten in this state, but in the developed world, the grains undergo further processing in which the pericarp, testa and aleurone layer are removed, leaving just the endosperm, which is then polished, giving *white rice*. This treatment to produce white rice removes valuable vitamins and minerals as well as some protein, so the nutritional value of brown rice is much greater than that of white, which lacks vitamin B_1, or thiamine, a deficiency of which causes beri-beri in humans.

Rice has been used to make beers and wines, such as sake, the national alcoholic beverage of Japan. Starch can be extracted from rice and rice powder is used in the cosmetics industry in the East. The hulls or husks are used for fuel, and the rice straw is woven into mats and baskets. The paddy fields are sometimes used for fish farming, as they can be stocked with young fish which will eat the weeds and insects. In these fields, rice yields are increased by about 6%, and the fish can be harvested as a second profitable crop.

Rice originated in India and Southwest Asia, where several wild species can still be found. Archaeological evidence suggests that the culture of rice began in India and China about 5000 BC, cultivation spreading to Japan by 200 BC. Rice was known in Europe around this time, as it had been brought by Arab traders. It was introduced into South America by the Portuguese and the Spanish in the 16th and 17th centuries, and into North America by the French, being grown first in North and South Carolina. Nowadays, California and Texas are the major growing areas and most of the crop is exported. Cultivation in Asia is still carried out using traditional, labour-intensive methods, the paddy fields being prepared for planting using ploughs drawn by buffalo or oxen and the seedlings transplanted by hand. Harvesting is carried out with sickles and knives, and the threshing and winnowing of the grain is usually done by women. In the USA, the whole process is more mechanised, with even the planting of the seed being carried out by aeroplanes.

There are thousands of varieties of rice divided into three groups or races (originally thought to be subspecies):

- *japonica* - short, rounded grains, about 5 mm long; grains go sticky when cooked; grown mainly in Japan and Taiwan; adapted to cooler conditions;
- *indica* - long, slender, flat grains, about 7 mm long; remain drier when cooked; grown mainly in Southeast Asia; adapted to tropical regions;
- *javanica* - fairly large grains; tall plants usually day neutral; grown in Asia but not as widespread as the other two.

The population in rice-consuming countries is still growing by 2% each year. It is important to increase rice yield, mainly by the use of new F_1 hybrids. Fertilisers have been used to improve yields, but the same problems have been encountered with rice as with wheat; the taller varieties tended to lodge more readily as the grain yields increase. This has led to the development of shorter-stemmed varieties, with an increase in harvest index. Other features which are being developed are a shorter dormancy period of the grains, larger grains, larger plants and insensitivity to the daylength.

Resistance to diseases is also important, as the rice plants are affected by a number of fungal, bacterial and viral diseases. Insect pests of rice crops include plant hoppers (especially the brown plant hopper which transmits viral diseases), and stem borers. Pesticides have been used widely to control the insect pests, but these have proved toxic to the fish populations in the paddy fields. A major consideration for the future is the development of varieties that will produce a greater yield in the poor growing conditions which exist where half the world's rice is grown. It may be necessary to persuade the farmers to try new varieties instead of continuing to use the traditional types to which they have become accustomed, but which are not very high-yielding. In fact, one new virus resistant variety is being grown on over 12 million hectares.

■ Maize (*Zea mays*)

Maize is a short-day, C4 plant which grows in warm temperate and subtropical regions. It requires:
- frost-free conditions;
- a minimum temperature of 9-10 °C for germination and growth;
- moisture at the time of pollination;
- prolonged sunshine and high temperatures for high yields of grain.

Maize is the third most important cereal crop in the world. The USA produces almost half the total

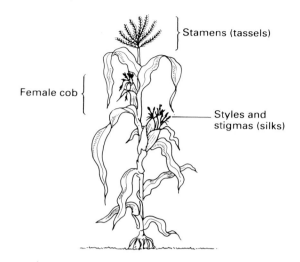

Fig.4.7 Maize plant

world tonnage of maize, and it is also grown extensively in Central and South America, where it is an important food plant. Originally, maize was grown exclusively for human consumption, but the grains are hard and need to be treated in some way before being eaten. In America, it was made into hominy by washing in wood ashes and quicklime, ground up to a coarse flour for making tortillas, boiled or eaten green. The American Indians ferment the grains to make a beer, or chicha, and it is used to make bourbon whiskey. Maize is called 'corn' in the USA and sweet corn, popcorn, cornflakes, corn syrup and cornflour are all products commercially derived from it. The term 'corn' in the UK refers to all cereals, so a cornfield could be a field of maize, wheat, rye, oats or barley.

When grown in the UK, maize has a short growing season because of the danger of frost, so the ears do not have time to ripen completely and contain soft, immature grains. Some of the crop is used for human consumption, but the majority is chopped up and made into animal feed and silage.

Nutritionally, maize resembles the other cereals, consisting mainly of carbohydrates with some 10% protein. It is low in the essential amino acids lysine and tryptophane, and lacks vitamin B_3 (nicotinic acid). A deficiency of this vitamin results in a condition known as pellagra, which is common among people with poor diets, who depend on maize as their staple food. Recent research has concentrated on using genetic engineering techniques to improve the nutritional value by increasing the lysine and tryptophane content.

Maize is different from most other cereals in that it bears separate male and female inflorescences. The male inflorescence is borne at the top of the plant and consists of a number of *tassels*, bearing large numbers of individual florets. Each floret has the typical structure common to the Graminae, except that there are no carpels present. Female inflorescences are referred to as *cobs* and occur in the axils of leaves lower down the stem. The florets lack male parts and the styles become very elongated during development. Large numbers of these styles protrude through the leaves surrounding the cob and are called the *silks*. Typically, the cobs have 8 to 24 rows of kernels with up to 50 kernels in each row. The pollen is windborne to the silks and after pollination and fertilisation, the silks shrivel and each ovary enlarges to become a maize grain, which is a one-seeded fruit, or *caryopsis*. When grown in hot climates, the grains ripen but remain attached to the axis of the cob, surrounded by the dry leaves, so natural seed dispersal cannot occur.

Most of the commercially grown maize is either yellow or white, but the maize cultivated by the American Indians has highly coloured grains with a floury texture.

Maize has been cultivated in the Americas for thousands of years, and was a well-established crop at the time Columbus found it growing in Cuba. However, the great Corn Belt of the USA did not come into existence until the mouldboard plough, capable of turning over the heavy prairie soils, was invented.

It is known that maize originated in Mexico, but its ancestors are unknown. All the known varieties are diploid, with a chromosome number $2n = 20$. There was little attempt to breed different varieties of maize until the mid-1800s when maize growers in the USA began to show their products at fairs and exhibitions.

At the end of the 19th century, attention had been drawn to the fact that crosses between two closely related varieties could result in increased yields, so attempts were made to improve maize yields by carrying out breeding experiments. A double crossing procedure was developed, which resulted in the production of very high yielding hybrids. When maize plants are self-pollinated, each generation becomes weaker, but when two inbred varieties are crossed, vigour is restored and the yield increases. Controlled crossings are possible because the male inflorescences can be removed from selected plants, before pollination has occurred.

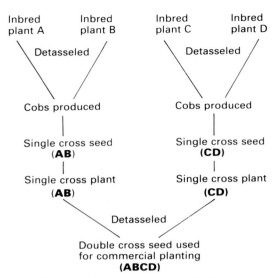

Inbred plant A Inbred plant B   Inbred plant C Inbred plant D

Detasseled   Detasseled

Cobs produced   Cobs produced

Single cross seed   Single cross seed
(**AB**)   (**CD**)

Single cross plant   Single cross plant
(**AB**)   (**CD**)

Detasseled

Double cross seed used
for commercial planting
(**ABCD**)

Fig.4.8 Diagram to show double crossing of maize

Double crossing (Fig.4.8) involves four inbred varieties: inbred A is crossed with inbred B, resulting in hybrid AB, which is crossed with hybrid CD, derived from a cross between hybrid C and hybrid D. The hybrids AB and CD show some hybrid vigour, but do not produce large quantities of seeds. The plants resulting from the AB and CD cross do produce large quantities, capable of growing into vigorous plants.

These double-crossed varieties were used in the USA until better selection of inbred plants made the double-crossing procedure unnecessary, and today nearly all the maize grown comes from single crosses. Special characteristics, such as tolerance to drought and resistance to disease, together with features such as the number of ears on the plants and the stiffness of the stalks, can be selected for, and varieties have been developed which are adapted to cultivation in different climatic zones. However, if high yields are to be maintained, the farmer must buy new seed each year, as seeds saved from one year's crop would give too much variety if planted the following year, i.e. hybrid plants do not breed true.

 Explain why hybrid plants do not breed true.

Maize has many uses in the developed countries. In addition to its inclusion in the diet as a vegetable and in products such as cornflakes and cornflour, much of the starch is now converted into syrups and sugars used in the food industry. Oil extracted

from the embryo, or germ, is used in cooking, salad dressings and in the manufacture of margarine. The glutens can be extracted and used in animal feeds and in the manufacture of plastics.

■ OTHER IMPORTANT CEREAL CROPS

■ Sorghum (*Sorghum vulgare*)
Sorghum is a short-day, C4 plant, adapted to grow well in dry areas where there are high temperatures. It can tolerate drought conditions better than most cereals, so it is grown in areas that would not support crops like maize. It is used for human food in China and a number of African countries. The grain and the foliage are important for animal feed.

■ Millet (*Setaria, Pennisetum* and *Panicum* spp.)
Millet is also a C4 plant and has a similar range to sorghum, but is even more drought tolerant. The grain is ground up and used to make cakes or porridge. Millet does not enter into world trade, but is an important source of food.

■ Rye (*Secale cereale*)
Rye grows in temperate regions, but is more hardy than wheat, so it can be grown further north and it will give a good yield on poor soils. It is the only other temperate cereal which has a use in bread making, although nowadays more of it is used to make crispbreads and in the distillation of rye whisky. Rye will hybridise with wheat to give *Triticale*, which combines the hardiness and greater lysine content of rye with the grain quality of wheat.

■ Barley (*Hordeum vulgaris*)
Barley was one of the earliest crops to be domesticated in the Near East, and was standard fare for Roman soldiers, serfs and slaves. It is a major cereal in the UK, with the same range as wheat. Its major uses are for malting and brewing, and for feeding cattle. Barley used for brewing beer and making malt whisky needs a high carbohydrate content but should be low in protein. The use of nitrogenous fertilisers to improve yields could result in too high a protein content, giving cloudiness in the beer, and consequent rejection by the maltsters. The grain would then have to be sold for less profit as animal feed. By contrast, in grain whisky manufacture, where a high proportion of maize may be used, the barley enzymes are used to break down the starch, so a high protein content is desirable.

■ Oats (*Avena* spp.)

Oats grow well in moist temperate climates and good yields are achieved on poor soils. Most of the crop is used for feeding animals; only a small proportion is eaten directly by humans as porridge and breakfast cereals. Oat straw provides valuable roughage for cattle.

■ STEMS

The main functions of stems are:
- to support the leaves in a suitable position for photosynthesis;
- to allow conduction of water and mineral ions to the leaves;
- to transport the products of photosynthesis to other parts of the plant;
- to hold the flowers in a suitable position for pollination.

If stems are green, they may photosynthesise, and all stems store some food substances. Some become modified as storage organs, accumulating large reserves of carbohydrates, often in the form of starch, which are used in the following growing season and enable the buds to grow rapidly producing leaves and flowers. These food stores can be exploited by humans, with the added advantage that the food plant can be vegetatively propagated, thus maintaining desirable characteristics. Two stems are extensively grown to provide food for humans: sugar cane for its sucrose, and the potato for its starch content.

■ Sugar cane (*Saccharum* spp.)

Sugar cane is a large perennial grass, belonging to the Graminae, which grows to a height of between 1 and 3 m. The stems are 25 to 40 mm in diameter, unbranched and divided into annular joints. The leaves are 1 or 1.5 m long, straight, flat and pointed. The stems contain a central, fibrous pith, which is white and spongy, containing the sugar-rich sap.

Sugar cane is a C4 plant which has a 3% efficiency at converting light energy to chemical energy, compared with 0.5% efficiency shown by most plants. It is thought to have originated in the tropics. Primitive people chewed the stems to extract the sweet juices, so the oldest cultivated species were selected for their sugar content and the softness of their stems.

Sugar cane plants

Sugar cane can grow in a variety of soil types but needs:
- a long, warm growing season so that the canes can increase in size rapidly;
- a cooler, drier ripening period, when vegetative growth rate slows and sugar accumulates;
- a rainfall of 150 cm per year.

Sugar cane is grown as far north as southern Spain and south to the northern part of Australia. The highest yields are in the tropical regions, where the growing season is the longest, but in the extremes of its range the growing season may only be nine months. The major cane-producing areas of the world are the Caribbean, India and Brazil. During the eighteenth and nineteenth centuries, the cultivation of sugar cane spread through all the tropical areas of the world as they were colonised by Europeans. Traditionally, the cultivation, harvesting and extraction of the sugar were all carried out on the plantations by hand, workers or slaves being imported to do the work, but nowadays mechanical harvesters are often used.

Sugar cane deteriorates very rapidly after it has been cut, so the processing has to take place soon after harvesting. The cut canes are first washed to get rid of the soil and then crushed between rollers to extract the juice. The juice is purified and concentrated by evaporation, then boiled. Crystallisation occurs and the raw brown sugar can be separated from the molasses. At this stage, the sugar is usually exported and refined in the importing country. The brown colour of the raw, unrefined sugar is due to oxidation and is similar to the browning of apples on exposure to air.

Most cultivated varieties are derived from *Saccharum officinarum*, the 'noble cane', which has a chromosome number of 80. Of several other species found in Borneo and the New Hebrides, *Saccharum robustum* is of interest as it is considered to be the ancestral form. Another widespread species, *S. spontaneum*, has a chromosome number which varies from 40 to 128 and is resistant to the mosaic virus.

Sugar cane is usually propagated by stem cuttings, and the breeding of new varieties is not easy because flowering, which causes the plant to stop growing, is not encouraged and has been selected against. Most varieties need long days before they will flower, so breeding programmes have to be carried out in controlled light conditions. Once the cross has been achieved, thousands of tiny plants are grown from which the selection is made. Root growth in the cuttings may be encouraged by using a synthetic growth hormone, NAA (naphthalene acetic acid). Plants are bred for resistance to disease, for high sugar content and for erect stems.

■ Potatoes (*Solanum tuberosum*)

The potato is a herbaceous perennial, which is widely grown in cool, temperate climates, particularly in areas where cereals do not grow well. In the UK, the plants are described as half-hardy, as the young leaves can be damaged by late frosts in spring and the stems are destroyed by the first frosts of autumn. Growth is best in areas where there is a mean summer temperature of about 20°C. *Solanum tuberosum* is an outbreeder, so sexual reproduction results in considerable variation. Potatoes are propagated vegetatively, choosing small 'seed' potatoes, or pieces of larger tubers containing at least one axillary bud, which will grow into a new plant using the food stored in the tuber (see Fig.4.9). Thus favourable characteristics can be maintained as there is no variation.

The tubers, which are modified underground stems, contain large amounts of carbohydrate, between 17 and 34%, but usually only about 1 to 3% protein, although some varieties may contain as

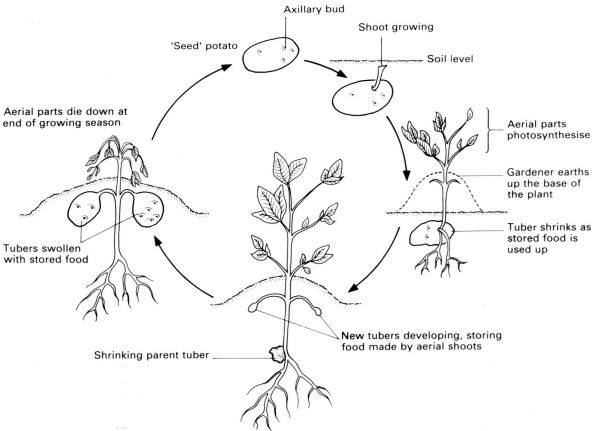

Fig.4.9 Diagram of the asexual reproductive cycle of the potato

much as 7%. Potatoes contain less protein than cereals, but the yield of carbohydrate per acre is double that of rice or wheat, and is an important energy source in many diets. 300 million tonnes of potatoes are grown annually worldwide, with Russia producing 40% of this total. Other major producers are India, China and the USA. In addition to large amounts consumed by humans in a variety of products, potatoes are used to feed animals, for the production of starch and in the production of alcohol.

Potatoes were first cultivated about 4000 years ago in Peru, at altitudes above 11 000 feet where maize would not grow. Wild tubers are bitter and toxic, due to the presence of alkaloids, so early selection would have been for the less bitter varieties, as well as for increased size. Potatoes were introduced into Europe around 1570, but did not become popular until the eighteenth century. The early varieties were not very productive and people were suspicious of their resemblance to the more poisonous members of the same family, the Solanaceae, e.g. deadly nightshade. By the nineteenth century, the potato was the dominant staple food for the Irish peasants, so the devastation of the crop in the 1840s by the potato blight fungus, *Phytophthora infestans*, was serious (Fig.4.10). About 1.5 million people died of starvation and a further million emigrated, mostly to the Americas.

Losses caused by the potato blight fungus can be reduced by selecting disease-resistant varieties of potatoes or by spraying with the appropriate fungicides. Neither eradicates the disease, because new strains of the fungus develop which can infect resistant varieties and others become resistant to the fungicide. Most farmers will use a combination of methods, together with good farming practices discussed in the previous chapter. In the UK, warnings are issued to farmers during the potato growing season, when weather conditions are favourable for the formation and dispersal of the fungal spores. So if the temperature is above 12.8 °C and the relative humidity is 75% for two days, the farmer is advised to spray the potato crop with fungicide. In areas prone to the disease, regular spraying is undertaken from mid-July.

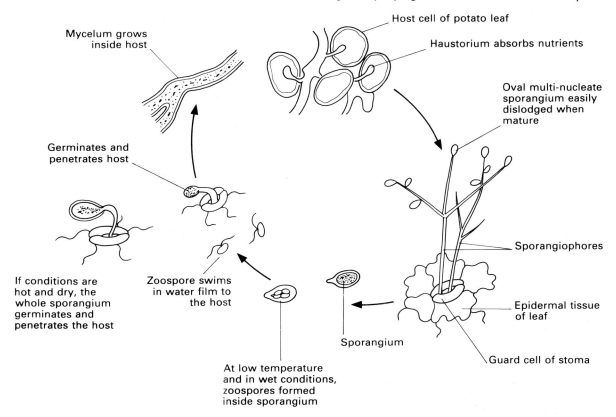

Fig.4.10 Diagram of the asexual reproductive cycle of *Phytophthora infestans*

Another serious pest of potato crops is the potato root eelworm, *Heterodera rostochiensis*. This nematode forms cysts which can remain viable in the soil for many years. The cysts consist of spherical females swollen with eggs, each of which contains an eelworm larva protected by an egg shell. If there are no potatoes in the soil, only a few larvae emerge each year, but if potatoes are being grown, a substance produced by the roots of the plants stimulates the hatching of large numbers of the larvae, so the crop is affected. Crop rotations involving a three or four year cycle are ineffective in getting rid of the larvae, so other means of eradication are necessary. *Nematocides*, special chemicals which have been developed to kill off the larvae, can be used on the soil, or a resistant variety of potato, such as Maris Piper, can be grown. Neither of these methods is particularly successful, especially as Maris Piper is only resistant to one strain of *Heterodera*, so the farmer is advised to grow a different crop on the land for at least seven or eight years.

The potato that was introduced into Europe in the sixteenth century, *Solanum tuberosum* var. *andigenum*, was badly affected by the potato blight, so potatoes from Chile were introduced in the late nineteenth century, and the varieties with which we are familiar today come from hybrids of *Solanum tuberosum* var. *tuberosum* with other species of *Solanum*, and are all tetraploids. The original South American species are short-day plants, producing their tubers very late in the long days of the European north temperate summer climate. Some varieties have been selected for their 'earliness', giving high yields of tubers in early or mid-summer. Crops are harvested early in some areas in the UK (e.g. Cornwall, Jersey) to obtain a higher price for a smaller yield.

The only other stem crop of major importance is the *yam* (*Dioscorea* spp.), which produces very large tubers. The crop grows best in humid areas in the tropics and the greatest production is in West Africa, where it is usually grown by farmers for their own use. Yams are also grown in quantity in the Caribbean. In the 1940s, some steroids used in the treatment of asthma, arthritis and skin conditions were extracted from yams, and in 1956 a drug derived indirectly from the plant tissue was found to prevent ovulation. This research led to the development of an oral contraceptive pill.

■ ROOTS

The main functions of roots are to provide anchorage for the plant and to absorb water and mineral ions from the soil. In addition, the products of photosynthesis are transported to the cortical tissues and stored. In some cases, large quantities of food are stored and the root swells up, forming a storage organ. Many of the roots eaten by humans are from biennial plants, such as the carrot, where vegetative growth takes place in the first growing season, and food is stored, to be used to produce flowering stems the following year.

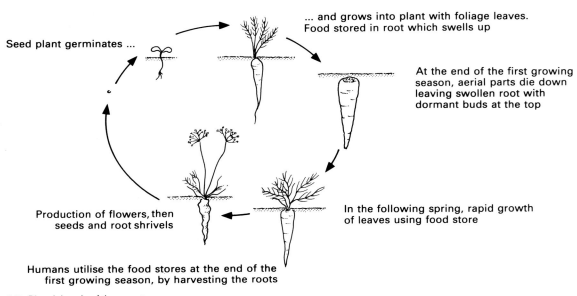

Seed plant germinates ...

... and grows into plant with foliage leaves. Food stored in root which swells up

At the end of the first growing season, aerial parts die down leaving swollen root with dormant buds at the top

In the following spring, rapid growth of leaves using food store

Production of flowers, then seeds and root shrivels

Humans utilise the food stores at the end of the first growing season, by harvesting the roots

Fig.4.11 Biennial cycle of the carrot

■ Sugar beet (*Beta vulgaris*)

Sugar beet is a biennial plant grown in temperate climates for the sucrose stored in its enlarged tap root. Beets have been in use since prehistoric times: the leaves have been used as pot herbs, Aristotle mentioned red chards and the Romans used sea beets as fodder for their animals in the winter. Red beet, or beetroot, was first mentioned as a vegetable in England in the fourteenth century, but it was not until the eighteenth century that the presence of the sugar sap in the roots was recorded. The first processing plant for the extraction and purification of the juice was built in Silesia in 1801, and sugar beet production is now a major industry in Europe, accounting for nearly half the total world production of sugar. Most of the crop is grown in Russia, the USA and Europe, but it can be produced in sub-tropical regions under irrigation. Perhaps the industry owes much to Napoleon, who encouraged its development in France, because the British disrupted the French imports of sugar cane from the West Indies. Beet sugar production is now entirely mechanised, whereas much of the production of sugar cane is still done by hand.

Selection of varieties of beet with higher sugar percentages began in the nineteenth century in France and Germany. Tetraploids were developed, but the diploid varieties seemed more successful. More recently triploid varieties have been developed, and these are widely grown in Europe. In beets, the fruits which develop from flowers are sown as 'seed' by the farmers. In monogerm plants, only one flower develops at each node, giving rise to a single-seeded fruit, but in the multigerm varieties the aggregate fruits have many seeds. The planting of monogerm varieties with mechanised seed drills, spacing the seeds the correct distance apart, does away with the need to thin out by hand the seedlings resulting from germination of the multigerm types and means that the whole cultivation procedure can be mechanised.

The original varieties of sugar beet were biennials, but if they are grown in northern areas, the increase in daylength and the cooler temperatures cause the initiation of flowering in the first season. This is described as *bolting* and the resulting plants have smaller, woody roots with a lower sugar content than non-bolters.

Extraction of the sugar from the bolters is more costly, because the yield is lower and because of the wear and tear on the machinery. Varieties have been selected for their resistance to bolting, enabling beet to be grown further north and to be planted earlier, thus producing bigger yields from a longer growing season. Sugar beet is susceptible to the curly top virus, transmitted by leaf hoppers, and to yellowing viruses transmitted by aphids. Resistant varieties have been produced with some success.

The extraction of sugar from sugar beet is carried out in a process similar to that for sugar cane, involving the crushing of the roots and purification of the raw sugar. The end product needs less refining than cane sugar and is whiter. The pulp left after juice extraction still contains 20% sugar and is fed to animals, being particularly good for ruminants as it contains a great deal of cellulose which they are able to digest. The wilted beet tops, in which the poisonous oxalic acid will have been broken down, can be fed to cattle, leaving very little waste from the crop.

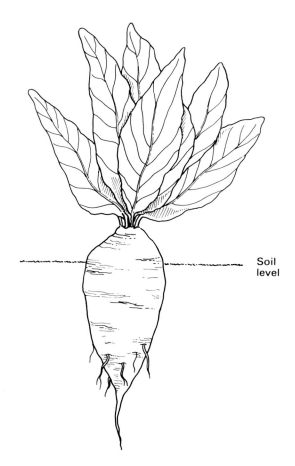

Soil level

Fig.4.12 Sugar beet plant

■ OTHER IMPORTANT ROOT CROPS

■ Turnips (*Brassica compestris*)

Turnips are important as forage crops for sheep and cattle, especially in northern Europe and in New Zealand, as well as being grown for human consumption. Leafy forms are used as salad in China (pe-tsai is Chinese cabbage, pak-choi is Chinese mustard). The stubble turnips, commonly grown for animal feed, are tetraploids. The animals graze the leafy tops, but do not readily eat the swollen roots, so plant breeders are aiming to develop varieties with an 80:20 leaf to root ratio rather than the existing 50:50 ratio.

■ Swedes and rapes (*Brassica napus*)

Swedes provide animal forage and vegetables, as do the turnips, and have a similar distribution. The leafy varieties are particularly valuable as fodder for animals.

Both *Brassica campestris* and *B. napus* produce oil-rich seeds called rape, and have been grown since the middle ages for their oil. The extracted oil is edible, having a low saturated fat content, and it can also be used industrially. Oilseed rape is grown mainly in Canada, China, India and parts of Europe. The familiar bright yellow fields in the UK indicate the increasing value of this crop much improved by the reduction in erucic acid due to modern plant breeding and selection.

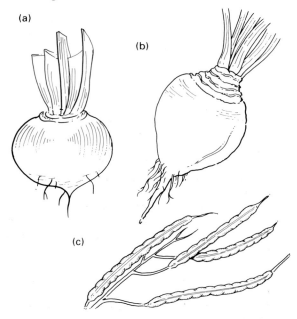

Fig. 4.13 (a) Turnip, (b) swede and (c) rape

■ LEAVES

Typically, leaves consist of a thin, flat lamina or blade, supported by a network of veins, and are attached to stems by a stalk, or petiole. They are green, due to the presence of large numbers of chloroplasts in the cells of the palisade and spongy mesophyll layers, and carry out photosynthesis. In some plants, such as onions, modified leaves act as food stores and remain underground during the winter. In the following spring, the stored food is used to enable rapid growth of buds and flower formation.

Leafy crops are grown both for feeding animals and for human consumption. In the middle ages, cabbages and other Brassicas were common vegetables, adding some variety to the diet.

■ Cabbages and kales (*Brassica oleracea*)

Wild cabbage is found growing, as an annual, along the coasts of north-west Europe and the Mediterranean, and it is thought that the cultivation of Brassicas began in the Mediterranean area several thousand years ago. The wild varieties contain several bitter-tasting substances, which have been linked with the incidence of goitre, an abnormal condition of the thyroid gland, so selection of early varieties would have been for the less bitter plants. As the cultivation of cabbages spread northwards, biennial varieties were developed for their winter hardiness, for a cold requirement before flowering (vernalisation), and for other desirable characteristics such as less fibrous and thicker stems.

Brussels sprouts, cabbages and cauliflowers are the result of selection for different organs, i.e. lateral buds, terminal buds and flower buds. They are grown in gardens and market gardens, while kale is widely grown as autumn and winter grazing for cattle. Different varieties have been developed for marketing at different times of the year, ensuring a more or less constant supply of leafy green vegetables, and there have been improvements in quality and disease resistance. Emphasis now is on breeding varieties with greater uniformity combined with vigour, so that harvesting can be carried out mechanically. F_1 hybrids from inbred lines are being produced, and there has been some success using three-way crosses and double-cross hybrids.

■ Lettuce (*Lactuca sativa*)

Lettuce is a major salad crop popularly grown, for the fresh market, in glasshouses, gardens and smallholdings in North America, Europe and Australia. It is a highly variable crop, with a great deal of variation in leaf length, size, texture, shape and colour. It developed in the Mediterranean and Middle East, where the first cultivated varieties were narrow-leaved and did not produce hearts. There are many references to lettuce in Greek and Roman literature, and the cultivation of lettuce appears to have spread to the rest of Europe with the advance of the Roman legions.

Nowadays, the most popular varieties are crisp with hearts, like Iceberg, and a visit to a large supermarket will reveal a range, such as butterheads with round leaves, crispheads with wrinkled leaves and the upright cos types, as well as loose-leaved, non-hearting varieties such as Salad Bowl with deeply indented ('Oak Leaf') and frilly ('Lollo') leaves, and also miniature varieties.

Commercially produced lettuces are grown all the year round in glasshouses, where the conditions can be controlled. They are prone to diseases such as downy mildew and botrytis. Current breeding programmes involve the development of greater uniformity, which could lead to mechanical harvesting, and disease resistance.

■ FRUITS AND SEEDS

Apples, plums, nuts and beans all produce valuable food for humans (Fig.4.14). After fertilisation, the ovary wall and the receptacle of the flower may swell up and become succulent, and the products of photosynthesis are stored up in the seeds.

■ FRUITS

Fruits, in the agricultural and horticultural sense, include the swollen, succulent receptacles of plants such as strawberries and apples, as well as the 'true' fruits such as the berries (gooseberry, blackcurrant, citrus fruits, date), drupes (plum, cherry, peach, apricot) and nuts (hazelnut). Many of our so-called 'vegetables' are in fact fruits: cucumbers, marrows and tomatoes are all berries.

■ Apple (*Malus* spp.)

Apples (Fig.4.15 overleaf), together with pears, are the most important fruit crops of the cooler temperate regions, and significant quantities are produced in Europe as well as in South Africa, South America, Australia and New Zealand. Both have been cultivated in Europe and western Asia for thousands of years, and references to different varieties of apples occur in the works of Cato and the elder Pliny.

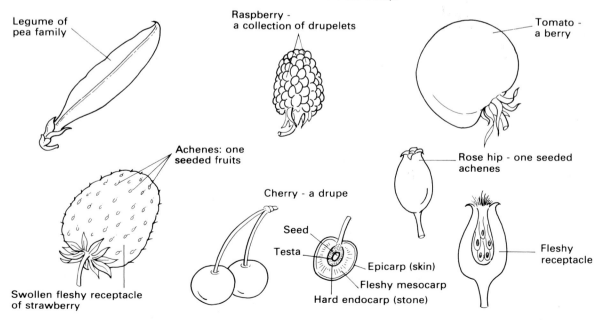

Fig.4.14 Plant reproductive structures used as food

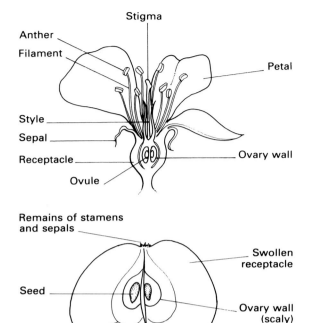

Fig.4.15 Apple flower and fruit

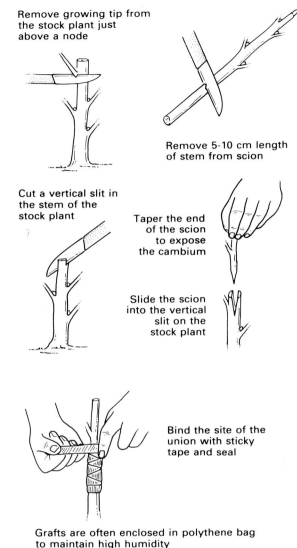

Remove growing tip from the stock plant just above a node

Remove 5-10 cm length of stem from scion

Cut a vertical slit in the stem of the stock plant

Taper the end of the scion to expose the cambium

Slide the scion into the vertical slit on the stock plant

Bind the site of the union with sticky tape and seal

Grafts are often enclosed in polythene bag to maintain high humidity

Fig.4.16 Grafting to a root stock

Varieties of apples such as Pearmain and Costard were grown in England in the thirteenth century, with Pippins being introduced from continental Europe in the sixteenth century. Since the seventeenth century, apples have been propagated by grafting, although in North America most of the initial distribution involved the planting of seed, with the consequence that the genetic diversity in the orchards of the New World was greater than in Europe.

Scions (cuttings) of the major varieties of apple are grafted on to rootstocks, because it is difficult to get cuttings to root (Fig.4.16). The rootstock can determine the eventual size to which the cutting, or scion, will grow and may also carry resistance to soil-borne diseases. Research carried out at Long Ashton and East Malling in the UK resulted in the identification of rootstocks with differing effects on the subsequent size of the tree. The fruit produced will depend on the variety from which the scion was taken, but the size of the tree will be determined by the rootstock. Malling *IX*, for example, is a dwarfing rootstock.

It is possible to produce apple trees by micropropagation (Fig.4.17), and the Plant Genetic Manipulation Group at the University of Nottingham, led by Dr J.B. Power, have produced clones of the original Bramley's seedling using this technique. An advantage of using micropropagation is that the plants produced will have exactly the same characteristics as the original tree from which the tissue was taken, and there will be no slight variations due to different rootstocks.

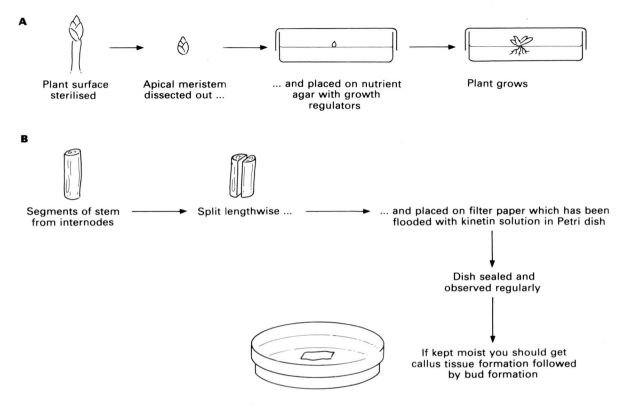

Fig.4.17 Micropropagation techniques

■ Tomato (*Lycopersicon esculentum*)

The tomato belongs to the same family as the potato, the *Solanaceae*, and has become one of the world's most important 'vegetables'. The small wild ancestors of the tomato, very similar in appearance to cherry tomatoes today, grow in Peru, but they were first cultivated in Mexico, where they were well-established when the Spanish arrived. Plants were introduced into Europe in the sixteenth century, but were not popular as the fruit, known to be related to the nightshades, was thought to be toxic. Most of the attempts to improve quality were rather haphazard initially, but more rapid progress has been achieved in the last 50 years. Major improvements include:

• increased yields with larger fruit size and more fruits per plant;
• improved ability to set fruit, more likelihood of self-pollination;
• greater uniformity of shape, colour, texture and flavour;
• pest resistance.

■ SEEDS

A seed is a reproductive structure consisting of an embryo and a food store, surrounded by a seed coat or testa. The food store can be quite separate from the embryo, in a tissue called the endosperm (endospermic seeds), or it can be located in structures called cotyledons, or seed leaves, which are attached to the embryo (non-endospermic seeds).

Seeds may be described as 'starchy', containing large amounts of carbohydrates (e.g. the seeds of cereals, peas, beans) or 'oily', from which oils containing unsaturated fatty acids can be extracted (e.g. the seeds of sunflower, rape).

Apart from the cereals, the other important group of plants producing seeds is the legumes. All members of the plant family Papilionaceae (the legumes) get their name from the seed pod, which is formed from a single carpel with the seeds arranged in a single row. They include peas and a range of beans, e.g. French, haricot, navy, butter (see *Biology Advanced Studies - Plant Science*).

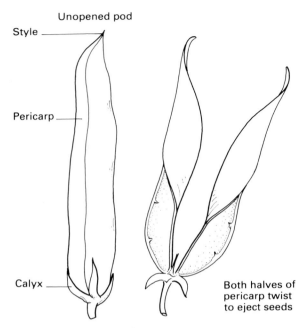

Style ⎯⎯⎯

Pericarp ⎯⎯⎯

Calyx ⎯⎯⎯

Unopened pod

Both halves of
pericarp twist
to eject seeds

Fig.4.18 A legume seed pod

In the uncultivated members of the family, the pods split down both sides, ejecting the seeds forcibly, often to considerable distances from the parent plant. Many of the cultivated species have lost this ability. In addition to the large amounts of carbohydrate, the seeds contain significant quantities of protein, and records indicate that peas and lentils have been cultivated almost as long as the cereals. Beans were amongst the earliest cultivated plants in South America and it is likely that domesticated varieties were being used in Peru around 6000 BC, before the appearance of maize. Legumes are high in the essential amino acids which the cereals lack, so they neatly complement each other in the diet, especially in areas of the world where the consumption of meat is not high for economic or religious reasons. As well as providing food for humans, the legumes provide animal fodder in the form of clover or lucerne, and are important components of a three or four year rotation of crops, as their roots harbour the nitrogen-fixing bacterium *Rhizobium* (see *Biology Advanced Studies - Environment and Ecology*).

The legumes were grown initially for their seeds (pulses), which when ripe could be dried and stored for cooking later, but the unripe pods of several varieties of peas and beans are harvested and consumed as fresh vegetables, and the seeds of

some species are allowed to sprout and the seedlings harvested. Of the cultivated peas (*Pisum sativum*), one main variety, the field pea, is grown for forage and dried peas, and the other variety, the garden pea, with its high sugar content, is a very popular fresh vegetable. The pods of the carob have a high sugar content, and so carob is used in the manufacture of chocolate substitutes.

■ Beans (*Phaseolus* spp.)

This genus originated in the New World and four cultivated species are recognised:
• *Phaseolus vulgaris* - the common, haricot, French or navy bean, which thrives best in warm, temperate conditions;
• *Phaseolus lunatus* - the Lima or butter bean, adapted to the tropical and sub-tropical climates;
• *Phaseolus coccineus* - the runner bean, which grows well in cool humid conditions;
• *Phaseolus acutifolius* - the Tepary bean, which can grow in dry, semi-desert conditions.

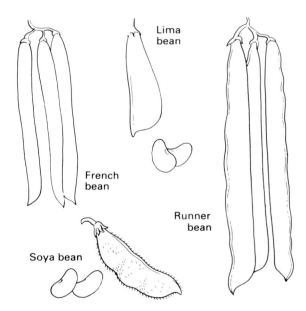

Lima bean

French bean

Runner bean

Soya bean

Fig.4.19 Different types of bean

The archaeological record shows that some of these beans were being cultivated before 6000 BC.

In the UK, the French bean, *P.vulgaris*, is grown mainly for the pods, which are eaten when immature. They can be allowed to ripen partially, then shelled to yield 'flageolets', which are green. If the pods are allowed to mature, the shelled, dry beans are known as haricot beans, and can be stored for winter use.

CHAPTER 5

CATTLE

◼ ORIGINS

Cattle are known to have been associated with human communities from early Neolithic times. The word *cattle* is derived from 'capital' (or chattel in the sense of property or belongings), and this shows how closely we have depended on cattle through the centuries. There is evidence of domesticated cattle in western Asia at least 8000 years ago and of milk production from cattle in Egypt and Mesopotamia 2000 years later. Pictures of cattle in ancient wall paintings or on pottery give clues about their form and indicate their symbolic and relgious significance in early civilisations.

Cattle in cave painting, Natal

The initial value of domesticated cattle was probably for their religious significance and use as a power animal rather than for food. Cattle have fulfilled a variety of purposes through the centuries: as draught animals for drawing a plough or cart; provision of food as meat or milk and dairy products (cheese, yoghurt and butter); clothing or leather from the hide; weapons, armour or artifacts from the bones and horns; and tallow from the fat (for candles and soap).

Using dung as fuel in an Afghan kitchen

The dung provides manure which has been important in maintaining the fertility of soil and is still valuable in some regions to make bricks for building and as a fuel. Even today for religious reasons a taboo against the eating of cattle persists in some countries.

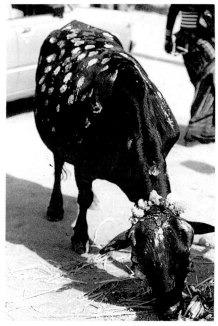

Cow decorated for religious festival in Kathmandu, Nepal

Domesticated cattle are believed to have the same ancestor, the now extinct aurochs or wild ox (*Bos primigenius*). During domestication, two distinct lines have emerged: the humped (zebu type) and the humpless, the latter being further subdivided into longhorned and shorthorned cattle. The humped forms probably developed from *Bos primigenius nomadicus*, recognised in fossil records from India. The humpless form, *Bos primigenius primigenius*, existed in Europe up to 1627.

The separation of the two lines is reflected today in their geographical distribution, though the different forms interbreed readily, produce fertile offspring and are considered to be the same species. The humped form (known as *Bos indicus*) is distributed predominantly in Asia and part of Africa, its main use being for cultivation with the plough, and to some extent for meat. The humpless form (*Bos taurus*) occurs throughout Europe, in northern Africa and northern Asia, regions with a much more developed dairy industry.

Humped (zebu) form of cattle

Humpless form of cattle

The humped form is probably physiologically better adapted to tropical and subtropical climates, yet UK dairy breeds, introduced within the last hundred years, flourish today in the highlands of Kenya.

Further evidence of the relationship between cattle and people is seen in the geographical distribution of people who are lactose intolerant, i.e. they lack the enzyme to digest lactose, the sugar in milk. Adults who lack the enzyme are found, for example, in the indigenous people in China, India and parts of Africa, regions where traditionally milking has not been part of the culture. However, new-born babies of all ethnic origins are able to digest lactose and it is suggested that retention of this character in adults living in areas based on a pastoral economy gave a selective advantage. Those able to digest milk products may have survived better in times of nutritional deprivation than those who could not. Lactose intolerance is still found today in southern Italy - this would suggest that their adult ancestors in Ancient Rome did not drink milk.

■ HOW BREEDS HAVE DEVELOPED

In studying modern breeds of cattle and their development, it may help to concentrate on those currently important in Europe, where the emphasis is on production of meat (as beef or veal) and milk. There has been some separation into those breeds best suited for the beef industry and those for the dairy industry, though dual purpose breeds are becoming increasingly important.

In the UK during the 18th century cattle were used as working animals and also provided tallow for candles, so animals were selected mainly for size and fatness. When horses became more commonly used for work, selection of cattle for production of meat and milk became a higher priority. Enclosure of common land to form discrete fields, particularly during the eighteenth and nineteenth centuries, allowed more control over the animals; adoption of gradually better feeding practices encouraged more sophisticated breeding programmes. The performance of the breeding animals and of their offspring began to be carefully documented, the beginning of record systems used extensively today.

The Longhorn was the dominant breed in the UK in the 18th century but has now become a rare, nearly extinct breed. The Shorthorn, useful for both milk and beef, took over from the Longhorn and remained important well into this century. In

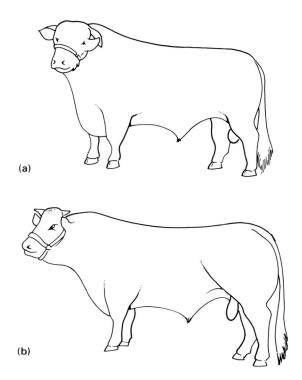

(a)

(b)

Fig.5.1 Different breeds of bull: (a) Hereford, (b) Charolais

1908, Shorthorns accounted for 64% of cattle in the UK but this fell to 50% by 1936 and has now dwindled to 1%, largely due to the introduction of black and white Friesians from Holland around the beginning of the twentieth century. Friesians became popular because they produce more milk and more beef than Shorthorns. Selection in the Holstein breed, in both North America and Europe, has been primarily for milk production, with some loss of yield and quality of its beef. Friesian and Holstein breeds and their crosses now account for the majority of cattle in the UK.

Other British breeds for beef include the Hereford and Aberdeen Angus. Both of these begin their fattening phase relatively early. This suits a fattening system based on grass, but with more intensive systems of feeding, involving cereal, Hereford and Aberdeen Angus develop too much fat at lighter weights. Increasing consumer demand for lean rather than fat meat led to a shift towards continental breeds, such as the Charolais and Limousin. These have become popular because they are larger, provide a high proportion of very lean meat and, even though they are late-maturing, they have the advantage of a high muscle to bone ratio. The Jersey and Guernsey, local breeds

originating in the Channel Islands, are well-known for the relatively high butterfat content of their milk, but currently represent only a small percentage of cattle in the UK. Local breeds do still exist in many countries throughout Europe, but there is increasing concentration on just a few successful breeds, which brings the potential danger of loss of genetic diversity.

 Explain the meaning of the term genetic diversity.

To some extent, breeding for competitive showing has become an end in itself, the animals being judged for excellence in appearance rather than on performance with respect to yield of milk or meat. There are breed standards, breed societies and herd books; elaborate records are kept and competitive breed shows are both serious and fun for the enthusiasts. The importance of maintaining stocks of rare breeds must be emphasised. Current advances in blood typing and DNA testing are helping to specify breed type and relationships.

■ Choosing a breed for the herd

In a commercial herd the initial choice may be between breeds for beef or milk, but other factors need to be considered, and these may fluctuate with changing conditions. For example, in the beef industry, a large calf is likely to develop a large body size with a potentially high yield of meat, but large body size may cause difficulties at calving. Survival rates (viability) of the calf are important and some breeds have a high calf mortality rate. Another consideration is the rate at which the calf grows, and the weight likely to be reached at slaughter, after a certain time of feeding. Efficiency may be measured in terms of the amount of lean meat produced from a given amount of food consumed by the animal, but the most efficient animal is not necessarily the one which reaches the largest size or grows most rapidly. The meat trader aims to satisfy the consumer market, by providing carcasses with a high proportion of desirable meat cuts and, to follow the trend of recent years, by offering quality lean meat rather than fat. The choice of the breed of bull is influenced mainly by the type of locally available feed (grass, cereals, etc.), local conditions (hills, lowland), and the time available for growth (finishing system used). Some effects of the breed of different bulls are illustrated in Table 5.1.

Breed of bull	Calf mass at 200 day/kg			Mass at slaughter/kg	Assisted calvings/%	Calf mortality/%
	Lowland	Upland	Hill			
Charolais	240	227	205	494	9.6	4.8
Limousin	215	204	186	454	7.2	4.4
Hereford	208	194	184	410	3.8	1.6
Angus	194	182	176	393	3.1	1.3

Table 5.1 Some effects of different breeds of bull. These are only some of the factors to be considered when choosing a breed for mating

Q Use the data in the table to explain the advantages of each type of bull: (a) as a Charolais breeder and (b) as an Angus breeder.

Dairy cows are selected primarily for their milk yield with respect to volume produced (per day) and length of lactation (the time when milk is being produced) and also for quality of the milk in relation to fat and protein content. The farmer also bases selection on certain physical features of the cow; the udder and its support, the length and angle of the teats (because this becomes important in machine milking). Choice from these different requirements must then be balanced with the regulations governing market prices and milk quotas. A herd of cows may yield the permitted volume of milk but be penalised if the fat content is too high.

Deciding on the most suitable breed for producing beef or milk is just the first stage in determining the quality of the herd. The breeder must consult detailed records to select individual bulls to sire or inseminate the cows in the herd. Records of the performance of the bull's calves are compiled from a series of matings, on different farms, with the progeny being raised in a variety of environmental conditions and under different systems of management. Ways of assessing the performance include gain in weight at 100 day intervals, quality and yield of milk per lactation, or ultrasonic measures of muscle and fat depth on the live animal. Progeny testing is inevitably slow because it takes time to rear the calf to an adult when the 'outcome' can be measured. It also becomes complex to test very large numbers of progeny. Information accumulated about each bull is continually updated and evidence of superior performance is likely to be reflected in a higher price for the semen offered for artificial insemination. Actual performance of a bull in a herd cannot be predicted precisely because of natural variation, the effects of environmental factors and management of the herd.

Choice of bull has become the major factor in promoting desirable characteristics in the offspring. The practice of artificial insemination (AI), established during the 1940s (see p.60), has made enormous contributions to the maintenance of successful herds. AI means that sperm from a desirable bull can be used by a wide range of farmers in different locations. By using frozen sperm from a well-tried bull, farmers feel more assured of success and consistency in their herd. Sperm from a desirable bull can be used long after the death of the donor.

One bull can be responsible for many thousands of offspring whereas a cow produces only a limited number of offspring in a lifetime. AI allows the spread of desirable genetic material on an international basis and helps in the coordination of a national breeding policy.

The more recently developed practice of embryo transfer also has the potential of allowing rapid reproduction of progeny showing the desired characteristics, avoiding the need for a long period of trialling. There is, however, the potential danger of using a limited number of bulls to perpetuate only desired characters, thus narrowing the pool of genetic diversity. Most of the breed societies maintain a stock of desirable bulls and a 'bank' of genetic variability in frozen semen. There are also commercial centres for AI. Stocks of rare breeds are important in contributing to this gene bank.

■ REPRODUCTIVE BIOLOGY

The reproductive system in cattle and the events occurring in the reproductive cycle from fertilisation through to the birth of the calf are essentially similar to those in other mammals. The following account describes those processes of particular significance to the farmer with a commercial herd.

■ Female reproductive system

The main parts of the reproductive system of the cow are shown in Fig.5.2. There are two ovaries and an oviduct leads from each ovary to the *uterus*. Note the two horns of the uterus which combine into a short uterine body. The muscular *cervical canal* separates the uterus from the *vagina* which opens to the exterior at the *vulva*.

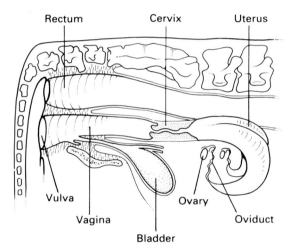

Fig.5.2 Reproductive system of a cow (side view)

In the ovary, the *ova* develop from the *oogonia* which arise by mitotic divisions from germinal cells during embryonic and fetal stages. Numbers of oogonia reach a peak before birth, then decline and only a minute proportion are ever likely to become fertilised.

■ Oestrous cycle

The oestrous (or ovarian) cycle (Fig.5.3) typically lasts 21 days. If a cow is not mated with a bull or artificially inseminated, the cycle will be repeated throughout the year, like the menstrual cycle in humans (see *Biology Advanced Studies - Human Systems*). There are effectively two phases within the oestrous cycle, the short *follicular* phase and longer *luteal* phase, and the various events of the

reproductive cycle are closely controlled by the action of hormones.

The follicular phase is stimulated by secretion of *follicle stimulating hormone* (FSH) and *prolactin* from the *anterior pituitary gland*. During the follicular phase, an oocyte becomes surrounded by a single layer of ovarian cells to form a *follicle*; cells of this primary follicle then divide to form a multi-layered structure. This fills with fluid to become the *Graafian follicle* which contains the ovum ready for release at ovulation. As the follicle matures, it secretes the hormone *oestrogen*, one function of which is to make the cow come into *oestrus*, the time at which she is receptive to the male, shortly before ovulation. A second effect of oestrogen is to stimulate the release from the anterior pituitary of *luteinising hormone* (LH) which is required to trigger ovulation.

Ovulation occurs on day 1 of the cycle. The ovum is released from the follicle which collapses, then undergoes development into a *corpus luteum*. This is the start of the *luteal* phase. By day 7 the corpus luteum is fully formed as a solid, almost orange, mass of tissue, its important function being to secrete the hormone *progesterone*. The level of progesterone rises to its highest between days 11 and 16 and secretion continues for at least two-thirds of the oestrous cycle. One function of progesterone is to prepare the reproductive tract for successful mating and subsequent nourishment of the embryo; another function is to *inhibit* the production of follicle stimulating hormone (FSH) which would initiate the next

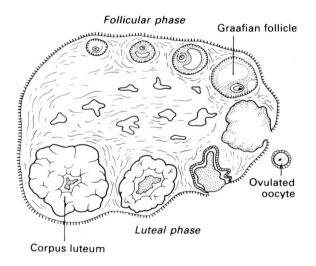

Fig.5.3 Section through the ovary of a cow, showing developments during follicular and luteal stages

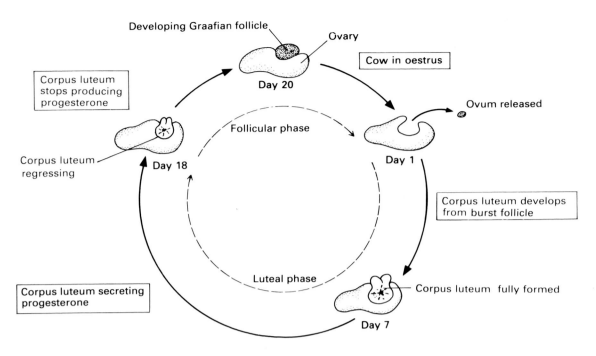

Fig.5.4 Changes in the ovary during the oestrous cycle

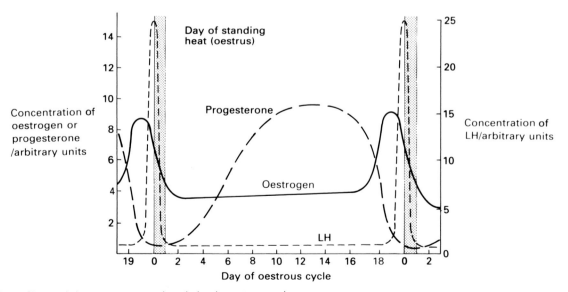

Fig.5.5 Changes in hormone concentrations during the oestrous cycle

follicular stage. This effectively prolongs the luteal phase, increasing the chance of the cow becoming pregnant. If fertilisation does not occur, the corpus luteum regresses (dies back) quite rapidly under the influence of the hormone *prostaglandin F2α*, secreted by the uterus. Regression of the corpus luteum results in a rapid fall in the level of progesterone, on about day 19, thus removing its effect of inhibiting FSH secretion, allowing release of FSH which stimulates maturation of a Graafian follicle and the whole cycle starts again (Figs. 5.4 and 5.5).

■ Controlling the timing of pregnancy

Hormones can be used artificially to influence the timing of ovulation. Precision in controlling the timing of ovulation means more reliable conception and the convenience of keeping a batch of cows together during their pregnancy. It allows, for example, synchronisation of suitable feeding programmes during pregnancy, birth of the calves at about the same time, and the convenience of rearing the group of calves together so that they have a common feeding programme and are cared for as a batch up to the time of marketing. Similarly, a group of heifers would be ready for bulling together and therefore calve and enter the dairy herd at the same time. Two approaches are used to control the time of ovulation, both of which are intimately concerned with the relative length of the luteal and follicular stages of the oestrous cycle.

The first approach attempts to maintain a high level of progesterone in the blood. This prolongs the luteal phase but when the progesterone level falls, the short follicular phase follows, leading to ovulation. This can be achieved by inserting into the vagina an artificial device (such as a plastic coil) containing a capsule which releases progesterone, thus mimicking days 7-18 of the cycle. When the device is removed the drop in the level of progesterone triggers the sequence of events which leads to the development of the follicle. Supply of progesterone can be adjusted so that a group of cows in a herd come into oestrus together, although the method may result in lower conception rates in the herd.

The second approach aims to cause regression of the corpus luteum. If no mating occurs this regresses naturally at the end of the luteal phase and leads into the follicular stage, then ovulation. Regression of the corpus luteum can be induced by supplying either prostaglandin F2α, a natural secretion from the uterus, or synthetic analogues of this natural hormone. If the hormone is injected after day 7, it advances the cycle so that in about three days the cow is in oestrus. However, in the herd, times of oestrus are liable to be random, so that some cows of the herd may not yet have a fully formed corpus luteum and would not respond to this treatment. A high rate of success has been achieved by giving two injections of the prostaglandin, the second 10 to 12 days after the first. It is then probable that about 90% of the cows will have a mature corpus luteum and are likely to respond to the second injection and lead into the short follicular stage. Such cows come into oestrus two to three days later, showing conception rates similar to that of the normal herd (Fig.5.6).

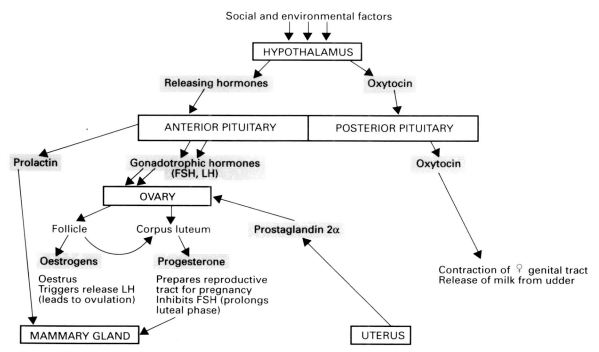

Fig.5.6 Major hormones (shaded) involved in the control of reproduction and related events in cows

Male reproductive system

The main parts of the reproductive system of a bull are shown in Fig.5.7. The testes lie outside the body cavity at a lower temperature because this is necessary for the development and ripening of sperm. The sperm pass from the testes along the very long epididymus, which may be over 30 m in length. The sperm suspension becomes concentrated; the sperms mature and acquire the potential for swimming and fertilising an ovum. Production of sperm can continue throughout the life of the bull, from puberty to old age and very high rates of production have been recorded. For example, nine million sperm have been produced during a 24-hour period from 1 g of testicular tissue!

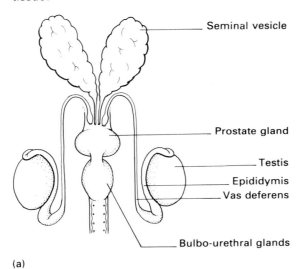

(a)

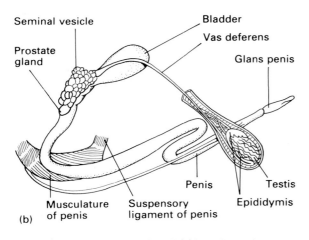

(b)

Fig.5.7 Reproductive system of a bull: (a) front view and (b) side view

Mating and artificial insemination

In cows, puberty is the age at which oestrus (or 'heat') is first detected and generally occurs between 8 and 17 months. The timing varies according to breed and is influenced by environmental conditions, especially the level of feeding. The presence of a mature bull amongst the young females has the effect of bringing on puberty and the farmer may use this to influence the timing of puberty in groups of females in the herd. Puberty can be detected by the female showing a degree of sexual excitement and becoming receptive to mounting and mating.

If a bull is allowed to run free with a herd of cows, mating is likely to occur when cows come into oestrus. Various signs indicate the onset of oestrus in the cow: there may be sniffing of the vulva or urine of other cows, a restlessness, bellowing, licking and mounting of other cows. The decisive and positive sign of oestrus is of the cow standing to be mounted. The bull is stimulated by the odours and secretions from the vulva. The bull mounts the cow, the penis is extruded and vigorous thrusting movements by the pelvis follow, which enable the penis to enter the vagina. Ejaculation occurs rapidly and the semen is deposited in the anterior part of the vagina. A bull with a herd can probably inseminate 3-4 cows per day, so there must be a sensible ratio of bulls to cows to ensure there is a reasonable chance of successful mating.

Methods of artificial insemination (AI) are becoming increasingly used for a number of reasons. AI makes it easier, for example, to shift the emphasis in production from milk to beef, and means the farmer does not need to keep several bulls to retain the required flexibility in the breeding herd. The advantages gained from the practice of synchronising oestrus in a group of cows in the herd are more easy to achieve with the use of artificial insemination. In the UK, about 80% of matings in 1992 were done by artificial insemination with a high success rate (70%) in relation to conception.

Semen destined for artificial insemination must first be collected. This can be done by exploiting the reaction of the bull to the vagina and its secretions. A 'teaser' female cow (one which is maintained in oestrus) may be used to stimulate the bull, the penis being directed into an artificial vagina which collects the ejaculate. Alternatively a 'dummy' which crudely resembles the shape of a cow is impregnated with urine or 'smells' which encourage the bull to mount it and ejaculate. The artificial vagina is a device which imitates the vagina of a cow, thus giving appropriate stimulus to the bull and also maintains a suitable temperature around the collecting vessel as sperm is highly sensitive to temperature changes.

The collected semen is examined in a laboratory and checked for contamination and for abnormalities. An estimate is made of the proportion of active (motile) sperm and of their concentration. A single ejaculate (3.5–$5.0\,cm^3$) may produce up to 15×10^6 motile sperm which is far in excess of the number required to give the chance of a successful fertilisation. The semen can be diluted with an *extender*, which increases the number of possible inseminations. The extender usually contains a sugar, salts (which buffer the sperm suspension against changes in pH and osmotic balance), a substance such as glycerol (which protects the sperm cells against the damaging effects of chilling), and antibiotics (which prevent the growth of bacteria). The sperm suspensions are packaged in disposable plastic straws containing about 0.25 to $0.5\,cm^3$ and stored in liquid nitrogen at $-196\,°C$. There is some slow deterioration of the fertilising ability of sperm stored in this way.

Artificial insemination is carried out by inserting a plastic or glass pipette into the cow's vagina, guided manually from inside the rectum so that the straw is deposited beyond the cervix. Provided the original semen was of good quality, that care has been taken over temperature changes and the correct time has been chosen in relation to ovulation in the cow, high rates of conception are achieved.

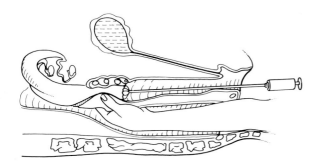

Fig.5.8 Artificial insemination in a cow. The vagina is manipulated from the rectum to ensure the straw deposits semen beyond the cervix

■ Fertilisation

For successful fertilisation in a commercial herd, it is important that oestrus is detected precisely so that mating or insemination occurs at the best time. Delay results in poorer conception rates. In the cow, oestrus lasts between 12 and 16 hours. The best time for insemination to occur is usually between five and 20 hours after the onset of oestrus. Ovulation occurs about 10-12 hours after the *end* of oestrus and this timing means the ovum has reached a suitable part of the oviduct.

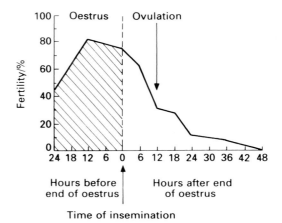

Fig.5.9 The best time for insemination is 12–18 hours before ovulation

Fertilisation normally takes place in the oviduct. The sperm reach this site by their natural motility and are assisted by contractions of the female genital tract which in turn are influenced by hormones, particularly oxytocin. Adrenaline acts antagonistically to oxytocin, therefore stress or fright may result in reduced conception rates. As the sperm move through the cervix and uterus towards the oviduct, there is a reduction in numbers from over a million at the site of deposition in the anterior vagina to about one hundred in the oviduct. When introduced by artificial insemination, deposition of a much smaller number is likely to result in successful fertilisation, because the straws are inserted well beyond the cervix. During their passage through the uterus, the sperm undergo the final stages of maturation, a process lasting about four hours, after which the sperm can penetrate and fertilise the egg.

The fertilised egg moves along the oviduct and reaches the uterus after three or four divisions. Attachment of the embryo to the endometrium of the uterus is not completed until about 22 days after fertilisation and occurs by means of a specialised region of fetal cotyledons which merge into maternal tissue to form the placenta.

Development of the embryo is similar to that in other mammals, the gestation period being about 40 weeks. Birth of a calf marks the start of lactation or production of milk (see p. 66).

■ Embryo transplantation

Recent advances in the techniques for embryo transplantation could have revolutionary effects when widely available commercially. A cow is stimulated to *superovulate* by treatment with FSH, which increases the number of follicles developing at the start of the follicular phase of the oestrous cycle. Several ova are released and artificial insemination with an increased number of sperm then allows these ova to be fertilised and the embryos start to develop. These embryos, ideally aged 6-8 days, are then flushed out from the reproductive tract of the donor cow and can be inserted into the uterus of the recipient cow, either through the vagina and cervix, or surgically, necessitating use of an anaesthetic. Flushing out of embryos from the donor cow is possible because of the delay in attachment of the embryos to the wall of the uterus. During this time, the embryos have been floating freely in a fluid environment and can therefore be transferred to a culture medium without harm.

Embryos need to be transplanted into the donor within a fairly short time of being flushed out or can be stored at -196 °C in liquid nitrogen (Fig.5.10).

Alternatively fertilisation and early stages of embryo growth can be carried out *in vitro* (in glass vessels). Ova are collected from the ovaries of cows at an abbatoir. These ova are cultured in the laboratory for about five days then fertilised with semen from a bull with desired characteristics. The resulting embryos are further cultured to the five- or six-day stage, then frozen until required for transplantation into the recipient cow.

It is likely that embryo transplantation will become available internationally, perhaps even replacing artificial insemination, and could thus have a comparable or greater effect on selection and control of characteristics of the herd. Recipient cows on local farms all over the world could nurture embryos derived from matings (or artificial insemination) between bulls and cows with chosen desirable characteristics. It is also possible to sex embryos in the laboratory: when this becomes available on a commercial scale, dairy farmers could, for example, choose to implant and rear only female embryos.

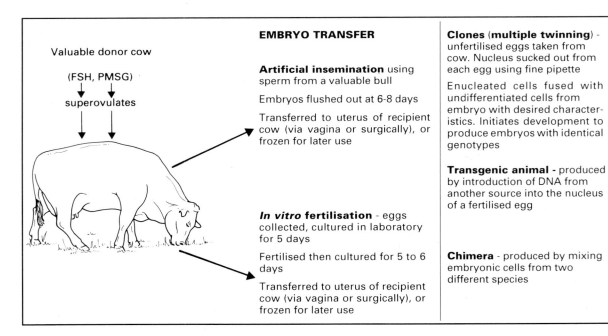

EMBRYO TRANSFER

Valuable donor cow

(FSH, PMSG)

superovulates

Artificial insemination using sperm from a valuable bull

Embryos flushed out at 6-8 days

Transferred to uterus of recipient cow (via vagina or surgically), or frozen for later use

In vitro **fertilisation** - eggs collected, cultured in laboratory for 5 days

Fertilised then cultured for 5 to 6 days

Transferred to uterus of recipient cow (via vagina or surgically), or frozen for later use

Clones (multiple twinning) - unfertilised eggs taken from cow. Nucleus sucked out from each egg using fine pipette

Enucleated cells fused with undifferentiated cells from embryo with desired characteristics. Initiates development to produce embryos with identical genotypes

Transgenic animal - produced by introduction of DNA from another source into the nucleus of a fertilised egg

Chimera - produced by mixing embryonic cells from two different species

Fig.5.10 Embryo transfer and other ways of manipulating reproduction in cattle

■ CALVES

A newly born calf would normally suckle milk from the mother cow, and then, after a period of several weeks, gradually be weaned on to solid food. In many farms calves are fed on artificial milk substitutes, or on milk taken from the cows in the herd, rather than allowing suckling to continue.

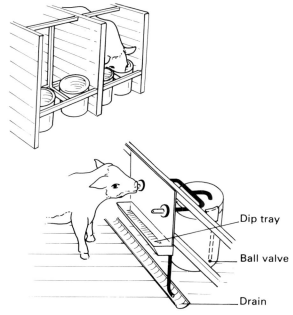

Fig.5.11 Young calves are usually fed on artificial milk either by teat or by bucket

The milk can be offered through teats from a 'feeder' or from a bucket. It is important for calves to receive the first milk, the colostrum, drawn from the mother cow during the first 24 hours. The calves should be fed colostrum within 12 hours of birth and continue for the first few days. Colostrum is valuable because of its nutrient composition, but its particular benefit is that it contains antibodies from the mother which protect the young calf against infections likely to be encountered early in life. At this stage, the large protein antibodies in the colostrum can be absorbed directly through the wall of the intestine of the calf.

Female calves will be kept for the dairy herd, to produce milk and give birth to more calves; some females will be reared for beef. Male calves are reared for beef but the number of male calves born is likely to exceed numbers that can be supported for feeding, or would be required in the meat industry. Some of these are, therefore, used for veal calves. In some cases calves are reared on the farm where they were born, but, particularly for rearing beef, calves are often 'bought in', having been transported from other areas, at the age of about one week. When calves are kept indoors, a high standard of hygiene should be maintained in the houses, to minimise losses from disease during the early vulnerable stages.

■ Veal

The term *veal* means calf meat. Veal production represents a relatively small part of the total meat production from cattle: less than 1% in the UK, though noticeably higher in certain continental countries (30% in the Netherlands, 20% in France, 14% in Italy). The calves used for veal are usually excess male calves and are raised almost entirely on milk substitutes, with little or no access to solid food. They are sold for slaughter at about 160 to 200 kg weight, at an age between 14 and 18 weeks. Typically the meat is pale in colour, due to a low level of iron in the diet, which reduces the haemoglobin content and myoglobin in the muscle. The practice of veal production was well established in peasant agriculture, probably originating as an ecologically sound way of using up surplus milk from the 'house cow', to produce a special fattened calf which, if killed young, did not compete with the mother for limited supplies of food.

Modern methods of veal production have developed from the 1950s, alongside pressure for intensification of livestock rearing and specialisation into dairy herds. This resulted in a large number of excess calves on the farm where they were born.

Veal calves are now generally transported to large rearing units, where they are placed either in small individual rearing crates, without access to bedding or solid food, or allowed limited freedom in the 'straw-yard' system. They are fed on a liquid diet, similar to that used for conventional calf-rearing, except that the iron content is restricted (though it is maintained above the minimum needed to prevent anaemia).

There has been concern over the welfare of veal calves and considerable pressure for more 'humane' conditions for rearing. These relate in particular to methods used for transporting partly grown calves, and provision of additional space for the calves to allow normal behaviour patterns (so that the calf is free to turn round) and to supply solid food with sufficient iron. Some of these points have been met in the UK in welfare regulations for calves effective from 1 January 1990. Different systems of rearing are also being investigated which take account of welfare requirements while remaining economically competitive.

Q There is some controversy about veal production. List the points that could be used in an argument, assuming that you represented a pressure group: (a) for veal production, and then (b) against veal production.

■ FOOD, DIGESTION AND DIET

Cattle are herbivores and because of their ruminant digestive system a high proportion of the cellulose in fibrous foods in the diet is digested and becomes available as energy. Benefits are also gained from features of their nitrogen metabolism and ability to synthesise water-soluble vitamins.

The alimentary canal is more complex than that of humans due to three additional compartments, the rumen, reticulum and omasum, which come before the true stomach, known as the abomasum (Fig.5.12). The *reticulum* has no digestive function and is concerned with the passage of boluses of food to the oesophagus and digested material from the rumen to the omasum. The *rumen* has a capacity of about 150 litres and is of considerable importance as the chamber in which fermentation of food material, due to activities of microorganisms, takes place. The *omasum* has a capacity of about 15 litres, produces no digestive secretions and its main function is to remove water and organic acids from digested material passed from the rumen. The *abomasum* functions as a 'true' stomach, secreting gastric juices, and digestion here and in the rest of the alimentary canal is similar to that in humans.

Mixed populations of microorganisms, mainly bacteria but including Protoctists and yeasts, are found in the rumen. They become established soon after birth when the calf begins to pick up solid food. The mixture of species depends on the food consumed so changes to the diet should be made gradually to ensure rumen microorganisms adjust accordingly. The microorganisms digest carbohydrates, particularly polysaccharides with β-links, hence their role in the breakdown of cellulose. Conditions are anaerobic, and the resulting hexoses are broken down to short-chain organic acids (ethanoic, propionic and butyric) with the release of the gases carbon dioxide and methane, as shown in the equation:

$$C_6H_{12}O_6 \rightarrow 2CH_3COOH + CO_2 + CH_4$$

Energy released in these reactions provides the energy required by the microorganisms for their own biosyntheses. The gases escape when the animal belches and are wasted. The acids, known as volatile fatty acids (VFAs), are absorbed through the walls of the rumen and are utilised by the animal to provide a significant contribution to the energy requirements. The proportion of the different acids varies according to the food source. High fibre foods rich in cellulose produce mainly ethanoic acid, whereas feeding of concentrates increases the proportion of propionic acid produced. In dairy cows, a shift towards more propionic acid results in deposition of body fat with a reduction in fat content of milk and a lowered milk production. Such factors need to be considered in formulating diets in relation to targets for milk in terms of yield and quality. The composition of the rumen microflora can be altered artificially so that the carbohydrate, when broken down, produces more or less methane.

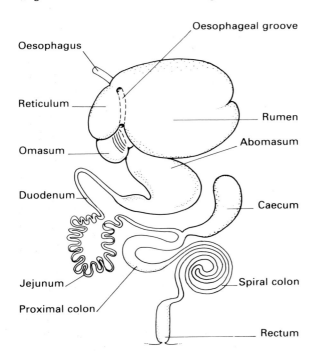

Fig.5.12 Part of the alimentary canal of a cow

Protein is also broken down in the rumen by microbial activity, first to amino acids then deaminated to release ammonia. Some ammonia is incorporated into microbial protein, the rest being absorbed into the blood of the animal. It may then either be excreted or recycled to the rumen by means of the saliva and thereby gain another chance of being synthesised into microbial protein. An advantage of the activities within the rumen is that non-protein nitrogen, in the form of chemicals such as urea, can be supplied with the diet and utilised by microorganisms to synthesise protein, which is then available to the cow. Protein synthesised by the microorganisms becomes available to the animal when it passes from the rumen into the abomasum. Some of the protein in the food bypasses the rumen and is then digested by the animal's digestive enzymes in the abomasum, duodenum and the rest of the alimentary canal.

Another benefit of having the microorganisms in the rumen is that they synthesise vitamins of the B-complex, so it is unnecessary to supply these with the food. Fibre slows down the passage of food in the gut and adequate amounts in the diet are essential for the functioning of the rumen.

■ Feeding systems for beef and for milk

The strategy used for feeding cattle depends among other things on the availability of food material which can be grown locally, to be grazed as grass or other leafy crops, known as *forage*. This may be replaced by or combined with artificially prepared 'concentrates' or other foods, which are often more expensive. The diet is adjusted depending on whether the animal is being reared for beef, for milking or for breeding stock. It will also be varied with the age of the animal, the time at which it was born, the season of year, and account must be taken of both the short- and long-term needs of the animal. For example, low conception rates may result from bulls and cows that have been poorly fed at an earlier stage of their life and improved milk yields can be achieved with better feeding in the early stages.

In the UK, the feeds used in the diets of farm animals fall into three groups: first, grass and forage; second, byproducts or other raw materials of plant or animal origin (which may or may not have been processed before being given to the animals); and third, concentrates, including cereals. Forage includes crops such as kale, turnips or beet which can be grazed and are a useful means of providing fresh food at times when grass is poor or unavailable. Cereal grains used in feeds are mostly barley and sometimes use is made of 'spent grains', discarded from breweries; field beans and residues from sugar beet and the processing of oil seed make an important contribution to concentrates. Concentrates are made up from a variety of ingredients, mixed in controlled proportions, with scope for providing high protein level and adding vitamins or minerals. Both hormones and antibiotics have been added to feed for different reasons. Hormones are now rarely included and antibiotics only in certain circumstances, usually with veterinary prescription.

Q Find out the advantages and disadvantages of using antibiotics and growth hormones in cattle.

Fresh grass can be conserved, either by drying (traditional haymaking or artificial drying) or by converting it to silage. The latter is a microbial fermentation, in which exclusion of air allows conversion of sugars in the grass to lactic acid. In terms of energy and protein, the nutritive value of well-prepared silage is higher than that of hay and is becoming increasingly important during the winter season. Grass for silage is cut early in the season when sugar values are high; several mowings may be possible, giving a high yield from the land, though increased input of fertiliser may be required.

Cows feeding on silage

Feed materials can be analysed into the energy fraction, protein fraction and ash, allowing suitable rations to be formulated. The diet provided should ensure that the intake of net energy, protein and other nutrients exceeds the basic maintenance requirement and gives the extra required for production (in terms of meat or milk).

In practice, it is difficult to arrive at precise values as any foodstuff will include a range of nutrients and itself be subject to variation. For example, grass will have a much higher energy value in spring (being close to that provided by concentrates) compared with later in the year, and the nutritive value and palatability of silage depends on the time of cutting and the conditions under which it has been fermented and stored. The cost of grazed grass is about half that of conserved grass and one quarter that of concentrates. In certain hill regions of the UK the quality of grass is adequate to support cattle reared for beef but not for dairy herds.

The following outline describes a *semi-intensive system* for rearing beef in the UK, and illustrates the way feeding practices may be altered through the life of the animal. Calves are born throughout the year and the feeding system aims to make best use of the summer growing season, alternating with conserved foods in different forms, with or without concentrates. Calves born in the autumn (from September to December) are likely to be slaughtered at between 14 and 18 months at a weight of 400 to 500 kg, depending on breed. During the first winter they are fed a mixture of forage and cereals and may gain about 0.7 kg per day to reach a weight of 180 to 200 kg by the spring. They are turned out on to grass for the summer, and, with an increased daily weight gain, reach 320 to 360 kg by October, when they are returned to yard enclosures. Here they are fed at a high nutritional level, usually including grass silage and cereals, to be 'winter finished' for slaughter and sale before the following spring.

Calves born in mid to late winter are likely to be older at slaughter, between 20 and 24 months, but this longer, slower growing period can result in a heavier, leaner body weight and consumption of a smaller quantity of the expensive cereals. They have two summers out on grass: by the end of the first, weights may reach 290 to 330 kg, then during the winter a relatively low level feed of silage with minimal supplements of minerals and vitamins is given. During the second summer, the cattle are again turned out to grass, and achieve high growth

rates of over 1 kg per day to reach a weight of between 440 and 540 kg.

Intensive systems for beef keep cattle housed throughout their lives, on a diet largely of cereals (barley) with or without silage. High daily weight gains are achieved (1.25 kg per day) with the animal being slaughtered after about 11 months at a weight of 430 kg. The costs of providing food are greater with increased risk of losses due to disease.

Levels of feeding are more critical in a dairy herd where high daily yields of milk are expected. In the UK, the majority of dairy cattle graze grass in the summer though they may receive additional concentrates at the time of milking. During the winter the bulk of the food comes from hay, silage or root crops, supplemented by concentrates.

There is a close correlation between energy intake and milk yield, so that higher levels of nutrition are required earlier in lactation when output is high. Disposal of slurry and silage effluents is a major problem with intensive and semi-intensive systems.

■ MILK - QUANTITY AND QUALITY

■ Lactation
A good dairy cow in a modern milking herd is likely to yield between 6000 and 7000 litres of milk in a year. There is variation with different breeds, the

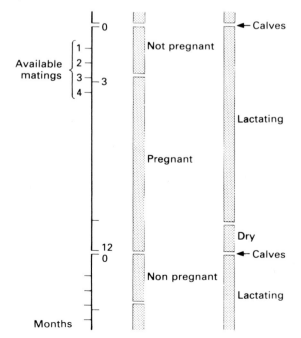

Fig.5.13 Typical breeding cycle for a dairy cow

highest yields (over 10 000 litres) being achieved from British Holsteins. Guernsey and Jersey cows yield much less (around 4000 litres), but their milk is valued for its higher milk fat. In 1991 in the UK, the average yield per cow was 5200 litres, a notable increase over the 1956 average of 3100 litres.

A lactation starts at the birth of a calf, and its length can be adjusted to give a desired calving frequency. An ideal length would be 305 days, followed by a 56-day dry period and this includes an 82-day interval between calving and mating. The actual frequency is determined by the time of successful conception of the next calf. Lactation can be prolonged by continuing to milk the cow, but once the cow becomes pregnant again, by the fifth month, daily yield begins to fall off sharply. The drying-off period allows the cow to recover physiologically from the heavy demands of producing milk (Fig.5.14).

The yield within a lactation varies, reaching a peak in the first few weeks then falling steadily. The yield is also influenced by the time of year at which calving occurs, the age of the cow and particularly by the feeding strategy. In the UK, cows are often turned out on to grass in spring, after wintering indoors, and the effect of young grass and other foliage can result in a 10-15% increase in daily yield. The daily yield can also be influenced by changes in the frequency in milking, for example increased yields can be achieved by milking three times a day (instead of the usual twice daily milking), provided adequate feed is available.

The cow has four mammary glands, contained in the udder which shows considerable increase in size during the later stages of pregnancy and lactation. Selection for high yields has led to grossly enlarged udders which can be awkward for the cow when moving and cause problems if inadequately supported by the suspensory ligaments which attach the glands to the body wall and pelvic girdle. Suitable shape of the udder as well as the positioning of the teats are characteristics that are considered in breeding and selection of dairy cows, otherwise there may be difficulties in applying teat cups during milking by machine. The condition known as mastitis is an inflammation of the udder, often due to bacterial infection but also resulting from physical damage to the tissues. Mastitis leads to lower milk yields and may be genetic in some cows which show greater susceptibility to the condition than others.

Milk is produced in the mammary glands, by the activities of milk-synthesising cells, using simple nutrients in the blood. Certain compounds are synthesised within these cells, such as the protein casein, and the sugar lactose, which are found naturally only in milk; other substances pass unchanged from the blood into the milk. The demand on nutrients is high: about 500 litres of blood pass through the mammary glands in the production of 1 litre of milk. Development of mammary tissue occurs during pregnancy, influenced by the hormones progesterone and prolactin. The milk-synthesising cells secrete their products into a series of ducts and cisterns leading towards the teat where it is stored until released either by the suckling calf or when milked.

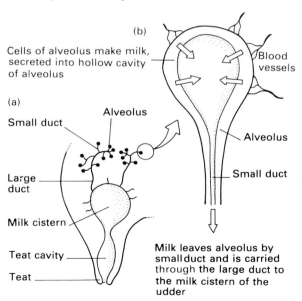

Fig.5.15 Synthesis and flow of milk in the udder showing the structure of: (a) the udder and (b) the alveolus (enlarged view)

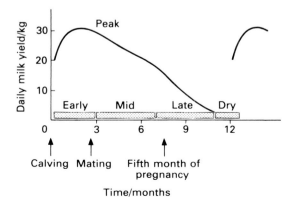

Fig.5.14 Changes in milk yield during a lactation

Machine milking

Release of milk from the udder is under both nervous and hormonal control. Sucking or mechanical stimulus of the teat which leads to the release of the hormone *oxytocin* stimulates contraction of the milk-synthesising cells.

Oxytocin may also be released in response to stimuli received through the eyes, ears or nose and indeed through the routine adopted prior to milking in the milking parlour. Cows are usually milked twice a day, and a familiar and undisturbed milking routine is important if successful release of milk is to be achieved in a relatively short time.

Machine milking of cows has become highly efficient, with the whole operation per cow being completed in about 6 minutes. A typical milking parlour consists of a series of adjacent stalls, which may allow the cow to be fed concentrates during the milking. The cow enters the stall, the udder is washed and the cluster of teat cups of the machine is attached. The machine, by its pulsating suction, both stimulates the flow of milk from the teat and withdraws it into the collecting jar. The milk from each cow is recorded individually. It is essential for all equipment to be kept clean by sterilising after each milking.

A number of factors influence the actual composition of the whole milk from a cow. These include breed, age, feed, health (of cow), season and stage of lactation. For the first few days of lactation, butterfat and protein content are high, dropping towards about week 12, during which time the yield is at its highest. Butterfat and protein then increase during the drying-off period and by week 44 have returned close to the level achieved at the beginning of lactation. Lactose content remains about the same throughout lactation (Fig.5.17). The average composition of whole milk from Friesian cows is compared with that from Channel Island (Guernsey and Jersey) cows in Table 5.2, an illustration of differences between breeds.

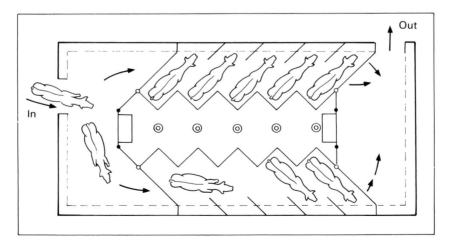

Fig.5.16 Organisation of milking machines in a herringbone parlour. The whole operation for each cow is completed in about six minutes. The cows are dealt with in batches of five. The worker can check the second batch of cows while the first batch are milked. The second batch are milked while the first batch are released and a new batch arrives

Nutrient	Freisian	Channel Island
Water/g	87.8	86.4
Fat/g	3.9	4.9
Lactose/g	4.6	4.6
Protein/g	3.2	3.6
Calcium/mg	115.0	131.0
Vitamin A/μg	53.0	60.0
Riboflavin/mg	0.17	0.19
Vitamin D/μg	0.03	0.04

Table 5.2 Composition of whole milk in mass per 100 g

Milk from most farms in the UK is collected in bulk in tankers and transported to a processing dairy or manufacturing unit. Milk intended for consumption as liquid is treated in different ways to reduce contamination by microorganisms and prolong the life of the milk. These are summarised in Table 5.3.

The quality of milk produced is carefully monitored, with respect to both composition and standards of hygiene. Samples of milk are taken from all farms and subjected to a range of routine laboratory tests. Results from these tests define the quality of the milk and may be linked to payments (or deductions) made for the milk from a particular farm.

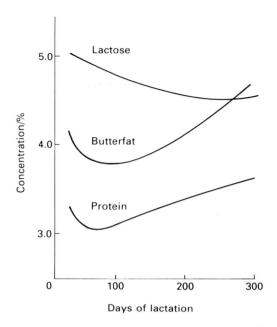

Fig.5.17 Changes in the composition of milk during a lactation

■ TESTING MILK

The composition of milk can be monitored by measurement of the infra-red absorption by the milk sample to give a direct digital reading of lactose, protein and butterfat content.

Process	Method	Effect
Pasteurisation	Either heat to 62.8 to 65.6 °C for 30 minutes or heat to 71.7 °C for 15 seconds then cool to about 3 °C.	Kills pathogenic organisms, does not affect flavour or nutritional value, extends keeping quality for several days.
Sterilisation	Pre-heat to 43 °C, filter, homogenise then bottle. Autoclave with steam under pressure to about 115 °C for about 20 minutes.	Destroys bacteria and microorganisms more completely than pasteurisation, though some spores may survive, keeps for several months. Processing changes taste and reduces nutritional value (reduced vitamin C, folic acid, vitamin B_{12}).
Ultra heat treated (UHT)	At least 1 second at 132.2 °C or above then cartons aseptically filled.	Virtually sterile, keeps for several months, flavour close to pasterurised milk, relatively little effect on nutritional quality.

Table 5.3 Different ways of treating milk

Bacteria in the milk can be estimated by mixing milk with nutrient agar and incubating this at 30 °C for three days. The number of colonies are counted automatically and recorded on a computer and give a measure of the total bacterial count (known as TBC). Presence of bacteria can be due to mastitis inside the udder or contamination from outside the udder, from dirty teats or milking equipment. An indication of the level of mastitis is given by the Cell Count Test. In this test, most of the cells counted are white blood cells which increase in number in response to the presence of mastitis-causing bacteria in the udder. Another test checks for brucellosis in the cow, by detecting antibodies in the milk.

Milk should be free from residual antibiotics which may have been given to cows suffering from disease, such as mastitis. The presence of antibiotics in milk is undesirable because they may lead to development of resistant bacteria in consumers and also because the antibiotics would destroy bacteria involved in cheese and yoghurt productions. Tests to detect antibiotics involve growing sensitive bacteria on nutrient agar with a small quantity of milk. An indicator dye (bromocresol purple) is incorporated in the growth medium. Inhibition of growth of the bacteria, as a result of antibiotics present in the milk, is shown if the indicator remains blue. Growing bacteria produce acid which changes the indicator to a yellow colour.

Other tests check the effectiveness of treatment of milk by pasteurisation, sterilisation and ultra heat treatment. The phosphatase test detects whether the enzyme phosphatase, present in milk, has been inactivated during the pasteurisation process. A test with methylene blue can be used to check the keeping quality of pasteurised milk. Sterilised milk is checked by the turbidity test. When milk is sterilised, certain proteins are denatured so their structure changes. Ammonium sulphate is added to the milk which leads to precipitation of denatured proteins. The filtrate gives a clear solution which remains clear on heating. If turbid, it is an indication that sterilisation has not been carried out effectively.

In the UK, a system of milk 'quotas' has been introduced in an attempt to regulate the production of milk. Farmers who exceed their allowed quota in terms of volume of milk and its composition, are liable to have financial penalties imposed. It is essential, therefore, to balance the various factors which interact in the production of milk: breed, feeding level, season, age and the economics of the business.

6 CHICKENS

■ ORIGINS

If you walk from a village in Thailand into the jungle, or choose many other locations from the Himalayas through Southeast Asia, you might be rewarded with glimpses of the colourful wild jungle fowl flying through the trees and hearing the familiar noise of its call. The untrained eye may be unable to distinguish it from domesticated cockerels in nearby villages or even bantams scattered today in backyards throughout the UK.

In a Thai village - a domesticated chicken closely resembles nearby wild jungle fowl

The red jungle fowl (*Gallus gallus*) is the ancestor of a range of modern forms of the domestic chicken (*Gallus domesticus*). When first domesticated, chickens were probably used for cockfighting and later assumed a religious significance in some communities. It was probably considerably later that they became important as a source of food, providing eggs and meat. There is evidence of domesticated chickens in Southeast Asia over 4000 years ago; the Greeks, 2500 years ago, kept chickens for cockfighting; the Romans built poultry houses, understood the need for hygienic conditions and kept chickens both for religious ceremonies and for food.

Any selection done by primitive people was probably for those chickens showing prominent spurs, or giving the largest eggs. Interest in controlled selective breeding developed in the latter part of the nineteenth century, resulting in the rapid evolution of a range of classes, breeds and varieties of poultry. The focus was on fancy, decorative and exotic breeds, for competitive showing. These breeders paid little attention to productivity in terms of eggs or meat. Show breeding became an end in itself and has persisted until today as a specialist hobby.

Showbred chickens (White Yokohamas)

Development of breeds for the production of eggs and meat, leading to the modern poultry industry, also started during the nineteenth century, particularly in the United States and the UK. Programmes of breeding and selection have concentrated on relatively few characteristics, notably mass production of large, white-shelled or brown-shelled eggs and of chickens raised for meat (known as broilers). White-shelled eggs come almost exclusively from commercial hybrids based on the variety known as White Leghorns; brown-shelled eggs come from other blends of breeds, such as Rhode Island Reds, New Hampshire or Barred Plymouth Rock.

Modern poultry stock - White Leghorns

Most of the chickens used for broiler meat come from crosses between White Cornish and White Plymouth Rock. By the 1980s, just a few very large multinational breeding companies had become responsible for providing and distributing stock on a world-wide basis. This has led to concern that the genetic pool has been reduced to a dangerously low level. It may be that show breeds, or those chickens which have persisted in village economies (or even the wild jungle fowl), may assume renewed importance in scientific and commercial fields, providing a reservoir of genetic diversity, a bank of genes with the potential for introducing new or desired characteristics into modern poultry stocks. (See *Biology Advanced Studies - Genetics and Evolution*.)

Q The colour of the shell has no relationship to its contents. What percentage of your friends assume that brown-shelled eggs are more nutritious?

Variety in eggshells - and a 'soft-shelled egg', the result of faulty calcium deposition

■ THE MODERN POULTRY INDUSTRY

The modern poultry industry shows a high degree of development of intensive systems, in which the commercial farmer concentrates on maximising productivity in terms of yield of eggs and meat. The swing to intensification occurred during the 1960s and 1970s, illustrated by the systems of management used for laying hens in the UK, shown in Fig.6.1.

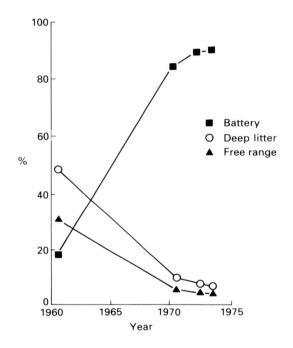

Fig.6.1 Systems of management for laying hens used in the UK

The size of flock (in terms of number of chickens) has also increased. In the UK, in 1957, 85% of the flocks of laying hens were under 1000 birds, whereas by 1971, 85% were over 1000 birds. By 1986, nearly half the flocks had over 50 000 birds, some holdings running to 2 or 3 million. Similarly, broilers reared for meat are kept in large flocks: in 1991 over half of UK broiler flocks had at least 100 000 birds. Battery production is currently showing some decrease in response to concerns about animal welfare with a corresponding increase in free-range and deep litter systems.

Development of a high level of automation has contributed to the rapid increase in intensive systems, though it involves considerable capital outlay in terms of housing and other equipment.

You can get some idea of the scale of automation by considering an estimate made for a farm in the United States with 300 000 laying hens. It was calculated that a single day sees the consumption of 35 600 kg of food and 73 000 litres of water, producing 34 000 kg of manure. The equipment includes 8 km of watering troughs, 23 km of feeders, 23 km of egg belts and only three people are needed to handle the birds - some farm!

Increased intensification has been accompanied by improved performance per bird, in terms either of an increase in the number of eggs over a period of time or a reduction of the time the broiler takes to reach the desired weight. This higher productivity can be attributed to genetic improvement resulting from selection of higher yielding strains, development of improved breeding techniques, understanding of nutritional requirements, better management and control of the environment (particularly housing), and measures to control disease. In 1954, average egg production per bird was 161. By 1972, this figure had increased to 233.

The bulk of chickens farmed intensively are reared in houses, under controlled environmental conditions, though there are outdoor systems, using yards or 'free-range', and also various types of semi-intensive small-scale operations. In global terms the USA and Europe account for about half of the poultry meat produced. Small-scale production is practised in rural economies with subsistence farming, especially in developing countries, where it is particularly valuable because of the low initial capital input and ability of chickens to scavenge and use local feeds.

Backyard chickens

■ BIOLOGY OF THE CHICKEN

In its natural state, the red jungle fowl is gregarious, often coming out of dense forest into fields or clearings in the morning and evening to feed, and roosting on branches off the ground. Its diet includes insects, earthworms, plant seeds and other vegetation, scratched and pecked from the surface soil. Persistent scratching of the ground and showy courtship displays by the cocks are characteristic behaviour patterns, familiar also in domesticated chickens. During the breeding season, a single cock maintains a territory with about five hens. A clutch of about six eggs would be laid in a nest on the ground, usually between March and May. The hen sits on the eggs during the 21 days of incubation leading to the hatching of the eggs and then shows characteristic protective behaviour towards the chicks before they become independent after a few weeks. Chickens very similar to jungle fowl are kept in many less developed countries where they scratch a living around the homes and villages - such chickens probably produce between 30 and 50 eggs in a year.

■ Behaviour
Certain behaviour patterns seen in wild jungle fowl can be recognised in small domesticated groups of chickens. Expression of these natural behaviour patterns has implications for birds kept under intensive conditions, partly because of welfare implications and because they can affect productivity (such as egg yield).

Within a group of chickens, a social order develops, known as the *pecking order*, and separate pecking orders may develop for males and females kept together. This hierarchy means that, for a group of hens, the dominant hen can peck all below, but none peck her. Similarly, the second in the hierarchy can peck all below but is submissive to the dominant hen, and so on. Such interrelationships are shown in Fig.6.2.

The evolution of a pecking order may be seen as a response to the need to share out space, allowing distribution of the birds within the space without the need to resort to fighting. Once the territory is established, there is no need for pecking. If space becomes limiting, aggressiveness may result. Communication between birds may be by a range of visual postures which reinforce the social status, including physical pecking. When new birds are introduced into a flock, there is a period during which their position in the pecking order is established.

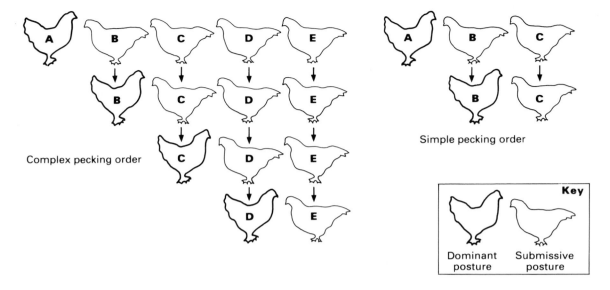

Fig.6.2 Pecking order in chickens. The dominant chicken is shown with a heavy outline, those in a lower pecking order are shown with a thin line. In the pecking order for a group of hens, the dominant hen **A** can peck hen **B** and hen **C**, but neither hen can peck her. Hen **B** can peck hen **C** and hen **D** and so on.

In a confined space, such as a yard or hen-house, chickens still try to establish a territory within which they move: straying beyond the arbitrarily defined limits may result in an increasing amount of pecking from other birds. In a large flock, subgroups become defined, within which the hierarchies are established. With laying hens in a confined space, those lower in the pecking order tend to produce fewer eggs, but this effect is avoided with layers kept in intensive battery cages. As light intensity becomes lower, as occurs towards dusk, demand for space required is reduced, hence the 'calming' effect of low light on birds.

Chickens also communicate by a range of calls, each of which may have a different meaning. These may indicate alarm, or are associated with finding food, with courtship and with egg laying, and broody hens have a series which allows elaborate communication with their chicks. Chickens show preference for social association rather than being kept in isolation. They also scratch the ground (or litter in artificial systems) and bath in the dust as a means of cleaning themselves. Deprivation of both space and suitable ground cover may lead to poor health, loss of feathers and extremes of behaviour.

■ LIFE HISTORY AND REARING OF CHICKENS

■ Female reproductive system

Two *ovaries* are present in the embryo but only the left ovary and oviduct develop to become functional in the mature hen. This ovary may contain 2000-12 000 or more *ova* of different sizes, but in modern poultry practices, probably only 200-300 of these are ovulated. The ova develop in sequence to be released in order of their relative size, the largest first. In a laying hen the largest are several millimetres in diameter and are visible to the naked eye in a dissected ovary. There are likely to be five or six large yellow developing egg yolks (follicles) and a large number of very small white follicles which represent immature undeveloped yolks. The relative sizes in the follicular hierarchy of successive ova in a hen's ovary are illustrated in Fig.6.4. The Graafian follicle, filled with yolk, contains the *ovum* together with its surrounding membranes. The follicular membrane, which attaches the follicle to the ovary, is well supplied with blood vessels. These bring the components of the yolk from the blood to the yolk. Part of the follicular membrane lacks blood vessels and is known as the stigma. At ovulation, the membrane ruptures at the stigma, and the whole structure is released from the ovary and develops into the future yolk of the egg.

Ova of different sizes attached to the ovary of a hen

Several different hormones are involved at successive stages of the reproductive cycle (Fig.6.3). *Follicle stimulating hormone* (FSH) from the anterior pituitary is responsible for initiating the development of the ovarian follicle. As the ovary reaches maturity it starts secreting *oestrogen* which leads to the development of the oviduct. Oestrogen also promotes formation of medullary bone tissue in the narrow cavity of the femur and some other bones. This acts as a store for calcium which is required at egg-laying for the formation of the shell. At the same time there is an increase in the blood levels of calcium, protein, fat and vitamins, which are needed for egg formation. Oestrogen also influences events leading to the softening and spread of the pubic bones and enlarging of the vent, ready for laying of the egg (oviposition). *Progesterone* produced by the ovary stimulates hormone releasing factors of the hypothalamus to release *luteinising hormone* (LH) from the anterior pituitary. LH is responsible for stimulating ovulation of the mature yolk from the ovary. *Oxytocin*, from the posterior pituitary, influences the expulsion of the egg after it has passed through the oviduct. *Male sex hormone* secreted by the mature ovary contributes to the bright red of the comb and wattles in a laying hen. The roles and interrelationships of these various hormones are summarised in Fig.6.3. The reproductive cycle is influenced by light: longer day length promotes the laying of eggs. Day length influences the timing mechanism which controls release of luteinsing hormone from the pituitary gland.

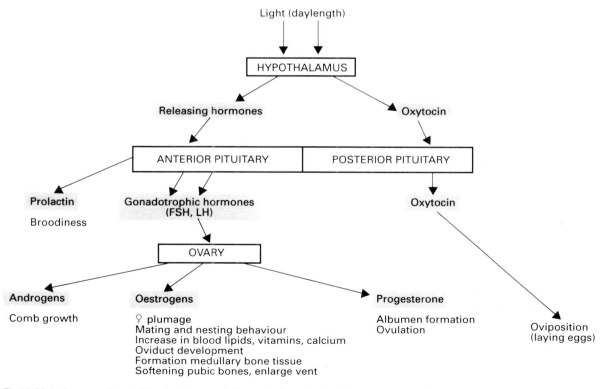

Fig.6.3 Major hormones (shaded) involved in control of reproduction and related events in female chickens

■ Ovulation to laying the egg

The *oviduct* (Fig.6.4) consists of six main regions, each with a different function in relation to egg-laying. At ovulation the yolk mass together with the ovum is released from the ovary into the *infundibulum*, then passes into the main portion of the oviduct. The infundibulum provides a short-term storage site for sperm, and fertilisation of an ovum may occur either here or as the ovum enters the *magnum*. The magnum is the longest and most conspicuous part of the oviduct. It is white, with thick walls and is of relatively large diameter. It has prominent mucus-secreting cells in the walls, including a large number of ciliated cells covered in albumen. In the magnum the albumen (egg white) is secreted in layers around the yolk.

The albumen is uniform as it is secreted, but becomes differentiated into thick and thin layers because of twisting movements of the ovum as it passes along the oviduct, and water is also added. Peristaltic movements carry the albumen-coated ovum into the *isthmus*, which is narrower than the magnum. The two shell membranes are produced in the isthmus. The *tubular shell gland* is involved in the transfer of calcium salts to the shell membranes.

The *uterus* (or *shell gland pouch*) is the region where the egg swells from a flaccid state, as a result of addition of fluid. The bulk of the hard shell material is added here, including calcium salts and finally pigment. The shell has an organic matrix consisting of a glycoprotein which forms a fine fibrous net into which salts are deposited to form the hard shell. The hard shell consists of 98% calcium carbonate with some magnesium, phosphate and citrate. Nearly 2 g of calcium is deposited in each eggshell, making very heavy demands on calcium in the diet. The *vagina* contains *sperm host glands*, responsible for providing nutrients which enable the sperm to remain viable before being carried up the oviduct by cilia and antiperistaltic movements. The completed egg leaves the oviduct through the *cloaca*.

The whole process of laying an egg, from the time of ovulation to the deposition of the egg in its hardened shell (oviposition), takes about 28 hours, with the bulk of the time (about 20 hours) being spent in the uterus. Ovulation usually occurs sometime after midnight so most eggs are laid during daylight, progressively later each day over a period of time, until darkness intervenes. After a gap of a day or so, a fresh 'sequence' starts. In highly productive hens, laying may continue for more days without a gap and the period of egg formation may be shortened to about 24 hours.

■ Structure of the egg

Eggs vary in size. Those laid earlier in a sequence are slightly larger than the later ones, and eggs from younger birds, starting to lay at 20 weeks of age, are smaller than those from older birds, say about 50 weeks of age. An egg is irregularly ovoid in shape (with one end more pointed and the other blunt) but are, on average, between 5 cm and 6 cm in length and weigh approximately 60 g.

The familiar outer shell has important biological functions and almost accidentally provides a solid (but fragile) packaging material. The shell consists of inner and outer membranes with calcium salts being laid down in the spongy layer (Fig.6.5). The

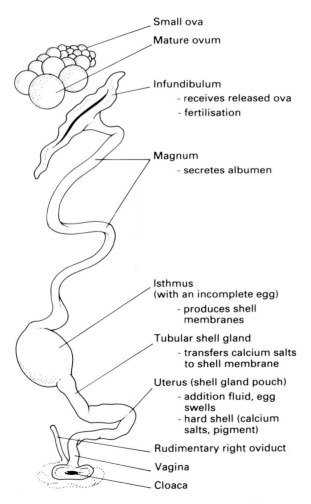

Small ova

Mature ovum

Infundibulum
- receives released ova
- fertilisation

Magnum
- secretes albumen

Isthmus
(with an incomplete egg)
- produces shell membranes

Tubular shell gland
- transfers calcium salts to shell membrane

Uterus (shell gland pouch)
- addition fluid, egg swells
- hard shell (calcium salts, pigment)

Rudimentary right oviduct

Vagina

Cloaca

Fig.6.4 Oviduct of a hen and the contribution made by different regions in the laying of an egg

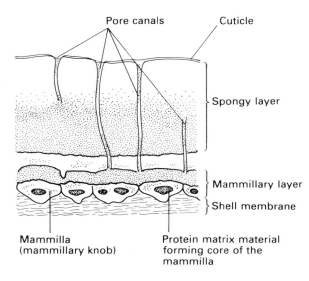

Fig.6.5 Section through the shell of a hen's egg. Calcium salts are laid down in the spongy layer and provide the hardness. The pores allow gas exchange and the cuticle reduces moisture loss and prevents entry of bacteria

membranes consist of the protein keratin, the outer being thicker than the inner. Both membranes are partially permeable, allowing passage of water and salts. The pores in the shell allow gas exchange and are partly closed with a cuticle, which helps reduce moisture loss and prevent entry of bacteria. The outer, thin, dense layer is mainly responsible for preventing entry of bacteria whereas the inner layer is more open and granular, providing strength and rigidity and also acts as a source of calcium for the growing embryo for calcification of its bones. During formation of the shell, calcium is drawn first from the gut of the hen, then from the medullary bone tissue.

In modern systems of egg production, high rates of lay, use of battery cages and mechanical methods for collecting eggs, tend to increase the likelihood of physical damage to eggs. Short cycles of light alternating with dark improve the quality of shells, probably in response to the level of calcium in the intestine. Mechanical washing of eggs for sale removes much of the cuticle, so eggs are sprayed with an oily mist to replace its protective properties. The brown colour of eggs is largely market-led: in the UK brown is more popular while white eggs are preferred in the United States.

Eggs when laid are not eggs in the biological sense of a female gamete capable of being fertilised. The egg when laid is either infertile and

the shell prevents fertilisation, or fertile and so no longer an egg.

The internal structure of the egg is shown in Fig.6.6. The bulk of the egg is made up of albumen (egg white), a complex mixture of about 40 different types of proteins. Albumen has a nutritional function for the developing embryo, but it also provides a source of water, acts as a bacteriocide, protects the yolk against mechanical injury and presents a surface for the deposition of the shell membranes. Within the albumen four layers of alternating thick and thin white can be distinguished, the thick white making up about half of the total. The *chalazae* are coils of twisted mucoid fibres, derived from the albumen, and they form a link between the very thin chalaziferous layer of dense white adjacent to the yolk and the main region of thick white. The turgidity of the albumen is important for providing support for the shell membranes.

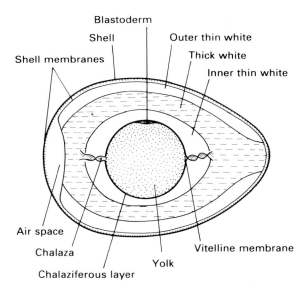

Fig.6.6 Internal structure of a fertile hen's egg

The yolk is held within the albumen by the chalazae. In a fertilised egg, the germinal disc or *blastoderm*, which has the potential to develop into the embryo, can be seen as a whitish disc, about 4 mm in diameter. It floats upright at the top of the yolk, held in position by the latebra (stalk) within the yolk. The yolk consists mainly of phospholipids, synthesised in the liver; its yellow colour is due to carotenoid pigments. Occasional double-yolked eggs result from two yolks moving through the oviduct at the same time, usually because two ova are ovulated together. Blood spots sometimes appear on the yolk, due to irregular tearing on the stigma of the follicle at ovulation. When the egg is laid, the surrounding temperature is cooler than the body temperature of the hen, so the egg contents contract, leaving the air cell at the blunt end, between the two shell membranes.

Q What variation can you find in commercially available eggs? Carry out your own investigations on size, colour, shape, yolk colour and taste.

■ Male reproductive system and mating

The reproductive system of the male bird consists of a pair of yellow testes (which remain within the body cavity), the epididymus and the vas deferens (Fig.6.7). A courtship display is followed by the mating process in which a cock bird grasps the hen by the skin at the back of the neck then mounts her. Sperm held in the vas deferens is ejaculated in semen into the entrance of the oviduct. The sperm move up the oviduct towards the infundibulum, where fertilisation normally occurs. A domesticated hen lays eggs without the need for mating and fertilisation - though, of course, these are infertile.

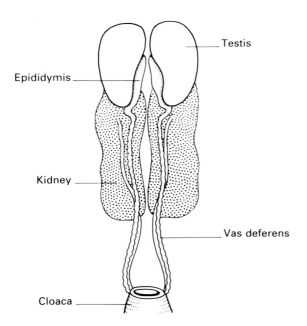

Fig.6.7 Reproductive system of a male chicken

In a *breeding flock*, seven to ten males are allowed for every 100 hens. Use of artificial insemination (AI) is still limited with chickens. This is due to labour costs rather than the lack of technological development. The extreme development of a heavy breast in turkeys bred for meat production has resulted in birds that are almost incapable of mating naturally, hence the extensive use of AI in the turkey breeding industry.

■ Development and hatching of the egg

The fertilised egg takes 21 days to develop until the chick hatches. During this time it must be maintained at a temperature of about 38 °C and a humidity in the region of 90%. In the natural state, the hen lays her clutch of eggs then becomes 'broody', signifying a change in her behaviour pattern which ensures that she sits on the nest and maintains the required conditions for incubation through to hatching. Broodiness is part of the natural reproductive cycle which starts with courtship and mating, followed by nest building and laying of the clutch of eggs. An increase in prolactin secretion from the pituitary gland occurs during incubation and a reduction during the parental phase, after the chicks have hatched. The first few eggs laid by the hen can be left for a few days before they start to develop. Sitting must then be more or less continuous to ensure successful development. A naturally broody hen turns her eggs several times a day which ensures the embryo and yolk are kept free from the membranes. She maintains the temperature with her body warmth and the feathers provide insulation and help keep the required humidity. In modern breeds of hens, if a broody behaviour pattern persists, the hen stops laying for a period of time leading to a reduction in the total yield of eggs from that hen. So it is an advantage to commercial producers that the broody characteristic has almost been lost in modern breeds selected for high egg yield.

Eggs required commercially for development into chicks are incubated in hatcheries under controlled artificial conditions. Eggs from laying hens are collected several times daily and can be stored for up to a week at 15 °C and 75% relative humidity. If they are kept longer, they should be turned to ensure the embryo and yolk are kept free from the membranes. In a commercial incubator, eggs are placed with the large end of the egg uppermost as this position allows the embryo to develop near the air cell, and also makes it easier for the chick to emerge from the egg.

The temperature is maintained at 37.8 °C with adequate ventilation to ensure even temperatures and allow for gaseous exchange. During incubation, short periods of cooling can be tolerated, as would occur in a naturally sitting hen, but embryos are easily damaged by cooling during the last two days (the time when a hen sits 'tightly' on her nest).

The embryo itself generates heat so adequate ventilation is needed to ensure excess heat is lost. The humidity in the air reduces loss of moisture from the egg which would lead to drying out of the embryo. Throughout the incubation, turning is done mechanically by automatic rotation of the trays of eggs through 90° every few hours. Levels of gases are monitored, particularly that of carbon dioxide, since hatchability is noticeably decreased if the level of carbon dioxide rises to about 2%. Reduced oxygen also decreases the percentage that hatch successfully. A very high standard of hygiene is required in the hatchery to keep down diseases, including those passed from hen to chick through the egg.

It is easy to observe the internal changes taking place within the egg (known as embryology), leading to the development of the chick. Development of a chordate embryo can be considered in four continuous stages: *fertilisation*, *cleavage*, *gastrulation* and *organogeny*. During cleavage, the fertilised egg (zygote) divides by mitosis, first into two cells, these each divide into two more, then double to eight and then to sixteen, and so on. These small cells or blastomeres form into a hollow sphere enclosing a central cavity (the blastocoel), and at this stage the embryo is called the blastula. The next stage, gastrulation, sees a rearrangement of the cells into layers which become *ectoderm* (on the outside), *mesoderm* and *endoderm* (inside). Already at this stage, cells in certain positions are destined to become future structures of the developing embryo. Cells of the ectoderm will (in the chicken) give rise to the skin, feathers, beak, claws, nervous system and the linings of the mouth and vent. The endoderm cells give rise to the respiratory and secretory organs and to the linings of the digestive tract, and the mesoderm to bones, muscles, blood, excretory and reproductive systems. Organogeny sees the development of organs and other structures in a controlled sequence.

The presence of the large yolk in birds distorts the early divisions which take place during cleavage, resulting in the development of a single layer of cells rather than a sphere. This appears as a cap, known as the *blastoderm*, which is clearly separated from the yolk by a small fluid-filled space. In the chicken, the ovum is fertilised within 15 minutes of ovulation and cleavage of the fertilised ovum begins during its passage through the oviduct. The first division takes place about five hours after fertilisation as the egg enters the isthmus; subsequent divisions take place so that it reaches the 256-cell stage about nine hours after fertilisation. These cells have arisen mainly by divisions in a vertical plane and form a single layer, the *epiblast* (or ectoderm); occasional horizontal divisions produce a second layer underneath, the *hypoblast* (or endoderm). The whole egg is generally laid during gastrulation.

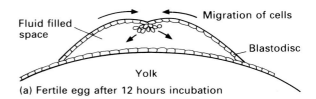
(a) Fertile egg after 12 hours incubation

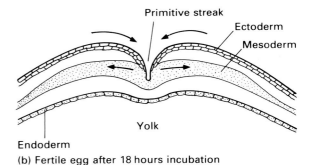
(b) Fertile egg after 18 hours incubation

Fig.6.8 The early stages of development of a hen's egg after fertilisation showing cell migration during gastrulation

Development resumes once incubation has started. Cell division continues and cells migrate from the edge of the blastoderm (cap) to the middle and rearrange themselves in other positions (Fig.6.8). At about 18 hours after the start of incubation a noticeable groove, the *primitive streak* (Fig.6.9) can be seen with the help of a hand lens, in the centre of a clear area. Towards the front end of the primitive streak, a bulbous swelling forms which appears to be the main organising area for subsequent differentiation of cells and areas.

Four membranes, the *extra embryonic membranes*, develop outside the embryo, forming sacs known as the *yolk sac*, the *amnion*, *chorion*

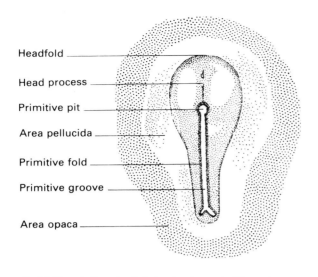

Headfold

Head process

Primitive pit

Area pellucida

Primitive fold

Primitive groove

Area opaca

Fig.6.9 The primitive streak during development of the embryo (surface view)

and *allantois*. These have important functions for the developing embryo (see Fig.6.10). The yolk sac forms from a layer of endoderm and mesoderm growing over the surface of the yolk. The yolk sac is well supplied with blood vessels which enable nutrients to be carried from the yolk into the embryo. The amnion and chorion develop from ectoderm and endoderm folding around the whole embryo. They contain a fluid, part of which is derived from the albumen. The fluid bathes the embryo, allowing it to float freely during development, giving protection from dehydration and mechanical shocks, and insulation from temperature changes. The allantois comes from mesoderm, is well supplied with blood capillaries and provides the respiratory surface for exchange of gases until the lungs take over the day before hatching. Waste nitrogenous material is passed into the fluid in the allantois.

Further development occurs rapidly, the sequence being summarised in Fig.6.10. For example, the heart is formed by the second day and the leg and wing buds together with the nervous system are becoming evident by the fourth day.

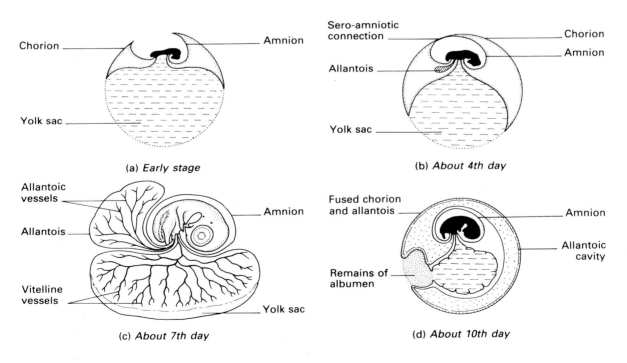

Chorion

Amnion

Yolk sac

(a) *Early stage*

Sero-amniotic connection

Chorion

Amnion

Allantois

Yolk sac

(b) *About 4th day*

Allantoic vessels

Allantois

Amnion

Vitelline vessels

Yolk sac

(c) *About 7th day*

Fused chorion and allantois

Amnion

Allantoic cavity

Remains of albumen

(d) *About 10th day*

Fig.6.10 Development of the embryo in a hen's egg. The extra-embryonic sac at an early stage and on about the 4th, 7th and 10th day

The embryo derives its nutrients mainly from the yolk sac. Just before hatching, the remains of the yolk sac are drawn into the body of the chick and this can sustain the chick for two or three days after hatching. Calcium required for the skeleton is absorbed from the shell, which becomes weaker, thus helping the hatching process. As the embryo develops, the air cell increases in size and it is probably the composition of the gases in the air cell which initiates the chick's urge to emerge from the shell. Oxygen in the air cell may fall to 15-16% and carbon dioxide may rise as high as 4%. The embryo starts to breathe air through the lungs on the twentieth day.

After 21 days of incubation, the chick is ready to hatch. To emerge from the shell, the chick repeatedly jerks its head, using the 'egg tooth' (a structure lost after hatching) to break gradually first through the allantois, then through the membrane separating this from the air space. Over a period of several hours, the shell fractures or 'pips', allowing the chick to escape. The newly hatched chick is wet and exhausted, but within a few hours it dries out to a fluffy chick, able to move around actively.

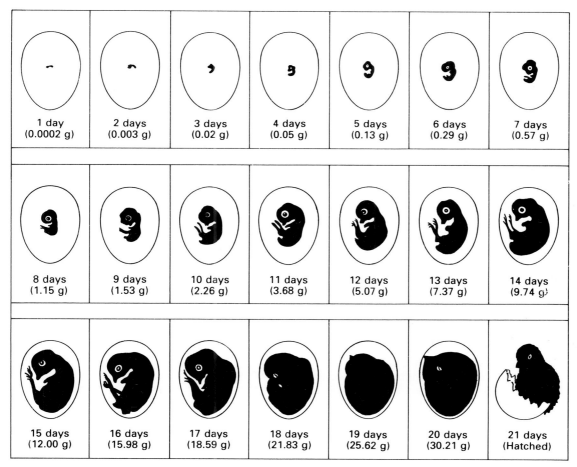

Fig.6.11 The chick hatches 21 days after the start of incubation. The diagram shows the changes and gain in weight of the embryo at different stages of development

Newly hatched chick

In commercial hatcheries, newly hatched day-old chicks are usually sexed either by examination of the vent or by use of sex-linked characters which are detectable at this age. These include feather-sexing (day-old females of some breeds having longer wing feathers than males) or making use of differences in down colour between the sexes. Future laying flocks require only females but even with broiler chickens, there are advantages in keeping males and females separate to ensure feeds are adjusted precisely to the requirements of each sex. Day-old chicks can be transported considerable distances, provided they are packed in suitable containers with reasonable temperatures. No outside food supply is required as the chicks use up the remains of the yolk sac. Large-scale hatcheries have become a specialised part of the poultry industry, supplying day-old chicks to intensive units either to become layers to produce eggs or to be grown into broilers for meat.

■ Growth and development of the chicks

A broody hen will naturally continue to protect her chicks, jealously guarding them against intruders, keeping them warm by spreading her feathers over them and leading them to food. Over a period of a few weeks the chicks gradually gain their independence. In commercial houses, the brooding conditions are artificially simulated. Growing chicks, reared from day-olds, need to be kept warm, at first requiring a temperature of 35 °C, then over a period of three weeks this is reduced in three stages to 24 °C. They should have free access to crumbs of food, which may be spread on belts on the floor with fresh water continually available at first from pipes with nipples and later from containers designed to avoid spillage.

■ LAYING HENS

Control over the environment together with selection of productive strains has resulted in a very high rate of egg-laying in the modern hen, averaging about 250 per year. Lengthening of each sequence of egg-laying is brought about by adjusting the light/dark regime, stimulating response to the photoperiod, and inducing moulting. Day-old chicks are usually given 23 hours of daylight, which allows them to find food and water. After one or two days this is reduced to an eight-hour day length. After 18 weeks, day length is then increased to reach the ideal day length of 17 hours which is suitable for maintaining hens in lay. Where natural daylight is being used, the day length can be extended, when required, using artificial light. Young hens (pullets) usually start to lay at an age of 20 weeks. A hen tends to lay for a period, then moults and egg production stops. Moulting can be induced artificially by changing lighting and feeding regimes. On recovery from moulting, the hen starts to lay again.

In the management of flocks on an annual basis, decisions must be taken as to when to replace the stock, or whether to extend the laying period by induced moulting. The main concern of the egg producer is to maintain a supply of eggs that matches market demands. Eggs may be marketed directly for consumption, or fertilised eggs hatched and reared into broilers for meat or kept to provide replacement laying hens.

A number of systems, from free range to highly intensive, are used for laying hens. The main differences relate to the space available, hence the degree of movement possible and association with other birds (see Table 6.1).

System	Space
Free range	370 birds per ha
Semi-intensive	1000 birds per ha
Straw yard	3 birds per m^2
Deep litter	7-10 birds per m^2
Aviary, perchery, multi-tier	20 birds per m^2
Laying cage	450-750 cm^2 per bird

Table 6.1 Space allowed per bird in different systems

Outdoor systems include free range, semi-intensive and straw yard, whereas deep litter, aviary, perchery, multi-tier and laying cage are

Free range hens

Battery cage hens

indoor systems. In free-range systems, birds must have access to open-air runs with suitable vegetation and be provided with housing for the night and for laying of eggs. There should be adequate supplies of fresh water and some shelter. A potential danger of free-range systems is that, as a result of over-use, the land becomes 'fowl sick', with a buildup or organisms causing disease. The vegetation can deteriorate, partly because of the pecking, dust bathing and other activities of the birds but also because of the excess of fresh poultry manure which is acid and very rich in nitrogen. These difficulties can be overcome by rotating the area of land being occupied and keeping careful control of the stocking density.

Precautions should be taken to protect the birds against predators such as foxes and even dogs and cats. In semi-intensive systems, outside access is available in wire enclosures. Straw yards are open to the weather but have the protection of a roof. Plenty of litter, usually chopped straw, must be provided, together with nest boxes and perches.

For indoor systems, the deep litter system gives the birds some freedom of movement in a house with the floor covered with a deep layer of wood shavings, peat or other material. Perches and nest boxes are provided. This system may be particularly useful for breeding flocks as the males can be included with the flock, allowing mating to occur. Disadvantages are that some eggs may be laid on the floor, becoming dirty and thus need special collecting. Pecking orders become established amongst the birds and, in the relatively confined space, some birds, low in the pecking order, may become deprived of food or even suffer physical injuries. The perches should be arranged so that most of the droppings fall into a pit or limited area and can then be removed, keeping the rest of the litter reasonably dry.

The battery cage system accounts for about 90% of the eggs produced commercially. A high degree of automation is used at all stages to increase efficiency and lower the costs of production. Attempts have been made to devise systems allowing more freedom of movement for the birds with a *get away* area offering a nest box and perch. Aviary and perchery systems give different arrangements for stacking of the cages. Cages may hold up to six birds and are arranged to allow adequate access and removal of droppings. Food is generally provided in troughs by a moving chain feeder and water is continually available from nipples or drinking troughs.

The floor slopes, allowing eggs, as they are laid, to roll onto conveyor belts which carry them straight to the cleaning, grading and packing area. Provision is made to remove droppings, either from a moving belt or from pits below the cages. In battery cage systems, there is complete control of the environment in terms of lighting (intensity and duration), temperature, humidity and ventilation.

Criticism of and public concern relating to the battery system on welfare grounds comes because the birds are extremely restricted in their movement. They are unable to take exercise, dust bath or form natural social associations with other birds; they lack the privacy birds normally seek for egg laying, and may suffer from breast blisters, lameness and loss of feathers. Lack of feathers removes the natural insulation provided, so temperatures in the houses must be higher to compensate. Arguments in favour of the battery system are that the birds are in a controlled environment and are not exposed to climatic extremes or predators and, under good management, disease risk is low. From the commercial point of view, the consumer can be offered eggs at a lower cost.

BROILERS FOR MEAT

In the broiler industry, systems are geared to producing birds of a certain weight in a certain time (say 2 kg in 41 days), keeping costs as low as possible. A number of units work in phase to provide a continuous supply of meat. The largest single annual cost is that of food and strict precautions must be taken to minimise losses due to disease.

Young chickens in a broiler house

In a chicken farm, birds are typically housed in single-storey wooden buildings. Several houses are grouped on one site, isolated from other nearby sites to reduce the risk of transfer of disease. The house provides a controlled environment for the birds from their arrival as one-day-old chicks until they reach the desired weight usually 41 days later. Ventilation is achieved by air inlets in the sides of the house and vents in the roof. Circulation may be enhanced by electrical fans and in hot weather air movement may need to be considerably increased. Ventilation helps remove moisture released from respiration, thus avoiding excessive condensation which would lead to release of ammonia from waste products accumulated in the litter. Houses should be well insulated to avoid temperature extremes, though artificial heat can be used when required. A range of materials, such as straw, wood shavings or straw pellets can be used as litter, which is important both to provide insulation and as a material to absorb the droppings from the chickens. A relatively low level of lighting is normally used throughout, though in some cases chickens are kept in darkness for a short period of, say, two hours in 24. In closed houses, a maximum stocking density of 20 birds per m² is allowed. One of the major problems is the disposal of vast quantities of poultry manure. It can be recycled as farm compost or even used as a fuel for power stations.

Chicken litter to electricity

A continuous supply of clean fresh water is essential, and the rate of consumption of water gives a useful measure of growth rate. Water may be provided in troughs or pipes with nipples. Food is supplied for day-old chicks on strips on the floor, then later from troughs or moving belts. 'Starter' crumbs are given to the chicks at first, followed by 'grower' pellets between three and four weeks and a 'finisher' up to the time of slaughter. The percentage protein changes as the chicks grow. The protein may originate from white fishmeal and different types of soya preparations. The feed also includes cereals (wheat, maize or barley) and mineral salts. After the required number of days most of the birds reach the desired weight together and the whole flock is removed from the house, and transported to the processing unit. Here, in a matter of minutes the birds are stunned, killed, plucked, eviscerated and prepared for the next stage. They may be chilled for immediate sale, frozen or processed for further 'value-added' products including pies, complete meals and pâté. The houses are completely cleared out, cleaned and disinfected, ready for the next arrival of day-old chicks a few days later and the cycle starts again.

CHAPTER 7

FISH

■ ORIGINS OF FISH FARMING

Fish farming has probably been practised for about 4000 years in China, where carp was the first species known to be domesticated. References to ponds stocked with fish appear in the Bible, in writings from ancient Egypt and from the monasteries of medieval Europe. Farming of seafish started in Indonesia about 600 years ago, and has shown considerable expansion, particularly in Japan and other parts of Asia, since the 1960s. In Europe, development of trout and salmon culture on a commercial scale began in the late 19th century, grew in importance during the first half of the 20th century and has shown a rapid escalation over the last 20 or 30 years, a response in part to declining stocks of wild fish.

The degree of domestication in fish is far less than in cattle and poultry and there is relatively little difference between wild fish and those bred and reared in captivity. Fish farmers are now actively looking for wild species showing characters with the potential for adapting to cultivation in an intensive environment, and there is future scope for development of controlled breeding for genetic change. There has been some artificial selection and change in domesticated carp, a species which has remained important in China and other Asian countries as well as in Europe, but the development of breeds of fish is in its infancy.

■ THE MODERN FISH FARMING INDUSTRY

Aquaculture, in the sense of farming of animals in water, now accounts for about 10% of the total fish harvest, the bulk of fisheries being geared towards catching wild fish, mainly from the sea. Less than half of the produce from aquaculture comes from farmed finfish, the majority being shellfish, especially mussels and oysters. Since the 1970s, there has been a steady increase in production of farmed fish and this trend is likely to accelerate into the 21st century. In Taiwan, for example, during the 1980s, there was a threefold increase in production of farmed fish due largely to development of inten-

sive systems. In 1984, the total estimated world production of farmed finfish was nearly 4 million tonnes (Fig.7.1). On a global scale, the bulk of the farming of finfish (about 75%) is concentrated in Asia, including China, Japan, Taiwan, the Philippines and Indonesia, with less than 20% in Europe and about 6% in the USA. Relatively little development of fish farming has occurred in Africa and Latin America where it could make a useful contribution to food production, whereas in South East Asia, small-scale subsistence fish farming has proved highly successful.

Within the fish-farming industry, there is a range of systems, for marine and freshwater fish from small-scale, semi-intensive (low input) through to highly intensive. The principles involved can be seen in methods used for production of intensively farmed freshwater rainbow trout (*Salmo gairdneri*). The closely related Atlantic salmon (*Salmo salar*) is now farmed extensively in the coastal waters, for example, of Scotland and Norway. Fish produced in these fish farms may be marketed for human consumption in a range of forms or used to provide live fish to stock rivers and lakes for anglers.

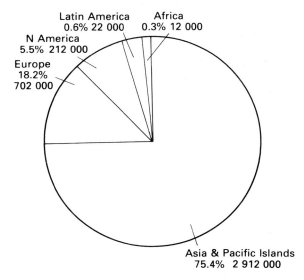

Latin America
0.6% 22 000

Africa
0.3% 12 000

N America
5.5% 212 000

Europe
18.2%
702 000

Asia & Pacific Islands
75.4% 2 912 000

Fig.7.1 Production (in tonnes) of farmed finfish in 1984 showing approximate worldwide distribution

■ BIOLOGY OF THE TROUT

The trout belongs to the family Salmonidae, native to temperate zones in the northern hemisphere, though wild stocks have been introduced to favourable waters in the southern hemisphere. In natural conditions, they are carnivorous, fast swimmers and slimly built. They spawn in fresh water, but can migrate for part of their life cycle to marine waters.

Compared with life on land, living in water has certain implications for the biology of fish. Fish are poikilothermic ('cold-blooded'), so their body temperature responds directly to that of the surrounding water. This means that the rates of metabolic processes, including growth and their physical activity, are strongly influenced by water temperature. It also means that energy is not used in maintaining body temperature and, because of the support provided by water, much less energy is required for support and locomotion. Fish are thus potentially more efficient than terrestrial animals at converting food into flesh.

The external surface (Fig. 7.2) of the fish is made up of two layers: an inner dermis and a thin outer epidermis which is continually sloughed off and contains mucus-secreting cells. The mucus makes the fish more streamlined and also gives some protection against entry of pollutants and microorganisms. The body scales arise from the inner dermis and, in the wild, show growth rings of varying thickness which result from seasonal variation, say in diet or temperature. These rings can be used to determine the age of the fish but such differences in thickness are less evident in farmed individuals that are raised under more uniform conditions.

Water is the medium through which exchange of gases occurs, as well as movement of salts and excretion from the fish. The amount of oxygen available in water is only about one-twentieth that in air and is affected by changes in temperature. Uptake of oxygen and release of carbon dioxide occurs through the gills which are richly supplied with blood capillaries and provide a very large surface area in contact with the water. Ventilation or flow of water through the gills is achieved by water entering the mouth then being forced out through the operculum due to up and down movements of the floor of the mouth. Because the gills are continuously in contact with water, movement of water and salts occurs through the gills. In fresh water, water is taken in by osmosis

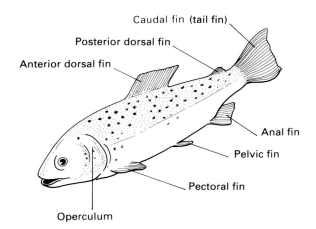

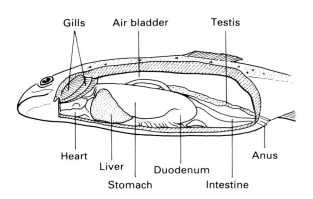

Body wall removed to show some internal features of a male trout

Fig. 7.2 External and internal features of a fish

and salts are lost by diffusion; in sea water, the opposite occurs. In both, some exchange also occurs through the body surface. To maintain the ionic balance, fish need to osmoregulate. In fresh water, fish actively take up salts through their gills and excrete large quantities of dilute urine, whereas in sea water, gills actively secrete salts and relatively little concentrated urine is excreted (see Fig. 7.3).

The main nitrogenous waste product is ammonia which is excreted through the gills into the water. Any deterioration of water quality, or the presence of particles in the water or infection from microorganisms could affect the gills, and in turn affect the respiration, maintenance of salt balance and excretion in the fish.

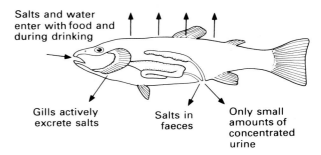

Water passively enters and salts are lost through gills and body surface

Salts enter with food

Salts actively taken up by gills

Some salts in faeces

Copious dilute urine

(a) *Fresh water*

Water is passively lost and salts enter through gills and body surface

Salts and water enter with food and during drinking

Gills actively excrete salts

Salts in faeces

Only small amounts of concentrated urine

(b) *Sea water*

Fig.7.3 Osmoregulation in fish

■ LIFE HISTORY AND CULTURE OF TROUT

■ Reproduction

The paired ovaries and testes lie dorsally in the body cavity and are very small in immature fish. Interaction of external factors with the hormones of the fish leads to the maturation of the ovaries and testes followed by spawning (release of eggs and sperm). The external factors include light, photoperiod and temperature, and these stimulate the release of hormones from the hypothalamus. This is followed by secretion of hormones (Fig.7.4) which act on the ovary and testis which in turn produce further hormones (mainly oestrogens and androgens, respectively). Both the ovaries and testes enlarge considerably as they mature, by which time the ovaries may occupy up to 30% of the body weight and the testes 10%. At ovulation ripe eggs are released into the abdominal cavity, where, in wild fish, they remain until courtship behaviour leads to their release through the urinogenital opening (vent).

In the wild, spawning is often an annual event, influenced by seasonal patterns of changing day-length and temperature, occurring at a time that is favourable for the subsequent development of eggs and young fish (fry). At the spawning season, trout swim upstream to shallow water where the stream bed is made up of clean stones. The female uses her tail to make a slight depression, known as a *redd*, into which she deposits her eggs. The male swims over, discharges sperm, and so the eggs become fertilised. The fertilised eggs are then covered over with gravel and left to develop.

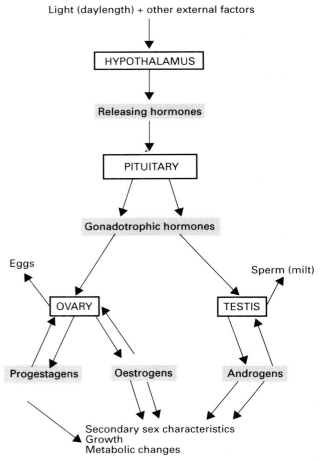

Fig.7.4 Major hormones involved in the control of reproduction in fish, leading to spawning

■ Control of spawning

In an intensive farm it is desirable to control the reproductive cycle so that production of marketable fish can be maintained regardless of the natural spawning season. An additional problem to overcome is that trout do not readily spawn in captivity.

Spawning time can be modified by changing the daylength (photoperiod). Keeping trout under a period of long days of 18 hours (with six hours of darkness) followed by constant short days of six hours (with 18 hours of darkness) can result in the spawning season being advanced or retarded by up to four months.

Spawning can also be induced by injection of hormones, derived from extracts of the pituitary gland. This practice alters the timing by only a few weeks so its main benefit is to enable broodstock to spawn under conditions of intensive cultivation. Some farms in the UK use eggs transported from the southern hemisphere (Tasmania or South Africa), thus taking advantage of their different spawning season.

■ Genetic manipulation of sex

The flesh of mature fish tends to lose quality and after spawning there is a high mortality rate, so fish raised for food are generally harvested before reaching sexual maturity. Males mature before females and they can cause problems due to their behaviour patterns and tendency to become aggressive at maturity. It is relatively easy to manipulate the sex of fish to produce single-sex or sterile stocks. In commercial farms stocks consisting wholly of females are preferred.

In most fish, females are homogametic (i.e. they have two sex chromosomes the same, XX) and males are heterogametic (i.e. they have two different sex chromosomes, XY). The genetic sex is established at fertilisation but determination of the actual sex occurs later during the development in response to hormone levels during the period of sexual differentiation. Sex reversal can be achieved by feeding hormones to the fish, thus overriding the genetic sex (as determined by the X and Y chromosomes). Male hormones or androgens will produce all males (with male sexual characteristics and testes capable of making sperm at maturity). Oestrogens will produce fish with ovaries and female characteristics. Hormones are administered in the feed to the young fish for a limited period only to ensure hormone residues are absent from the flesh at the time of harvest.

Sex reversal can be extended to the second generation of fish to produce all female fish. Genetic females (XX) are 'masculinised' by treatment with male hormones so that all sperm contain an X chromosome, rather than a mixture of X and Y. Fertilisation of X eggs with X sperm then results in all female (XX) offspring (Fig.7.5). There are some practical difficulties in separating the masculinised females and in obtaining sperm from them, but potentially this method avoids the objection of feeding hormones to fish raised for human consumption.

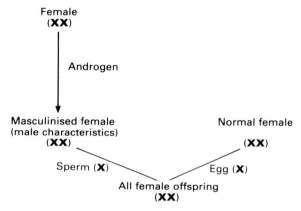

Fig.7.5 Sex reversal to produce stocks of all female fish

■ Sterilisation

Sterilisation allows the fish to continue their growth beyond the size at which they would normally mature. Sterilisation can be achieved either by hormone treatment (supplying higher doses of male hormones in the feed) or by inducing changes in the chromosome number. Triploids can be produced by subjecting the eggs to environmental shock at a critical stage during fertilisation. In trout, the temperature is raised to 28 °C for about 10 minutes during the period 20-40 minutes after fertilisation. The final division of the egg nucleus fails to occur, resulting in a diploid egg nucleus ($2n$) which becomes triploid ($3n$) when fertilised by the haploid (n) sperm. When grown separately these triploid fish show improved growth performance, do not spawn and avoid the deaths normally associated with maturation.

■ A TROUT FARM IN OPERATION

Fish farming tends to be specialised into *hatcheries* which produce and hatch the eggs through to fry (young fish) and *growing-on farms* which raise the fish (from fry) to marketable size.

■ Fertilisation and development of the young trout

The parent fish used to provide the eggs are known as the *broodstock*. Ripe females are recognised by their swollen bellies, due to the release of eggs at ovulation into the abdominal cavity. In the farm, the eggs are removed by a process known as *stripping*. The abdomen is stroked gently but firmly by hand, moving towards the tail, so that the eggs flow out through the vent and are collected in a container such as a bowl or bucket. Males are stripped in a similar way to provide sperm (known as *milt*).

Both eggs and sperm are kept dry at first, then water is added after 5-10 minutes. The sperm is then mixed with the eggs, using a finger or feather, to allow fertilisation to occur. The fertilised eggs are rinsed and allowed to harden.

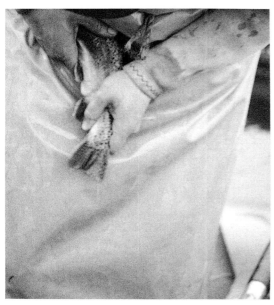
Stripping eggs

Immediately after fertilisation, eggs are extremely sensitive to disturbance and considerable losses can occur at this stage. Unfertilised eggs and milt are less sensitive and so can be transported to allow distribution to other farms, and eggs can be

Troughs for rearing young fry

stored at low temperatures (2-3 °C) for a few days.

The fertilised eggs develop through to hatching in an incubator, which usually consists of long troughs, holding large numbers of eggs in perforated trays. A flow of water is maintained through the incubator to ensure adequate oxygenation for the developing eggs. Dead eggs must be removed regularly to avoid growth of fungus; this can be done by hand or sometimes automatically. During incubation, eggs are normally kept in darkness as blue or violet light is damaging to them, though orange or yellow lights are safe to use.

The time taken for eggs and fry (young fish) to develop depends on the temperature of the water and is referred to as 'day-degrees'. Trout eggs require about 300 day-degrees to hatch, so, at a temperature of 8 °C, eggs would hatch in about 38 days (i.e. $38 \times 8 = 304$ day-degrees).

During incubation, eggs should continue to be kept in darkness (later semi-darkness) until the hatched fry are ready to feed. Part way through the incubation period (about 160 day-degrees for trout), the larval eyes become prominent as dark spots. At this stage the developing eggs can be safely transported from hatcheries to farms for growing-on into adult fish.

Newly hatched fry (known as *alevins*) swim through the perforations in the tray into larger troughs, leaving behind the remains of the eggshells and other debris. They remain in these troughs for a few weeks, but the rate of flow of water must be increased to allow for their higher oxygen demand. At first, the alevins derive nourishment from the remains of the yolk sac of the egg, but as this is used up they begin to swim up

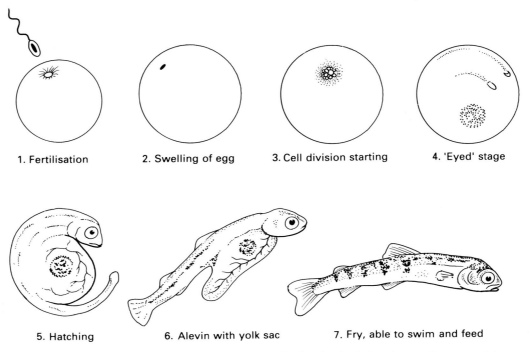

1. Fertilisation   2. Swelling of egg   3. Cell division starting   4. 'Eyed' stage

5. Hatching   6. Alevin with yolk sac   7. Fry, able to swim and feed

Fig.7.6 Stages in the development of the egg, from fertilisation to freely swimming fry (not drawn to the same scale)

towards the water surface, ready to take their 'first feed'. This is a critical stage for fish farmers to ensure feeding becomes established otherwise heavy losses may occur. Fry are generally reared in small tanks, less than 1 m deep. When fry reach a weight of approximately 5 g (200 fry per kg), they are generally sold on to growing-on farms.

■ Growing-on farms

The water quality is crucial to the success of a fish farm and several physical and chemical factors need to be monitored and controlled.

Fish may be affected in different ways by changes in temperature. Under natural conditions daily fluctuations in water temperature occur, the temperature rising to a peak during early afternoon with the lowest temperature a few hours before sunrise. Activity and growth rate of fish are both influenced by temperature. The optimum range for any particular fish species is likely to vary at different stages of the life cycle. Trout growers favour a temperature range of 0-20 °C, with an optimum of about 16 °C, though trout can survive under ice at 0 °C. Above 21 °C they can survive only for short periods and show extreme distress above 25 °C.

Temperature also affects solubility of oxygen and the level of free ammonia in the water. Fish depend on dissolved oxygen in the water for respiration.

Temperature/°C	0	10	20	30	40
Oxygen solubility /mg dm⁻³	14.6	11.3	9.2	7.6	6.6

Table 7.1

The solubility of oxygen in water decreases as the temperature rises (see Table 7.1) but the demand for oxygen by a fish increases with rise in temperature. The oxygen demand also increases with increased food intake and with increased activity. In relation to body mass, demand for oxygen decreases as the fish grows. Inadequate oxygen at any stage leads to suffocation of the fish, so adequate aeration is essential and the stocking density must be controlled.

Excretory products of the fish include carbon dioxide from respiration and nitrogenous material. Carbon dioxide in the water can affect pH, though normally carbon dioxide levels do not become critical. The bulk of the nitrogenous waste is ammonia. In its free state, ammonia is highly toxic, though it is far less toxic as the ammonium ion (NH_4^+). The balance between ammonium hydroxide and free ammonia depends on both pH and temperature: at a pH of 6.5 dissociation into the non-toxic ammonium ion is favoured, whereas at a pH of 8.5 there is a considerable increase in toxic free ammonia. At higher temperatures (15 °C and above) the level of toxic free ammonia increases and can very quickly become dangerous.

For trout, the preferred pH range of the water is just below neutral to slightly alkaline (6.4-8.4). Fluctuations in pH can cause considerable stress. Changes in the pH of the water supply may result from inflow of organic acids leached from soils, though hard water (associated with limestone areas) has some buffering capacity which helps to maintain a more stable pH.

Suspended solids and particles including silt and faecal material, when present at high levels, can cause damage to fish, particularly the gills. If polluted water enters a fish farm it may bring harmful effects to the fish. Run-off from agricultural land may carry a high level of nutrient, resulting in algal blooms which seriously deplete the available oxygen supply, due either to respiration of the algae during the night or to an increase in biochemical oxygen demand (BOD) if the bloom suddenly dies. Death of fish from oxygen depletion due to algal blooms is most likely during the night or early morning.

Organic matter from, say, sewage, farm waste or silage effluent, also increases the BOD, thus lowering the available oxygen for fish. Blue green bacteria are known to produce toxins and fish suffering from toxic algal bloom are likely to die during peak hours of sunlight. Dense growth of algae may interfere physically with the fish, particularly the gills, and may also lead to the blockage of pipes and machinery in the fishpond. Certain heavy metals, such as copper, lead and mercury, are toxic to fish and may occur in water originating from industrial effluents. Non-metals, such as ammonia and chlorine, and complex organic compounds, including those derived from herbicides and insecticides, may also reach toxic levels.

Mass mortality of fish, known as a *fish kill*, may occur quite suddenly, within a few hours of the fish feeding and behaving normally. Fish kills occur most commonly from lack of oxygen, though there may be other causes. (For further details of pollution and the environmental effects of fish farming see *Biology Advanced Studies - Environment and Ecology*.)

■ Layout of the fish farm

Ponds used for growing fish to market size are typically dug into the earth, though they may be lined with concrete, fibreglass or other materials. The size can vary considerably and an important factor is ease of access for maintenance, and feeding and monitoring the fish.

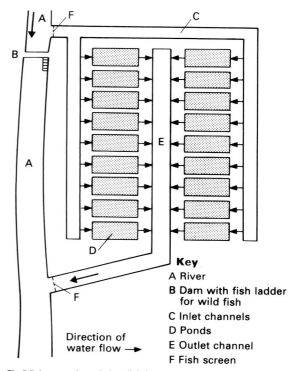

Key
A River
B Dam with fish ladder for wild fish
C Inlet channels
D Ponds
E Outlet channel
F Fish screen

Direction of water flow →

Fig.7.7 Layout of ponds in a fish farm

Pond in a typical trout farm, showing provision for netting and system for aeration of water

A series of ponds are arranged in sequence, surrounded by walkways to allow access for feeding and cleaning, and linked to common inlet and outlet channels for water flow. The layout usually allows a fresh water supply to each pond. There must be some means of controlling the water level and emptying the pond at intervals for cleaning and removal of accumulated sand or silt. Screens in the form of mesh or bars are essential: at the inlet they prevent entry of wild fish, leaves and other debris and at the outlet they stop fish escaping. Ponds are often covered with netting to protect against predators including birds such as herons.

The flow rate of water through the ponds needs to be adjusted to ensure adequate oxygenation, and this also influences the rate at which ammonia and carbon dioxide (from the fish metabolism) are dispersed from the water. If the flow rate is too high, fish will expend unnecessary energy in maintaining their position against the current; if the flow rate is too low the water stagnates, though mechanical devices are often used to improve the aeration.

Generally it is not economic to heat the water, except during early stages of growth, unless warmed water is available, say from a factory outlet. The level of oxygenation is probably the most critical factor in determining the stocking density, hence the profitability of the farm. The quality of effluent from the farm must be carefully monitored to ensure it is acceptable with respect to standards required by river authorities or equivalent bodies.

If water supplies are insufficient to meet the requirements of the fish, water may be recirculated. Such systems must include ways of restoring the water to the required quality, and may involve biological or ion-exchange filtration. Despite the higher costs of such operations, they may be appropriate on a small scale or where alternative sources of protein (for the consumer) are scarce.

An alternative to ponds is to grow fish in cages, in freshwater lakes or in the sea. Advantages of using cages for the culture of fish are that there is less chance of problems with water supply or oxygenation, though it is important that cages are strong and securely anchored in sheltered water, particularly when in the sea. There is risk of pollution from outside sources (e.g. oil tanker spills) and also from the fish themselves if the water movement is insufficient to remove their own waste products.

▪ Growing on and feeding

Feeding requirements depend on the size of the fish and the temperature of the water. Relatively higher rates of feeding, in relation to body weight, are required by fry, and the rate decreases as the fish grow larger. Feeds are usually supplied as pellets, the size and formulation being adjusted as the fish grow, and can be delivered by hand or automatically. Young fry require almost continual feed, in fine pellets, whereas mature broodstock fish can take their whole day's ration at once, as large pellets.

Fish cages in a Norwegian fjord

Trout are carnivores and there is a heavy demand in the diet for protein, up to about 70% during the rapid growing stage. Preference is for animal protein though small amounts of vegetable protein can be utilised. Protein is the main source of energy, but incorporation of lipids, and to a lesser extent carbohydrates, lowers the cost of the feed. Too much carbohydrate has harmful effects, leading to swollen bodies and an excess of glycogen being stored in the liver. To ensure healthy growth of the fish they are also given minerals and vitamins.

The red or pink colour of the flesh in salmonids is due to a fat-soluble pigment of the carotenoid group which, in the wild, is obtained from eating other animals, such as crustaceans. In response to consumer demand for pink-coloured flesh in both trout and salmon, this colour can be achieved in farmed fish by feeding with prawns or shrimps (dried or fresh), though this can be expensive. The artificially synthesised pigments canthaxanthin and astaxanthin (which also occurs naturally) may be added to the food, but there is some concern over the safety of canthaxanthin with respect to human foods. To overcome this, these additives are supplied in the diet for only part of the life of the fish.

■ Growth to harvest

Within a pond, fish feed and grow at different rates so fish are graded at intervals during their growth by passing them through bars set at a distance to allow certain body sizes through. This allows fish of about the same size to be reared together and, at harvest, to provide uniform sizes to suit the retail market.

In Europe, trout are usually prepared for marketing at between 180 and 280 g, though in Norway much larger fish (2 kg or more) are sold. The rate of growth depends on temperature: the 180-280 g size is likely to be achieved at the age of about 18 months. Care must be taken in handling the fish at capture to avoid damage and bruising because such fish are then unsightly and deterioration occurs. Before harvest, fish are starved for up to 48 hours as this helps to 'firm up' the flesh and they are kept in clear water to ensure that the flesh has a good flavour. The subsequent gutting,

Farmed salmon and trout in the supermarket

cleaning and transport of harvested fish is now linked to mass markets and must be carried out quickly and efficiently to retain the fresh quality of the fish flesh.

■ SALMON FARMING

In principle, methods used for the farming of salmon are similar to those used for trout farming. The Atlantic salmon (*Salmo salar*) is *anadromous*, which means that its juvenile stages are spent in freshwater followed by migration to the sea where the fish grow to their full adult size. They remain in the sea from 1 to 5 years before returning to freshwater rivers to spawn. The migrations between seawater and freshwater entail internal changes in the salt-regulating mechanisms, accompanied by changes in the appearance of the body and behaviour. When migrating to the sea, the salmon must swim with the current rather than against it as they do when returning to the river. Many show a strong homing instinct and return to the same river for spawning. Salmon farms are thus sited in the sea for the growing-on stages. The young stages, however, are carried out in freshwater. The eggs develop and the salmon become eyed at about 245 day-degrees and hatch at 510 day-degrees so have a longer development stage than the trout. Acclimatisation to seawater takes place over a period of several weeks with fish being kept in water of intermediate salinities. The physiological shock of any sudden changes would mean fish cease feeding for a few days and this would lead to a reduction in growth rate. (See *Biology Advanced Studies - Environment and Ecology* for further details of fish farming.)

BEES - A SPECIAL CASE STUDY

Bees have not been domesticated in the same way as cattle, pigs and chickens, but there has been a long-standing association with human communities and exploitation of their activities. In the Bronze Age, honey and other products were collected from wild bees, and in medieval times, beekeepers tended colonies of wild bees found in hollow trees in the same way as in some societies even today. The position of a beekeeper carried responsibilities and privileges, one of which was the right to carry a crossbow in case of attack from bears while collecting the honey. Later, the beekeepers moved the hollow trees nearer to their houses, making it easier and safer to collect the honey and so the practice of *apiculture* began. One famous beekeeper and breeder was the Czech monk Gregor Mendel.

Honey is an easily digestible food and was the only sweetener available in any quantity before the extraction of sugar from sugar cane and sugar beet was developed, so it was a valuable commodity and the colonies of wild bees were important. The Babylonians and Egyptians used honey for the treatment of wounds and infections of the eyes and the skin as it acts as a disinfectant and counteracts inflammation.

Traditional cylindrical beehive in a tree at Faroum, Egypt

There are some 20 000 known species of bees, most of which are solitary, but members of the genus *Apis*, the honeybees, are social insects, living in permanent colonies where there is a high degree of organisation and caste differentiation. Each colony consists of a single, reproductive female (the queen), a large number of sterile females (the workers) and a much smaller number of males (the drones).

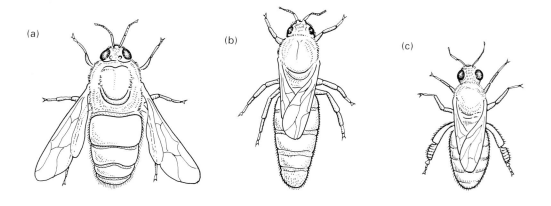

Fig.8.1 Different castes of bee: (a) drone, (b) queen and (c) worker (with pollen baskets)

The genus *Apis* has four species, three of which are native to South East Asia. Two of these species, *Apis florea* and *Apis dorsata*, typically nest in the open and build single combs, which may hang from the branches of trees or under overhanging rocks, making the collection of the honey a precarious business.

Two other species of *Apis*, *A. mellifera* and *A. cerana*, build their nests in enclosed sites, each nest composed of a series of parallel combs. It has been found that these two species can adapt to using hives and, as they build bigger combs storing larger amounts of honey, their exploitation is more profitable. *Apis mellifera* is found throughout Africa, the Middle East and temperate regions of Europe, and it has also been introduced into North and South America and Australasia. The large stores of honey and pollen, together with the preference for enclosed spaces in which to build combs, enable the colonies of this species to survive adverse environmental conditions, especially the cold winters of temperate regions.

A typical colony of honey bees in the summer will be made up of a single queen, about 50 000 workers and a few hundred drones, together with a number of combs containing eggs, larvae, pupae and stores of honey and pollen. The part of the hive in which the young bees develop is called the brood nest, and it is here that the queen lays eggs into the cells. The brood nest is surrounded by cells containing pollen, and then the cells containing the stored honey are around and above the pollen.

The queen, who mates with several drones on her nuptial flight, lays eggs at the rate of about 2000 a day. She can lay two types of eggs, fertilised and unfertilised. The unfertilised eggs will develop into haploid male bees (the drones), which produce haploid male gametes by mitosis when they are mature. The fertilised eggs develop into diploid female bees. Depending on their feeding regime and the needs of the colony, these eggs can develop into sterile worker bees or fertile queens. The offspring of one queen are all genetically similar. The males can only pass on their genes to the females and any genetic recombination is restricted to the queens. The workers perpetuate their genes by looking after the queen's offspring, which have the same genes as they have. This state of affairs could be considered altruistic behaviour on the part of the worker bees, but some scientists think that the queen manipulates the workers through the production of pheromones - chemicals which she produces and which are thought to control the behaviour of the workers.

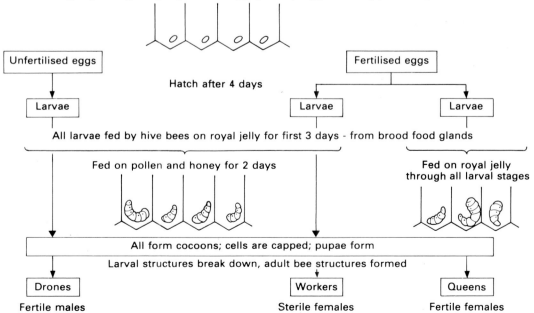

Fig.8.2 Development of different castes of bees

Drones	Workers	Queens
Fertile males	Sterile females	Fertile workers
Big, broad body	Smaller body than drone or queen	Larger, longer body than workers
Well-developed wings	Small wings	Shorter wings than workers
No sting	Barbed sting	Unbarbed sting
Reduced mouthparts	Mouthparts modified for sucking up nectar and moulding wax	Poorly developed mouthparts; fed by worker bees
Only function is to mate with queen	Variety of functions within hive and as forager	Function is to lay eggs and swarming
Lives 4-5 weeks; killed or driven out of hive in autumn	Lives 4-5 weeks in summer, longer if over winter	May live 5-6 years

Table 8.1 Differences between the different castes of bees

Days after hatching	Activities in the hive	Activities outside the hive
1 to 3	Fed by other workers; cleans out cells of recently-hatched bees	
3 to 5	Feeds older larvae on pollen and honey	
5 to 12	Hypopharyngeal glands secrete brood food (royal jelly); feeds young larvae and queens; helps to keep brood warm	
12 to 20	Wax glands on abdomen become active; can secrete wax for comb building and repair. Collects nectar and pollen from foraging bees; processes nectar. Cleans hive; may act as a guard bee	Begins to leave hive for short flights
21 to 40	Communicates position of sources of nectar to other foraging bees using 'round' and 'waggle' dances on the combs	Becomes a foraging bee; daylight hours spent collecting water, nectar, pollen and propolis

Table 8.2 Timetable of activities of worker bees. **Note:** This is not a rigid schedule as older bees have been observed doing duties in the hive and younger bees have been seen foraging

It is difficult to carry out selective breeding of bees under natural conditions because of the nature of the mating process. The nuptial flights can take place anything up to 5 km away from the hive and the males could come from different colonies. In addition to his work on garden peas, Gregor Mendel became interested in crossing different strains of bees, but he is recorded as observing that he found it difficult to persuade the bees to mate under controlled conditions. Any attempts at selective breeding have been confined to isolated colonies kept on moorland, in enclosed valleys or on off-shore islands. An alternative is to use artificial insemination with the queens, a practice which has been used for about 70 years.

The majority of the eggs laid by the queen will be fertilised and develop into worker bees. A few will be laid in special queen cells which hang vertically from the comb and which are larger than the worker cells. Once hatched, the worker bees perform various tasks about the hive, depending on their age. The young workers remain inside the hive, helping to rear the larvae and keep the cells clean, but older bees leave the hive and forage for nectar and pollen. Workers live for about six weeks, but most of those that emerge in the autumn will probably survive until the following spring.

It has been recognised for many centuries that bees were able to communicate with each other in some way, especially about the location of rich food sources, but it was not until Karl von Frisch carried out his experiments that the precise nature of this communication was discovered. If a foraging bee discovers a rich source of nectar a short distance from the hive, when she returns she performs a 'round dance' on the vertical comb. The other worker bees follow her movements and the vibrations of her body, picking up clues from the odours on her body and the taste of the regurgitated nectar. They know from the nature of the dance that the food is within 80 metres of the hive and they fly out of the hive and search for the source. If the food had been further away, the returning forager would have performed a different dance, a 'waggle dance', in which precise information about the distance and direction of the food source is given (Fig.8.3). Bees recognise colour and also communicate this information.

(a) *Round dance*   Indicates that the source of food is within a radius of 80 m

Worker bee moves rapidly round in a circle, first to the left, then to the right

The faster the dance, the richer the source of food and the closer it is to the hive

(b) *Waggle dance*

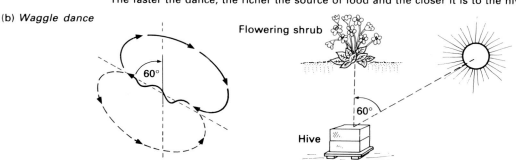

Flowering shrub

Hive

This dance indicates food is further away. The tail end is 'waggled' on the straight part of the dance; the slower the wagging, the further away the food source.
The location of the food source is indicated by the angle of the straight part of the dance on the vertical surface of the comb, which corresponds to the angle between the sun, the hive and the food source.

Fig.8.3 Round dance and waggle dance

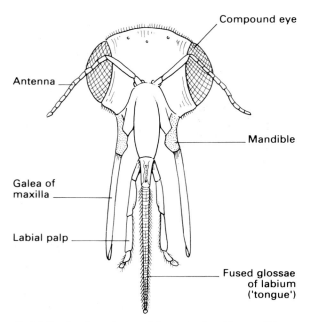

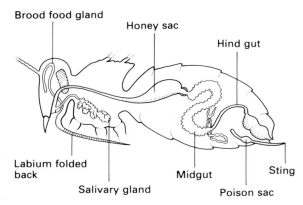

Fig.8.5 Digestive system of the worker bee

Fig.8.4 Head and mouth parts of the worker bee. The mandibles are used to chew pollen, manipulate wax and in the defence of the hive. Nectar is drawn up the grooved surface of the labium

Honey is made mainly from nectar collected by the foraging worker bees. The nectar is a sugar solution, containing mostly sucrose, secreted by the glandular tissue in some flowers in order to attract pollinating insects. The areas of glandular tissue are called nectaries and are usually situated at the base of the petals or on the receptacles of the flowers. The visiting bee has to push past the male and female reproductive structures in order to get to the nectar and in doing so, cross-pollination is achieved. Pollen from the anthers of the flower is deposited on to the body of the bee, and pollen from a previous flower visited gets brushed on to the stigma. The sugary nectar is drawn up the grooved surface of the labium of the bee, partly by capillary action and partly by the pumping action of the muscles of the head. The nectar passes to the honey sac where it is stored until the bee returns to the hive. It is then regurgitated, either into a cell of the comb or to another bee. The bees repeatedly swallow the nectar, mix it with enzymes and regurgitate it, until the enzyme action and the evaporation of water results in its conversion to honey.

The enzymes present in the bees' saliva,

secreted from the hypopharyngeal glands, contain sucrase, which speeds up the conversion of sucrose to glucose and fructose. Other sugars may be present in the honey, depending on the source of the nectar. The bees' saliva also contains the enzyme glucose oxidase, which oxidises glucose to gluconic acid. Gluconic acid helps to keep the pH of the honey low and also prevents the growth of bacteria. Hive bees deposit the honey into cells of the comb, where further processing goes on until the water content is reduced to 17 - 20%. At this stage, 70% of the honey consists of monosaccharide sugars (40% fructose, 30% glucose), 10% disaccharides (sucrose and maltose) together with small amounts of amino acids, minerals and vitamins. Full cells are sealed with a wax cap.

In addition to the nectar, foraging bees collect pollen, which supplies protein to the colony and is especially important in the feeding of the developing larvae. The foraging bees' bodies become covered in pollen as they move past the anthers of the flowers, and this is brushed off, using the hairs on their legs, and packed into special pouches, called pollen baskets, on the third pair of legs. On returning to the hive, the bee strips off the pollen into an empty cell, where a hive bee will pack it down for storage. Pollen can be harvested from a hive, using a pollen trap, but care must be taken to ensure that no more than 10% is taken, otherwise the development of the larvae will suffer. Harvested pollen is used to feed colonies and is also of value as a health product because of its high protein and vitamin content.

Other marketable products from bee hives include beeswax, bee venom, royal jelly and propolis. Royal jelly and propolis are claimed to be health foods and there is an increasing demand for them. Royal jelly is secreted from the hypopharyngeal glands of young worker bees and is fed to the laying queens and to larvae. Propolis is a sticky brown substance, which the bees use to seal cracks in the hive and also to cover objects which are too big to remove from the hive, even dead mice!

In North America, China, Australasia and parts of Europe, honey production is a highly developed industry and the rearing of large colonies of bees is big business. In developing countries, apiculture is a useful form of agriculture, because it is not too expensive to set up and can provide valuable food. A wild swarm can be collected, hives can be constructed from local materials and the hives can be located on land which is unsuitable for other purposes.

Beekeeping is an all-the-year-round activity, although there is less to do during the winter months. In September, winter food is provided for the bees in the form of a sugar solution, so that enough is stored in the hive to enable the remaining bees to survive the winter. Maintenance of the hives can be carried out during this time, and it is important to check equipment. In the spring, the beekeeper needs to check the hives to establish whether queens are present. Worker bees that survived the winter will die off and need to be replaced by young ones. At this time of year, the brood nest gets bigger and there is much more activity as sources of nectar and pollen become available from early flowering plants. The hive needs to be weighed to ensure there is sufficient food for the increasing numbers. In May, the colonies reach their full strength and it is at this time that swarming can begin to occur when new queens leave the colony with a number of workers. It is in the beekeeper's interests to prevent this by destroying queen cells or relocating the colony. If swarming does occur, then the swarm must be caught as quickly as possible and housed in spare hives.

In good summer months, there is plenty of nectar and pollen around for the bees and so the beekeeper can start to harvest honey. In the UK, important food plants for bees include rape, red clover, raspberry, blackberry, heathers and fruit trees.

Modern beekeeping - a hive in the Peloponnese, Greece

To extract the honey, the honeycombs are removed from the hive and the wax caps are cut from the cells. The combs are then placed in an extractor which pulls the honey out by centrifugal force. The honey collects at the bottom and runs through a tap. It is strained to remove pieces of wax and other debris, then filtered through cloth. It is allowed to settle for a few days before crystallisation starts. To ensure even crystallisation, the honey is stirred a little each day. It can be packed into sterile jars and stored or sold. Some of the honey from a hive can be used to feed the bees in that hive should their natural food sources become scarce. It is usually diluted with water and fed to the colony in the evening, when the bees have stopped flying.

Colonies of bees are susceptible to diseases which can spread rapidly in the conditions within a hive. The parasitic mite, *Varroa jacobsoni*, has recently spread to England from the continent, and it is causing great problems to beekeepers. It lives on the surface of the adult bees, as well as on the larvae, and it feeds on the body fluids. In most cases, the disease will subside on its own as the bees remove the dead larvae and clean out the cells. The use of chemicals to get rid of the pathogens is not recommended as it can affect the honey.

■ INVESTIGATIONS

(a) What food plants contribute to a honey sample?
To identify the pollen grains, a sample of honey has to be dissolved in warm water, centrifuged to concentrate the pollen grains, then examined on a slide using a microscope. Pollen grains from the various food plants are fairly easy to identify, and it is possible to work out the percentage of the different types of pollen present in a sample. This technique can be used to verify the source of honey - we would not expect 'Pure English Honey' to contain pollen from Australian flowers.

(b) Identify the sugars present in honey
Identification of the sugars in honey involves the use of a chromatographic technique. Solutions of known sugars such as sucrose, maltose, glucose and fructose (the standards) are required in addition to a solution of the honey. Spots of the standards and the honey solution are placed on the bottom of a piece of chromatography paper and allowed to dry. The paper is rolled into a cylinder and placed in a tank containing the solvent (iso-propanol in water). The solvent is allowed to rise to within 1 cm of the top of the paper, the paper is then removed from the solvent and allowed to dry. In order to show up the various sugars and identify those present in the sample, the paper is dipped into a solution of the locating agent (usually aniline diphenylamine) and heated for a few minutes. The spots of sugars show up in different colours and it is possible to identify the sugars in the honey by comparison with the location of the spots of the standards.

POSTHARVEST BIOLOGY

■ FRUIT AND VEGETABLES

When you pick an apple off a tree, it does not die; living metabolic processes continue for days, weeks or even months. Internal physiological changes occur which affect its chemical composition, colour, texture, taste and weight, leading eventually to deterioration, spoilage and decay. In the home or traditional rural communities, techniques were developed which conserve or preserve fresh food to be eaten at a later date, usually to tide over seasons when food would be scarce or unavailable. In communities that were largely self-sufficient, this was simply a means of survival. Out of this a whole range of specialist foods have developed, which add variety to the diet and tempt the appetite: some are treated as delicacies or even classed as gourmet foods.

In the modern food industry, considerable attention is paid to postharvest conditions and treatment for fruit and vegetables, which are sold without further processing. The aim is to ensure that 'freshness' is maintained from the initial handling at harvest, during transport and storage until the produce is sold to the consumer and eaten. The development of the food industry is largely a result of the shift from rural to urban society, reflecting a greater dependence on professional food producers and processors with a corresponding decline in home cooking and its replacement by 'convenience' or partially prepared foods.

Trade on a worldwide basis for certain commodities, such as spices, dates back to ancient civilisations. Recently, we have seen a surge of international exchange of perishable goods, bringing, for example, tropical fruits fresh to the supermarket shelves in Britain, out-of-season salad crops, unusual vegetables and 'new' potatoes throughout the year. All this has led to an increase in consumer choice. The control of postharvest processing and retailing is now dominated by a few giant companies, channelling their goods to supermarkets where we expect to call in and pick up a wide range of fruits and vegetables throughout the year.

Olives and gherkins - examples of preserved foods which have now become speciality or gourmet foods

Postharvest processing has brought fruits and vegetables from all over the world

Considerable crop loss occurs after harvest, with estimates for fresh fruit and vegetables varying between 20% and 80%. This may be the result of fungal or bacterial diseases, infection by viruses, attack by insects, mechanical damage in the form of bruising or splitting leading to discoloration and changes in flavour, or deterioration due to unsuitable storage conditions. These losses mean that time, energy, labour and other resources which were used to boost the initial crop yield are wasted. There are thus strong economic reasons for understanding the postharvest biology to minimise these losses.

■ The story of an apple... and other fruits

Apples can be stored for several months in a cool place without any special treatment: the skin colour changes from green to yellowish or red, the texture softens, the apple becomes sweeter and other subtle changes develop in the flavour. Gradually the apple shrivels, brownish patches become evident and eventually decay sets in. Different apple varieties vary considerably in the length of time they will keep successfully in storage: amongst apple varieties in Britain, Discovery or Worcester Pearmain keep only a few weeks, whereas Bramley's Seedling or Blenheim Orange can be stored several months. We will take a closer look inside the apple to see what is causing these changes and how the life of an apple is prolonged in the commercial world.

Apple blossom, attractive to pollinators

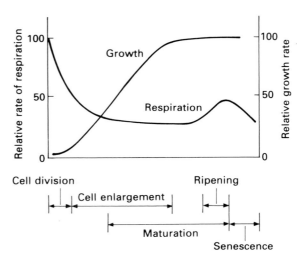

Fig.9.1 Changes in respiration rate in an apple or pear from early development of the fruit through the stages of ripening and senescence

When an apple is harvested, respiration continues: oxygen is taken up, carbon dioxide, water and heat are lost. Further loss of water occurs by transpiration. When attached to the plant, water and respiratory substrates are replaced from active metabolic processes occurring in the rest of the plant: once detached, various physiological changes associated with ripening and senescence (ageing) become evident.

The rate of respiration, shown in Fig.9.1, reflects the series of changes which take place from the time of petal fall throughout the development of the fruit. During the growth stage, cell division and enlargement occur, resulting in rapid increase in size. Ripening involves a complex series of physical and biochemical changes and effectively changes an inedible plant organ into a food that is attractive to eat in terms of appearance, taste and texture. Ripening is itself a relative term depending on the requirements of the consumer: different conditions of ripeness are, for example, required for eating and for juice extraction, and some fruits, such as courgettes, are eaten when botanically underripe.

Senescence describes the phase when catabolic (breaking down) processes take over from anabolic processes, leading to degradation rather than synthesis. The increased rate of respiration accompanying ripening is known as the *climacteric*, a feature shown in some but not all fruits and vegetables. Linked with the climacteric peak in respiration rate is an increase in the production of *ethylene*, a plant growth substance, known to be closely associated with the processes of ripening. As ripening proceeds, pectic substances in the middle lamella break down, resulting in a softer texture in the fruit. Chlorophyll is degraded, leading to loss of the green colour so that the yellows and reds of carotenoids and other pigments become visible. Levels of organic acids fall, accompanied by an increase in sugar content. A range of volatile substances, present in minute quantities, contribute to the characteristic flavours.

Some of the changes occurring during the ripening of a tomato fruit are summarised in Fig.9.2. The main thrust of postharvest treatment is thus directed at reducing respiration, postponing ripeness and slowing the onset of senescence.

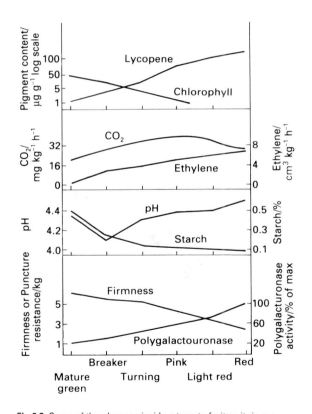

Fig.9.2 Some of the changes inside a tomato fruit as it ripens from green through to red

■ Postharvest treatments

A low temperature reduces the rate of respiration (hence the disappearance of carbohydrate, the respiratory substrate), which would result in a loss of weight. For storing apples, a temperature between 1 °C and 4 °C is suitable, and this also diminishes attack by fungi and bacteria. Below 0 °C, the tissues may suffer from irreversible chilling injury; because frozen tissues may fail to resume metabolic processes when thawed, resulting in permanent browning and damage. Lowering the temperature decreases both the rate of ethylene production and the response of tissues to the effects of ethylene, thus delaying the onset of ripening. Other reactions, such as the development of the aroma in ripe fruit and the green colour turning to yellow, are also slowed down at lower temperatures. The actual temperature of the apple is likely to be higher than that set for the storage chamber due to the heat generated in respiration. The design of the store should provide continual cooling, if necessary by air circulation with fans, to ensure the desired temperature is maintained.

Modification of the gases in the atmosphere in which apples are stored has led to considerable success in prolonging the storage life. The terms *modified atmosphere* (MA) or *controlled atmosphere* (CA) are used to describe systems in which the atmospheric composition is different from normal air. The practice probably has ancient origins: the burying of apples or carrying them in unventilated holds of ships resulted in a much longer storage life. The effect was probably due to low oxygen and high carbon dioxide levels in the atmosphere, modified as a result of respiration in the tissue.

In modern storage systems, the atmosphere is deliberately manipulated, with levels of oxygen, carbon dioxide, nitrogen, ethylene and carbon monoxide being controlled. In apples stored at 5 °C, the oxygen level must be reduced to 2.5% to achieve a 50% reduction in respiration, and care must be taken to ensure anaerobic conditions do not develop as these may result in development of undesirable flavours. At higher temperatures, anaerobic respiration would increase. Increased carbon dioxide levels also affect respiration: for apples a storage atmosphere of between 5% and 10% is often used but again, at higher carbon dioxide levels, anaerobic respiration can occur. Changes in oxygen and carbon dioxide levels affect other processes involved in ripening, senescence and deterioration. High carbon dioxide levels reduce the breakdown of pectic substances in the middle lamella, resulting in a firm texture being retained for a longer time. Microbial activity is also reduced by high levels of carbon dioxide, thus delaying the onset of decay.

In practice, different products vary considerably in their tolerance to reduced oxygen and increased carbon dioxide levels. Within the storage atmosphere, ethylene tends to accumulate, thus encouraging the onset of ripening. Inside the storage chamber there should be adequate ventilation to remove ethylene, and fruits at different stages of ripeness should not be stored together, since ethylene produced from the more ripe fruits would affect the less ripe.

Q What happens if you store unripe tomatoes in a plastic bag with a red apple? Try it!

Water loss, due to transpiration, can be controlled by increasing the humidity of the storage chamber. The decreased water pressure gradient between the apple and its surroundings reduces the rate of water loss through the stomata. This can be achieved by spraying water as a fine mist inside the store, though this may increase the likelihood of growth of microorganisms. Any damage to the skin surface naturally increases the rate of water loss. Artificial waxes have been developed which are applied as a film on the outside of fruits to help reduce weight loss. These are used with apples and particularly citrus fruits and avocado pears. Other substances such as fungicides and inhibitors of senescence can be incorporated into the wax formulation. These coatings affect the gas exchange, allowing oxygen to diffuse into the apple but retaining some of the carbon dioxide produced in respiration, effectively modifying the internal atmosphere and thus prolonging the life of the stored apple. These coatings also allow the fruit to be polished, a practice used to increase the sales appeal on the supermarket shelf and market stall. However, the use of some waxes has been questioned on the grounds of safety to the consumer.

Various plastic films are now used for the packing of fruit and vegetables because they modify the environment and have proved to be a successful means of extending shelf-life, particularly for short-term storage. The ideal substance would be permeable enough to allow some gas exchange and reduce water loss, but avoid development of the high humidity which encourages growth of microbial spores. In practice, films are usually more permeable to carbon dioxide than to oxygen, but their permeability does not alter with temperature, whereas the rate of respiration does. Experiments with Discovery apples wrapped in low-density polyethylene film and kept at a temperature of 20 °C showed that the atmosphere inside the packages was modified within one to two days, giving 3-5% carbon dioxide and 5-6% oxygen, with a noticeable slowing down in softening and yellowing of the fruit. Discovery apples have a relatively short shelf-life and the optimum conditions for storage with respect to film properties and temperature can be worked out.

Modified atmosphere storage linked with plastic film packaging technology and combined with controlled temperature has now been adopted for a wide range of fruits and vegetables as a means of extending storage times and shelf-life. Containers wrapped with appropriate partially porous plastic films have been used for mushrooms, tomatoes, strawberries, leeks and asparagus to delay development followed by senescence.

Plastic films used for packaging mushrooms can modify the atmosphere inside the container and give increased storage times

Bunches of bananas can be sealed inside polyethylene bags, on or off the plant, to delay the ripening process. This is a relatively simple way for the subsistence farmer to create a modified atmosphere on the farm, though ethylene tends to accumulate and this encourages ripening. Inclusion of potassium permanganate (which destroys ethylene) inside the bag can result in the shelf-life of bananas and avocados being noticeably extended (see Table 9.1).

Treatment	Shelf-life/days
Air control	up to 7
Sealed polyethylene bags	14
Sealed bags, with potassium permanganate	21

Table 9.1 Simple treatment to extend the shelf-life of bananas

Lettuces and other salad crops can be stored for four weeks in containers with an atmosphere of 10% carbon dioxide, 10% oxygen and 80% nitrogen. In future we are likely to see development of a wider range of plastic packaging materials, the conditions for use being closely matched to the particular pattern of postharvest metabolism of the different products, providing a convenient means of extending storage time while maintaining qualities of freshness and presenting the produce attractively to the consumer.

Another aspect of postharvest storage is the use of inhibitors, for example to delay the sprouting in potatoes and onions. If stored below 4 °C, sprouting rarely occurs, but at this temperature starch is converted to sugar, which is undesirable. Certain chemicals, such as maleic hydrazide, may be used to prevent sprouting at higher temperatures, but their use brings concern over permitted residues in the produce. When used, maleic hydrazide is applied by spraying or dipping some weeks before storage starts, and successfully prolongs storage without sprouting for several months.

■ A tomato for the future?

Botanically, the tomato is a fruit. Gene technology with tomatoes promises to take our control over ripening a stage further. *Transgenic* tomatoes have been created by modifying the genes involved in the ripening processes, thus delaying the onset of spoilage associated with ripening yet retaining the colour, aroma and desirable flavour. In the UK, such tomatoes cannot be eaten, but the research has revealed more of the inside story relating to ripening processes. We will now look at this process in more detail.

Ethylene has an important role in the switching on and off of genes involved in the ripening programme, by activating genes controlling colour, texture and flavour. The sequence of events is summarised in Fig.9.3.

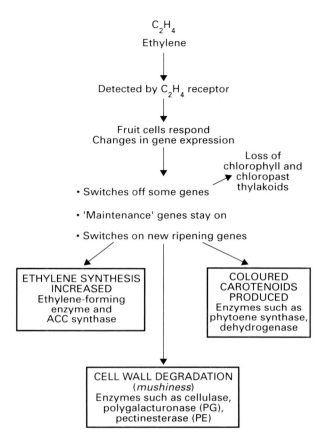

Fig.9.3 Ethylene has a key role in switching on and off the genes involved in the ripening process

Ethylene is derived from the amino acid methionine, by a pathway in which the compound abbreviated as ACC is an intermediate, involving the enzyme ACC synthase. Pectinesterase (PE) and polygalacturonase (PG) are enzymes involved in the stages of breakdown of pectic substances in the cell wall, through the pathway:

$$\text{Protopectin} \longrightarrow \underset{\text{acid}}{\text{Pectinic}} \overset{\text{PE}}{\longrightarrow} \underset{\text{acid}}{\text{Pectic}} \overset{\text{PG}}{\longrightarrow} \underset{\text{acid}}{\text{Galacturonic}}$$

Breakdown of the pectic substances is largely responsible for the changes in texture leading to 'mushiness' in the overripe tomato. The enzyme PG is absent, or present in only very low quantities, in unripe fruit but is found in large quantities in ripe fruit. It acts by reducing the chain length of pectin molecules in the middle lamella and primary cell wall. An *'antisense'* PG gene has been inserted into strains of tomato with the result that the production of PG is reduced and the tomatoes stay firm while ripening (Fig.9.4). Such tomatoes can be kept longer on the plant before picking which can mean improved development of colour and of the aroma which contributes to flavour.

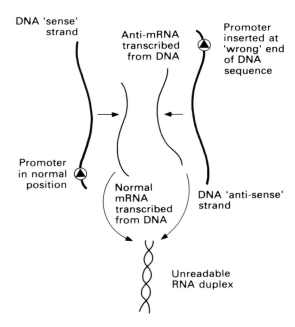

Fig.9.4 How to produce antisense genes which block the action of mRNA

A second approach with tomatoes has come from identification of a gene controlling the synthesis of ethylene. This gene, called pTOM13, appears to control the enzyme concerned with the synthesis of ethylene from ACC. Antisense technology has been applied to the production of transgenic tomatoes containing this pTOM13 gene. These tomatoes produce far lower amounts of ethylene during ripening, less than 5% of the normal amount (see Fig.9.5). When left attached to the plants, these tomatoes ripened slowly and, after picking, developed the yellow colour but did not ripen fully unless ethylene was artificially supplied.

These advances in gene technology allow different parts of the ripening process to be unravelled independently. Gene technology allows precision in the development of a breeding programme and application of these findings could be used to improve both the shelf-life and appeal of the product for the consumer.

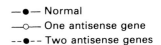

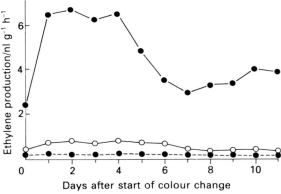

Fig.9.5 These transgenic tomatoes produce far less ethylene during ripening compared to normal tomatoes

■ MEAT

Meat is derived from the muscle of the animal, together with associated connective tissue and fat, though the term is used to include liver, kidneys, heart and other products from the animal. The term *killing-out percentage* is used to define the proportion of liveweight represented by the carcass weight (excluding hide, head, feet, internal organs, body fluids and gut contents). The quality of the meat, when offered for sale, depends on a number of factors, starting with the breed of the animal, the feeding strategy used, its sex, age at slaughter and the treatment immediately before and after slaughter. The aim of the farmer is to produce a carcass with a high proportion of desirable lean meat cuts, with minimum bone in relation to muscle and high killing-out percentage.

As cattle grow heavier and fatter, nutrients contribute preferentially first to bone, then to muscle and finally to fat. Thus a young animal has a higher proportion of bone in its body weight and a mature animal has a greater deposition of fat (Fig. 9.6). The breed can affect both the distribution of muscle and the rate at which growth occurs. In early maturing breeds, there is a low rate of liveweight gain as a result of small skeletal size, and fatty tissue is laid down at an early age. In late maturing breeds, there is a higher rate of liveweight gain linked to a larger skeletal size and muscular development, with fatty tissue being laid down at a later age.

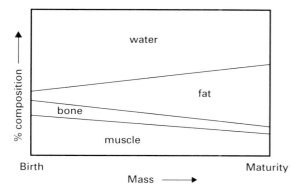

Fig.9.6 Changes in carcass composition during growth

British breeds, such as Angus and Hereford, have a relatively early fattening phase compared to continental breeds of cattle, such as Charolais and Simmental, which are leaner with a later fattening phase. Limousin have a particularly favourable muscle to bone ratio. Variations in feed intake will affect the carcass weight at a particular time. Reduced intake, due, say, to seasonal fluctuations in availability, are to some extent compensated by a longer maturing period. In conditions of low nutrient, fat is used first as the source of energy; conversely, excess or use of high-quality feed has the effect of diverting a substantial proportion of the energy intake to become fat and such animals would need to be slaughtered at an earlier age, but lighter weight.

Muscles of male meat animals tend to be larger than the equivalent muscles in females, so inherently males yield more meat than females. Castration of males actually reduces the efficiency of weight gain because the benefits of anabolic hormones originating in the testes have been removed. Hormones, including steroid hormones and growth hormones, can be used to influence growth and development of muscle. Steroid hormone pellets have been implanted under the ear and this practice results in increased daily weight gain, improved efficiency of conversion of feed and leaner carcasses. Oestrogens give best results in male cattle and androgenic hormones in females.

To a lesser extent, use of the growth hormone bovine somatotrophin (BST) also stimulates leaner more efficient growth. However, the use of hormone implants (naturally occurring and synthetic) has aroused considerable controversy because of concern over residues in the meat, and pressure from consumers led, in 1986, to a ban on using hormones in the EEC. Another group of substances, the β agonists, are similar to adrenaline and improve the efficiency of food conversion, resulting in increased lean percentage relative to fat. However, the effects appear to be short-term only and produce lower quality meat from the carcass. A future possibility for manipulation of growth and development may lie in an immunological approach, for example, by stimulating cattle to produce antibodies which interfere with the release and interaction of different growth hormones.

Up to the moment of slaughter, the cells of the muscle destined to become meat have been carrying out living metabolic processes, notably respiration. When the animal is killed, a series of irreversible biochemical changes occur which affect the eating quality of meat and, if not controlled, these would lead to deterioration and finally spoilage. Practices adopted on the way to and at the abbatoir, and subsequent handling, packaging and distribution aim to provide meat of high quality for the consumer.

The level of glycogen in the muscle before slaughter is important, to achieve the desired pH of about 5.6 in the meat: if higher, the meat is likely to have poor colour and reduced water holding capacity. It will also be more susceptible to attack by microorganisms and will not keep well. Pre-slaughter treatment can directly affect glycogen levels. Any form of stress, perhaps during the loading and unloading of animals for transport, fighting, struggling or other exercise, leads to depletion of glycogen reserves. Similarly, poor nutrition of the animal particularly in the period before slaughter would also mean glycogen levels were low. Pigs are more sensitive than cattle to depletion of glycogen and in some cases the animals are rested after transport or fed with sugar before killing to allow replenishment of glycogen reserves.

In the living animal, contraction of muscle involves the proteins actin and myosin. The process needs a supply of energy released from ATP, which is replenished from glycogen reserves in the muscle. Energy is also needed to maintain the temperature and organisation of the cells. At the moment of death, blood circulation ceases as does supply of oxygen to the muscle. At first, glycogen continues to be broken down and glycolysis results in the anaerobic production of lactic acid. Accumulation of lactic acid causes a fall in pH, leading to inactivation of the enzymes involved in ATP release. In the absence of ATP, actin and myosin combine to form rigid chains of actomyosin, and the muscle contracts but is unable to relax again. This condition is known as *rigor mortis*. If muscle is cooked while in this condition, the meat is tougher and darker in colour than it would be if cooked before the condition sets in (when it is always tender) or after it has passed through rigor. In the present-day systems of commercial distribution, meat is not available to the consumer before rigor. After rigor mortis, the muscle goes through a period of *ageing* or *conditioning*, which allows development of flavour and the meat becomes more tender. Changes occur in the proteins of the muscle, resulting in their becoming more pliable (hence more tender on cooking) and this is accompanied by some enzymatic breakdown of protein into peptides and amino acids. The meat is kept at low temperatures (around 5 °C) in clean conditions to reduce the chance of microbial infection at this stage.

Tenderisation of meat can be hastened by the use of protease enzymes. The practice is not new and was probably carried out at least 500 years ago by Mexican Indians who wrapped meat in pawpaw leaves during cooking. An enzyme known as *papain*, extracted from the latex of the pawpaw plant (*Carica papaya*) is now the most widely used proteolytic enzyme, and shows activity with actomyosin, collagen and elastin.

Other proteases are also used, for example, *ficin* from the fig plant, *bromelin* from the pineapple and others of bacterial and fungal origin. These enzymes can be administered by injection, shortly before slaughter. They appear to have little or no effect on the live animal because the pH of the blood is well above their optimum, the oxygen tensions (in the living animal) are unsuitable and the enzymes do not reach their optimum temperature for activity until about 70-85 °C, a temperature which is achieved during cooking. The injection of these enzymes reduces the time needed for post slaughter storage. Alternatively, enzymes can be applied after slaughter, and a range of treatments, including salting and marinading with wine, lemon juice or vinegar, owe their success as tenderisers to their effect on meat proteins.

Colour is another attribute which contributes to the attractiveness of meat to the consumer. The red colour, characteristic of certain meats, is due primarily to the myoglobin in the muscle, rather than the haemoglobin of the blood, and the colour of the meat surface depends on the type of myoglobin molecule and also on its chemical state. There are species differences in the myoglobin, for example, between beef and pork, and in the myoglobin content of different muscles within an animal. The myoglobin molecule consists of one *haem* unit joined to one protein molecule (see *Biology Advanced Studies - Human Systems*). It is the iron within the haem unit which is the key to the colour changes. In myoglobin, the iron is present as Fe^{2+}, giving a purplish-red colour. Oxygenation, by binding a molecule of oxygen within the haem unit, gives oxymyoglobin, which is bright red. Oxidation of myoglobin or oxymyoglobin, which converts Fe^{2+} to Fe^{3+}, gives metmyoglobin which is brown. The reactions are reversible, so myoglobin is formed by reduction of metmyoglobin or deoxygenation of oxymyoglobin. The bright red colour on the surface of fresh meat is due mainly to oxymyoglobin. To retain this colour, which is attractive to consumers, fresh meat requires oxygen, but at the same time water loss should be minimised. Packaging materials used for fresh meat need to allow passage of gases but reduce the loss of water. The dull brown colour, sometimes seen on the lower side of fresh meat standing on a container, results from development of metmyoglobin, due to lack of oxygen. The bright pink colour of *cured* meat is due to nitrosomyoglobin, formed by the combination of myoglobin with nitrogen II oxide (nitric acid) produced from nitrates and nitrites used in the curing process. In this case, oxygen is not required to maintain this colour, so packaging materials for cured meat products can be impermeable to oxygen.

Spoilage may take place because of microbial contamination of the meat after death. Infection of the consumer may be caused by bacteria (e.g. *Salmonella*) or parasitic worms (e.g. beef tapeworm, *Taenia saginata*) present in the living animal. Meat inspection should detect the presence of the tapeworm parasite as 'measly' beef. Infection can be avoided by adequate cooking of the meat (rather than serving underdone 'rare' beef) and good hygiene (for example by ensuring human faeces are not disposed of in the areas where cattle feed).

10 FOOD PRODUCTION - SOME PERSPECTIVES

■ ENOUGH TO EAT?

Throughout the history of the human race there has been a precarious balance between human population numbers and the amount of food produced. In early history, provision of food was mainly a localised community activity, but, as population numbers grew and trading patterns became established, exchange of food occurred over increasingly longer distances. Now, towards the end of the twentieth century, all nations are dependent on others for at least some of their food requirements, moving away from the pattern of small-scale self-sufficient communities. It is appropriate, therefore, to consider issues relating to quantity of food produced on a global scale.

In 1800, the world population was about 1 billion. By 1930 it had doubled to 2 billion, reached 3 billion in 1960, 4 billion by 1974 and 5 billion just before 1990. Further increases are projected into the 21st century. This escalation of world population in recent decades has increased enormously the pressure on available land resources and sharpened the need to maximise the capacity for production of food. By 1985, the population in developed[1] countries was about 1.2 billion, but was about three times that figure (3.7 billion) in developing[2] countries. Looking at the distribution of food in different regions of the world, in particular between developed and developing nations, and also at changing patterns of consumption, we can see there is no simple equation balancing the number of people and the amount of food produced.

During the 30 years between 1950 and 1980 the total world population showed a 76% increase, but the rate of growth was faster in developing countries (average rate 3.1% per year) than in developed countries (average rate 1.25% per year). During these same 30 years, total world production of food more than doubled. In Fig.10.1 you can see that developing countries showed a larger percentage increase in production than developed countries.

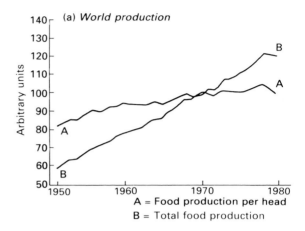

(a) *World production*

A = Food production per head
B = Total food production

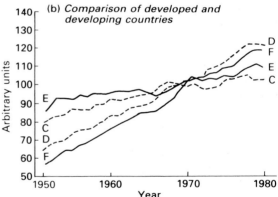

(b) *Comparison of developed and developing countries*

Developed countries { C = Food production per head
D = Total food production

Developing countries { E = Food production per head
F = Total food production

Fig.10.1 (a) Total world production of food more than doubled between 1950 and 1980. (b) Developing countries showed a larger percentage increase than developed countries. The year 1970/71 is given an arbitrary value of 100.

[1] Also referred to as the *economically more developed world*.
[2] Also referred to as the *economically less developed world*.

If this is expressed in terms of the average production *per head* of population, divergence between developing and developed countries is apparent: developing countries showed an increase of only about 15% in production whereas in developed countries it was about 50%.

Increased demand for food arises from population growth, but also from growth in income as this generally leads to increased consumption per head. During the 30 years from 1950 to 1980, developed countries showed a relatively higher consumption per head than developing countries, and consumption increased faster than population growth. Growth in income is also occurring in developing countries and is likely to lead to similar increased demands in consumption. By the 1990s, the general pattern which emerges is that of overproduction and over consumption in the developed countries in contrast to underproduction, accompanied by threat (and reality) of hunger, malnutrition or starvation in developing countries, though within these broad categories the position varies considerably.

To some extent redistribution of food can be brought about by trade. In effect, this would mean exports from developed countries with surpluses or 'mountains', and imports into developing countries with deficits. In some cases, the need to generate cash to pay for basic food imports has led to gross distortion of the agriculture or of the economy of the country. For many individuals in developing countries, the money is simply not available to pay for imported food. So another way of bringing relief is through 'aid' to developing countries, though distribution of aid may encounter problems, associated with transport or perhaps because the food is unacceptable in relation to traditional diets. If this imbalance is to be adjusted to ensure adequate levels of food throughout the world, there are economic, political and cultural barriers to be overcome.

In many developing countries cash crops (instead of much-needed food crops) have to be produced to pay off foreign debts. As more countries produce these crops the supply becomes too great and the price falls. These countries then have to import food crops (often as 'aid') which it could otherwise produce itself.

One way of increasing production is to bring more land into cultivation. Historically, demand for more land prompted mass migrations of people or expansion of empires. Systems of shifting cultivation also exploit fresh land. The area is cleared and cultivated for a few years until

depleted, then abandoned: such systems have been practised since the earliest times and account for a substantial area of the land surface today.

In the late twentieth century, there is still some scope for bringing fresh land into permanent cultivation, though a substantial proportion of the land surface is unsuitable for cultivation, because of its topography, the nature of the soil or the climate (particularly rainfall). Social factors may also deter people from using land, say in remote areas. Estimates during the 1970s suggested that in Europe and Asia, a very high proportion (over 80%) of potential arable land was already under cultivation, whereas in South America and Africa a much smaller proportion was under cultivation (about 11% and 22% respectively). In such areas it is still possible to increase the area of land that can be cultivated for food production.

Water is a key factor in the successful growth of crops. Systems of irrigation have been used for many centuries to cultivate areas with inadequate rainfall, making fresh land available.

Traditional systems for irrigation are often simple in structure but can be very effective

Agricultural land may be lost in the areas where it is most valuable. Successful cultivation in, say, a narrow fertile mountain valley or irrigated strips beside a water course, invariably leads to an expanded population in the area, followed by building of houses, roads and other supporting infrastructure on the very land that brought success. Larger scale urbanisation, accompanied by land being taken up by industrialisation, plus provision of a transport network in the form of roads or railways, have led to substantial losses of good quality agricultural land. In China, between 1957 and 1977, estimates suggest that about 30% of the arable land was lost in this way and suburban

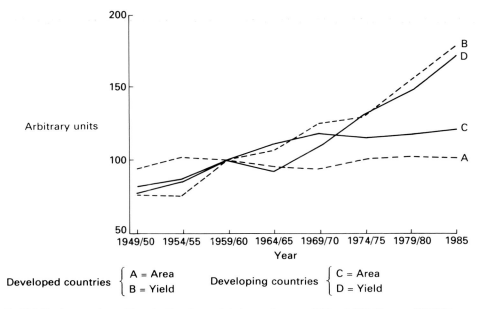

Arbitrary units

Developed countries { A = Area, B = Yield }   Developing countries { C = Area, D = Yield }

Fig.10.2 The increase in world production of cereals between the years 1950 and 1985. The year 1959/60 is given an arbitrary value of 100.

development (for example around Beijing and Shanghai) led to a damaging decline in local vegetable production.

Examine Fig.10.2 which refers to cereals and note how production has increased from 1950 through to 1985 in both developed and developing countries. Some of the increase can be attributed to expansion of the area of land under cultivation (more in developing than in developed countries), but the main contribution has been from an increase in yield per unit area of land. Some of this has resulted from use of chemicals in the form of fertilisers, herbicides and pesticides. Similar trends have been recorded in other major crops. Increased yield has also come from genetic improvements resulting from controlled breeding programmes. Developing countries in particular have benefited from the introduction of high yielding varieties of rice and wheat, and potential losses have been reduced by the use of disease-resistant varieties.

Annual productivity can also be enhanced by more effective use of the land. *Intercropping* is used extensively in some countries, allowing two or more crops to be grown simultaneously on the same land even though they may mature or be harvested at different times. The practice saves space but may have other advantages: for example, the presence of a second crop may reduce competition from weeds and if a leguminous crop is included there are the benefits of nitrogen fixation.

Multiple cropping, which refers to the number of crops per year on an area of land, is also a means of increasing the yield from a given area of land. Egypt has the highest degree of multiple cropping, on average approaching two crops per year, due

Intercropping in Sichuan, Western China

111

mainly to successful irrigation schemes and favourable climate. Parts of Asia (China, Taiwan and Bangladesh) also achieve a high level of multiple cropping. Extension of the growing season, particularly for horticultural crops, has been achieved by the use of glasshouses and polythene tunnels, although this increases costs. Such practices also allow the environment to be controlled artificially, say by increasing carbon dioxide levels, thus boosting yield. Clear polythene laid on the ground is now being used increasingly, its main benefit being to raise soil temperature, allowing earlier establishment of the crop. Artificial systems such as hydroponics allow intensive growth of crops (for example tomatoes and cucumbers), regardless of the suitability of the soil or climate.

Intensive systems for raising animals save space and, because of the high stocking densities used, have led to high yields per unit area. Use of artificial housing allows close control of the environment as a means of optimising conditions and the rearing units can be located on land unsuitable for extensive rearing because of climate, soil or other factors.

Intensive systems in agriculture and horticulture require a high input of energy. This energy is used as fuel for farm machinery, manufacture and application of fertilisers and pesticides, building of housing and automation systems, maintenance of controlled conditions, irrigation systems and finally to transport the food from the sites where grown to the consumer. Linked to these energy inputs are the economic considerations in terms of capital cost of housing and machinery and the reduced demands on labour because of the high level of automation.

Availability or cost of energy may become a constraint which prevents further increases in production through intensification, particularly in those developing countries lacking a natural supply of oil and unable to pay the price of imports. As production becomes more specialised and more distant from the consumer, the need for effective postharvest processing and storage, and an efficient distribution network becomes critical and raises the cost of production. If wastage due to post-harvest losses could be avoided, this would contribute to an increase in the quantity of food available for consumption.

In countries faced with overproduction, measures are taken to regulate production and avoid surpluses. In the UK, regulation can occur through a variety of strategies: the set-aside scheme enforces deliberate reduction of existing agricultural land; quota systems are used to limit milk production; subsidies may encourage diversification into other crops or activities. However, such measures have not yet solved the problem of excesses.

Despite national and international efforts to regulate and improve distribution of food, there is still a widening gap between developing and developed countries. As an example, in 1984 the average number of eggs consumed per person per year was equivalent to 35 in Africa, 60 in Asia and 256 in western Europe. Figures 10.3 and 10.4 illustrate the worldwide variations in average daily energy intake and average daily protein intake.

■ THE QUALITY OF FOOD

Let us think about an apple you may have picked off a tree in your garden, or the tomatoes, lettuces, beans or potatoes you raised with some care in your glasshouse or vegetable plot. The apples and tomatoes may well be misshapen, the skin of the apple may be a little rough and blemished and there might even be the odd maggot inside; your tomatoes are perhaps unevenly coloured or beginning to split around the stalk. The lettuce, cabbage or potatoes may show traces of slug damage, perhaps a snail still lodged in the inner leaves. Despite the imperfections, you believe you are enjoying the elusive qualities of flavour of fresh, home-grown food. By contrast, your supermarket packs offer you produce that has been subjected to a high degree of quality control at all stages of production. It is all clean and probably wrapped. The tomatoes will have been graded to a uniform size, the dimensions stated on the pack label. The label also records the 'sell by' or best before' date and often includes a guide as to the nutritional content.

You can be sure that ripening of fruits is even, controlled (often artificially induced to provide a predictable display shelf-life) and that any produce showing pest damage has been discarded. On some items you may see the Soil Association symbol which testifies that it has been grown in a way that satisfies the standards for organic food. There is unlikely to be any guarantee regarding taste, even though for many people this is one of the delights of eating!

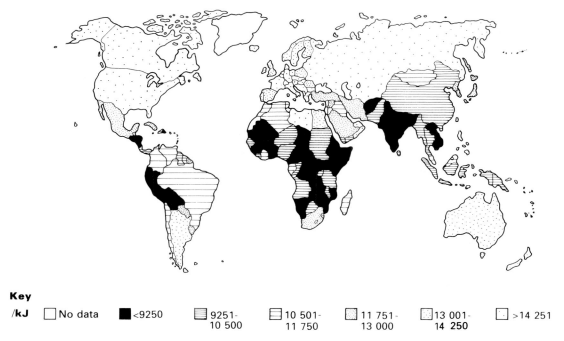

Key

/**kJ** ☐ No data ■ <9250 ▤ 9251-
10 500 ▤ 10 501-
11 750 ▨ 11 751-
13 000 ▨ 13 001-
14 250 ☐ >14 251

Fig.10.3 Worldwide variations in average daily energy intake. The basic daily energy
requirement is taken as 9600 kJ per day for a young woman and 13 400 kJ per day for
a young man (U.N. FAO). Data from years 1979 to 1982.

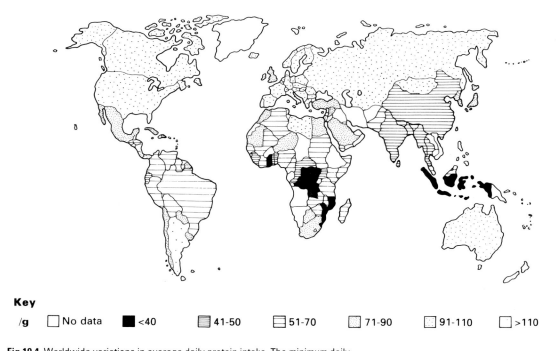

Key

/**g** ☐ No data ■ <40 ▤ 41-50 ▤ 51-70 ▨ 71-90 ▨ 91-110 ☐ >110

Fig.10.4 Worldwide variations in average daily protein intake. The minimum daily
requirement is taken as 50-70 g per day. Data from years 1979 to 1982.

Fig.10.5 The Soil Association symbol shows that the produce has been grown in a way that satisfies the standards for organic food

It is difficult to arrive at a precise definition of *quality* in relation to the food presented to the consumer. It may be viewed in terms of value for money, appearance (including size, colour, uniformity), the level of microbial contaminants, the nutritional value, the presence of unnatural substances in the form of residues or additives, the anticipated storage and 'shelf-life', or the organoleptic qualities (flavour, aroma, colour and texture).

The commercial producer aims to satisfy the consumer and still make a profit. To achieve a high quality of marketable produce, crop varieties have been selected for their success in cultivation with respect to yield, disease resistance, consistent ripening within a short time-scale and ease of harvesting without loss or damage.

When picked by hand, ripe produce can be individually selected, the same area of crop can be harvested on several occasions, it is possible to take appropriate care with handling, and unsuitable or damaged produce can be discarded or put aside for sale at lower prices. Use of machinery means that the whole crop must usually be harvested together. Survival in the harvesting process is important so, for example, tomatoes are selected for firmness of texture, toughness of skin and simultaneous ripening. Because of the need for consistency in packing and processing, produce is cleaned, sorted and graded after harvesting.

Labelling of food offered for sale gives the consumer information about the quality of the product. The label is expected to give the name of the food together with date and statements regarding quantity and ingredients and to refer to the country of origin. The composition of the food may be specified by reference to energy, protein, carbohydrate and fat, and sometimes saturated fats, sugars, fibre and sodium. Further information

may be given about mineral and vitamin content and, in processed foods, the presence or absence of 'additives'. The description given may make claims about the nutritional value of the food in diets and so become a way of educating the consumer.

Traditional 'organic' yoghurt and milk

To be effective, the information stated on the label must not be too complex nor must it make false claims, implied or actual. Since food is derived directly from living organisms, it is inevitably subject to the variation expected in biological material. Only a limited number of samples are tested and composition will be affected by the timing of harvest or slaughter, the degree of ripeness or maturity, conditions of storage or freshness, and, if processed, the nature of processing. Values given are useful only if considered in relation to the whole diet or food intake of the individual. The increasing use of labels on packaged foods has helped to make the consumer more aware of the composition of the food and provides some measure of quality control. Interpretation of the information may, however, require expert knowledge.

A label that gives an indication of *how* a crop was grown or *how* animals were reared is the Soil Association symbol used on organic produce. Use of this symbol gives an assurance that the food has been produced in systems which avoid chemical inputs in the form of synthetic fertilisers, pesticides and herbicides, show respect for the welfare of livestock and minimise damage to the environment.

Despite the higher premium usually commanded by organic food, there has been increasing demand for such guarantees. This demand is linked to concern over the safety of food with respect to current agricultural and processing practices, the health implications, welfare of animals and the effects on the environment of intensive farming in the short and long term.

Intensive methods for rearing animals for the production of meat and fish are increasingly being questioned and to some extent this is taken into consideration by the consumer in judging the quality of food. Part of this is the *ethical* concern, for the welfare of animals, because when kept in crowded conditions animals are unable to express their natural behaviour and may suffer physically. For example, in broiler houses, as the chickens grow in size and space becomes minimal, feather pecking and cannibalism are liable to occur; in battery chickens, the lack of exercise and cramped space often leads to weak and broken bones or deformed feet, and the skin and feathers become damaged from rubbing against the wires of the cage.

There are also worries over conditions used for transport and slaughter of animals. The Farm Animal Welfare Council has proposed five 'freedoms' for animals reared in farming systems and these are incorporated into codes of practice which control the standards to be adopted. These include freedom:
• from starvation and malnutrition;
• from thermal or physical discomfort;
• from pain, injury or disease;
• from fear or distress;
• to express most normal socially acceptable patterns of behaviour.

An area of concern connected more directly to food quality relates to a range of substances incorporated into artificial feeds used for intensively reared animals. Antibiotics are added on a routine basis to lessen the chance of disease which spreads so readily in intensive conditions; antibiotics can also promote growth by improving feed conversion. A danger is that strains of disease organisms develop that are resistant to the antibiotics used and also that residues may persist in the meat sold to consumers, with consequent risks to human health.

Hormones have been used to promote growth and anti-obesity drugs can be used to produce animals which are leaner at the time of slaughter. There can be knock-on effects from residues remaining in the meat. For example, in Puerto Rico, occurrence of a condition, in which girls develop secondary sexual characteristics and start menstruation at a very young age, has been linked to high levels of hormones in chickens. In some cases an insecticide is included in feed used for chickens to reduce infestation by flies in the droppings below the cages, but when kept on litter, chickens peck at the maggots which help to keep flies under control. Intensive rearing of both chickens and fish, without access to the natural diet, usually results in pale yolks in the chicken eggs and pale flesh in the fish. In both cases, canthaxanthin has been used in the diet to improve the colour.

Despite regulations concerning the use of these and other chemicals, particularly the obligation to withdraw them from the diet at a specified time before slaughter, residues do persist and there are concerns with respect to their effects on human health. In some countries certain chemicals have already been banned from use. Since the early 1980s, despite strict measures regarding hygiene, there is concern over the increase in the incidence of infection from *Salmonella enteritidis* and the possible link with eggs and chickens produced from intensive systems.

Another area of criticism in relation to quality of intensively reared meat and fish is the uniformity and blandness with respect to taste and texture. Although some of this may be the result of deliberate steps taken to tenderise meat, say by injection of the enzyme papain just before slaughter, much can be attributed to the consistency of a closely controlled balanced artificial diet compared with the variety which would be available in a natural diet. Today many consumers demand information regarding rearing systems so they are at least in a position to make a choice when purchasing their food.

The nutritional benefit or quality of any food should be assessed in relation to the whole diet of the individual. Yet actual requirements vary: a young child should have more protein than an adult (in relation to body weight), a man uses more energy than a comparable woman and an active person more than a sedentary one. Our perception of a 'good' diet may be guided by cultural customs or beliefs, such as vegetarian diets for Hindus or prohibition of pork for Jews and Muslims. Dietary recommendations with respect to health have shifted over the years. During the 1950s we were told starches were the fatteners and that we should not eat too much bread and potatoes; by the late 1980s, we were being positively encouraged to eat potatoes and pasta but warned that sugar, salt and saturated fats were dangerous to health.

Recommendations and health-promotion

strategies undoubtedly influence people's eating patterns and farmers have responded by altering their crops or other products (for example, the trend towards meat with less fat). Tradition also plays a part in determining eating patterns, as illustrated in Fig.10.6.

Many people are obsessed with slimming and healthy eating, yet these fads, fashions and changes are irrelevant luxuries to certain social groups, particularly in some developing countries (but also within some affluent societies), where malnutrition, undernutrition and even threat of starvation dominate their lives.

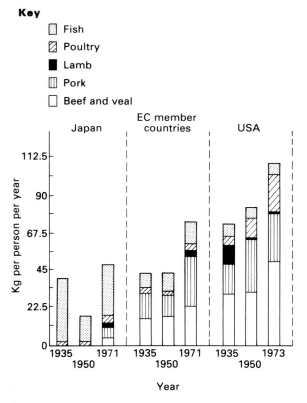

Key
- Fish
- Poultry
- Lamb
- Pork
- Beef and veal

Fig.10.6 Meat and fish consumption in Japan, EC member countries and the USA between 1935 and 1973. You can see how the pattern varies in the different countries and how it has changed during the 40 years. The Japanese ate mainly fish, the Europeans preferred pork and the Americans ate mostly beef and veal

■ FOOD PRODUCTION AND ITS EFFECTS ON THE ENVIRONMENT

A consequence of food production is its effect on the landscape. About 11% of the world's surface is used for growing crops and about 25% for grazing animals. In the UK, a high proportion of the land is used for agriculture and the familiar scenery is of fields and hedges.

Fields and hedges in England

In the USA and Canada vast areas are dominated by uninterrupted prairie land, and in Asia many mountainsides are terraced to create cultivatable land. Natural ecosystems have therefore been lost or confined to limited areas, often replaced by monocultures or agricultural systems comprising a very limited range of species.

Intricate terracing allows cultivation on steep mountains in Nepal

The loss of natural ecosystems or habitats leads to a reduction in biological diversity and this may have serious repercussions in the short and long term for food production. Out of an estimated 10 000 potentially edible plant species, humans have probably used about 3000 species at different times during their history. Of these, 150 species have been cultivated on a large scale but a mere 29 species currently account for 90% of the world's food products. These include eight species of cereals which supply about half of the total kilojoules required in food by the whole human population. Within the narrow range of species used, there is continual discarding of varieties. This further reduces the pool of genetic diversity, as the following examples show: in Indonesia, 1500 local varieties of rice disappeared in the 15 years leading up to 1992; in the USA, half of the wheat grown comes from only six varieties, and over the last 100 years the number of apple varieties in France has dwindled from over 2000 to about a dozen.

With the prevalence of monoculture, there is danger of agricultural uniformity and an increasing likelihood of devastation and disasters resulting from large-scale crop failure. The Irish famine in 1846 was due to the infection of the potato crop by blight (*Phytophthora infestans*); in 1970 corn leaf blight caused considerable losses in the maize harvest in the USA; and in 1991 severe losses of oranges in Brazil occurred because of outbreaks of citrus canker. Such disasters might have been avoided if a wider range of varieties had been in cultivation, because this increases the chance of some being resistant to disease or of the crop species itself being able to adjust or adapt to environmental change.

A wild species may be low yielding but precious because it provides a genetic reserve which is potentially useful for improving commercial stock by introducing desirable characteristics such as in-built resistance to diseases. These benefits can be illustrated by tomatoes: a wild species cross-bred with the cultivated species allowed selection for improved resistance to parasitic fungi and viruses, and two wild species found in Peru in the early 1960s were used to improve the pigmentation and solid matter content of commercial tomatoes. In some cases localised traditional crops show better performance on marginal or unimproved land compared to 'conventional' varieties geared to large-scale production.

Richness of animal species in natural habitats may similarly provide a genetic reserve which could be used for improving domesticated animal stocks. These habitats may also harbour a range of predators with the potential for reducing the numbers of pests in crops. Biological control techniques give renewed importance to these natural reservoirs of species. In the UK, some farmers now deliberately leave permanent strips sown with grass around and within their fields. This allows insects, spiders and other natural predators to overwinter and this helps to control pests such as aphids on the crop the following year.

Conscious efforts are being made to conserve species and varieties through the establishment of *gene banks*. Material may be kept as dehydrated seed or as living tissue (in cold storage or the living crop), which from time to time needs to be cultured, grown and replanted to maintain its viability. Similar attempts are being made to protect wild animals or conserve rare breeds of domesticated animals. A worldwide network of gene banks is at least an attempt to reverse the effects of losses in habitat and species, but undoubtedly the natural habitat is the most important reservoir of genetic material, some of which may be useful to food production in the future.

Removal of natural ecosystems, particularly large-scale deforestation, affects climate. This in turn influences the type of crop that can be grown and the likely yield. The noticeable increase in carbon dioxide in the atmosphere over the last 150 years, and particularly in recent decades, has been linked to the effects of land clearance for agriculture, combined with overgrazing and burning of fossil fuels.

Increases in carbon dioxide in the atmosphere may result in increases in the net photosynthetic rate and affect the heat balance of the earth, through what is known as the *greenhouse effect*, resulting in global warming. The warming could bring the risk of altering wind and rainfall patterns; changes in the distribution of water resources could lead to shifts in agricultural zones and currently productive land might become too arid for agriculture. In response to warmer temperatures, the geographical range of crops might extend to more northerly latitudes (or more southerly in the southern hemisphere), or higher in mountainous regions. A warmer climate could bring a greater variety of crops to the colder regions and an increase in crop yields. The pattern of pests and diseases is also likely to alter.

Destruction of vegetative cover can lead to environmental degradation in terms of loss of quality of the land by erosion. This may occur as a result of deforestation and also on agricultural land that has been over-used, poorly managed or heavily exploited. During heavy rains, erosion may result in the loss of topsoil with its nutrients and valuable humus. The sediment produced from erosion may accumulate in streams, rivers and artificial water channels, sometimes altering the water course and often upsetting established irrigation or drainage systems.

Desertification is a more extreme form of environmental deterioration in regions of low or inadequate rainfall. The precursor or trigger to desertification usually develops from pressure of human and animal population on natural resources, which becomes critical in drought conditions. Low rainfall means the region can support only limited vegetative cover, so grazing of animals and gathering of fuel spreads over yet a wider area, giving less chance of recovery. Demands by existing herds then exceed the carrying capacity of the land. Lack of vegetation means that the surface reflects more of the solar radiation, thus disturbing the balance between transpiration and evaporation and reducing the likelihood of further rainfall. A downward spiral ensues.

Deterioration of the soil as an environment for growing crops may arise directly from practices of agriculture. Soils can become excessively salty, through the processes of salinisation, particularly in arid or semi-arid regions. The underlying soil and ground water may hold high levels of soluble salts and this water rises to the surface by capillary action. High rates of evaporation and transpiration associated with dry areas result in accumulation of salt deposits at or near the soil surface. Inappropriate irrigation systems may exacerbate the situation. Irrigation brings more water to the area, and if drainage is insufficient it leads to a rise in ground water levels, so bringing more salts towards the surface. If waterlogging occurs, the land is rendered unsuitable for growing crops. There are examples of successful ancient irrigation systems where drainage was sufficient and the water-salt balance was not upset.

Pollution arising from agricultural practices also affects both the environment and the food produced. Chemical fertilisers applied to the soil disturb the nutrient level in the soil; excesses may be leached from the soil, resulting in eutrophication of water supplies. Raised levels of nitrates have aroused concern in relation to concentration of nitrate in foods (particularly vegetables) and water quality. Pesticides can enter food chains and accumulate in carnivores. Another problem comes from disposal of wastes from intensive animal units: animal slurries if dumped give rise to pollution and also waste valuable nutrients that could be recycled. In the UK, the poultry industry produces more than 1.5 million tonnes per year of waste litter from broiler farms. Rather than being discarded, positive steps are being taken on a commercial scale to convert this to compost in a form that can be used on the land or in horticulture.

Gathering brushwood for fuel in denuded desert area in Afghanistan

An alternative enterprise is to utilise poultry litter for the generation of electricity: the first commercial power station opened in eastern Britain in 1992, and is able to provide electricity for 12 500 homes. A by-product is a nitrogen-free fertiliser rich in phosphate and potash.

■ A SUSTAINABLE FUTURE?

Agriculture in any form interacts with and disturbs natural ecosystems. Growing of crops or grazing of animals prevents the natural climax of vegetation being achieved and reduces the biodiversity in terms of the plants and animals remaining in the area. Crops are removed from the site of cultivation and products from livestock are taken away after rearing, so the soil nutrients need to be replenished if the land is to retain its fertility or potential for producing food. In the long term, an ecological equilibrium must be maintained and a balance must be achieved between the human population and the carrying capacity of the earth. Increasingly there is interest in developing *sustainable* systems in agriculture which minimise the environmental impact of crop and animal production, and which meet the needs of society yet ensure an economically viable future for the farmer.

Traditional systems of agriculture, as practised through the centuries, are more or less self-sufficient or biologically self-perpetuating, putting back into the soil what was removed. Equilibrium is maintained through the recycling of biological wastes in the form of manures or composts, by regeneration through natural cycles

■ CASE STUDY - THE ARAL SEA

A specific example of an attempt at irrigation on a vast scale is seen in the Aral Sea, but the story illustrates how misjudgement and mismanagement can have far-reaching and damaging consequences on the environment and on the people living there.

Modern irrigation channel near the Aral Sea

The Aral Sea is a large inland lake, lying east of the Caspian Sea in Central Asia, to the north of Iran and Afghanistan. For centuries there had been relative stability in the level of water in the sea. The two rivers bringing water to the sea (the Amu and Syr) had also supported irrigation networks which allowed crops to be grown in the region that would otherwise have been desert. The sea itself yielded large catches of fish and the surrounding land included reed beds, rich pasture land and forests.

During the 1950s, large-scale irrigation systems were constructed, intended to enable cotton to be grown in the area. The water from the two rivers was diverted hundreds of kilometres away from the natural basin and did not drain back into the Aral Sea. By 1988, the level of the sea had dropped more than 12 m and is still falling; the main fishing port is now stranded 60 km from the water. Levels of salinity in the water have almost tripled and about half the former surface is dry land, salty and subject to wind erosion. Salt blown from the dry sea bed contaminates fruit and vegetable crops around Tashkent, Bukhara and Samarkand, about 1000 km away.

The once fertile soil around the lake is exhausted, prompting heavy applications of chemicals, and has become salty as well. By now it is unsuitable for growing cotton and no longer supports growth of other crops. People living in the area suffer from pollution from salt, toxic chemicals used on the crops, and residues in food from pesticides and untreated waste; health problems are becoming increasingly apparent. The reeds, pastures and forests are rapidly disappearing, there is a loss of animal species and no fish to catch in the sea. There are larger daily temperature fluctuations and stronger winds because the sea no longer provides a protective climatic barrier. The land is scarred by derelict machinery, disused buildings and other signs that an ancient ecological equilibrium has been destroyed, perhaps irreversibly.

(such as the carbon and nitrogen cycles) and by growing a diverse range of crops in mixed farming systems with some means of fixing nitrogen, usually by use of legumes. People from the community are closely involved; food production is part of their way of life. Even slash-and-burn systems of shifting agriculture do no long-term harm to the environment, provided there is a time space of a few years for the fertility of the soil to recover.

Modern conventional agriculture has developed into a large-scale industry, with the products being sold on the local or international market for profit. It relies strongly on inputs of energy and of chemicals, and on machines and automation with relatively few people involved to provide labour. It has developed and changed in response to scientific discoveries and applications of scientific principles leading to increased yields. A high degree of control over plants and animals allows mass production to be geared to consumer markets. The greater quantity of food produced goes some way towards keeping pace with increases in world population and feeding more mouths. But there are criticisms of current agricultural practices, including damage to the environment and to soil structure, concerns about the reduction of food quality and potential health hazards in food, and ethical concerns about intensive animal production systems. By the 1990s, an increase in extensive systems is becoming evident for a variety of reasons and perhaps marks the start of a swing away from intensive systems.

The organic farming movement has grown considerably since the 1960s and offers a potential alternative to conventional intensive systems. Methods used in organic agriculture are dependent on maintaining ecological balance and developing biological processes to their optimum for the production of food. Traditional systems were usually totally organic and in some parts of the world continue to be so. It is neither desirable nor feasible to put the clock back but modern organic farming methods attempt to integrate an understanding and application of science with traditional methods.

A few examples can be used to illustrate how this is achieved. Soil structure, fertility and required level of nutrients may be maintained by use of green manures, crop rotation (including a nitrogen-fixing legume) and use of manures or composts. Weed control can be achieved mechanically, by use of mulches or by under-sowing with another crop that does not compete adversely with the main crop. The undersown crop can be chosen to bring benefits in the form of nitrogen fixation or by attracting natural predators which help control pests. An example is the deliberate sowing of the blue-flowered plant *Phacelia*. Its pollen is particularly attractive to hoverflies, the larvae of which are voracious feeders on aphids. Strips of *Phacelia* sown around or amongst crops have led to a useful level of control of aphid numbers. Maintenance of areas of biodiversity in other ways is a valuable way of providing biological control by encouragement of natural predators.

Compared with conventional farming, organic systems are usually more labour-intensive and probably lower yielding. The relative costs in terms of expenditure and income are a matter for debate: with organic systems probably less is spent on agrochemicals and more is likely to be spent on labour, but the food produced may command higher market prices.

In developing countries the 'Green Revolution' from the 1960s achieved considerable success in terms of increases in output, through the use of high-yielding varieties and chemicals in the form of fertilisers, pesticides and herbicides, but it has not solved the problems of distribution. In some situations, it has brought wealth to a few but worsening conditions of poverty to many, thus accentuating the inequalities. Simple transfer of technology based on practices used in the

Chicken litter to compost

developed countries is not necessarily appropriate for the local climate, conditions, economics or expertise of the people.

A more positive approach to improving the level of food production in developing countries in the future may be by small-scale projects, integrated closely with the people in the community and the immediate environment. As one example, we can look at attempts to stimulate productivity of chickens as a means of providing more available protein for food. In most developing countries the bulk of poultry production remains in small-scale units. An increase in output could be achieved through intensive broiler and egg-laying units, but this requires capital investment, technology, expertise and may depend on imported feedstuffs. In Bangladesh there is a programme of poultry development which exploits the natural scavenging behaviour of chickens. A high percentage of households, whether they own land or not, already have a flock of between five and 15 chickens. A government-backed strategy aims to increase the productivity of these local chickens by the introduction of improved genetic stocks, to bring some enhancement of feeding through supplementing the naturally scavenged feed, to provide better protection of young chicks to avoid losses, and to provide vaccination against disease. The overall potential increase in protein and cash for poor rural families is considerable and there is no need to divert food which is suitable for human consumption to the chickens.

To return to a global view of food production, projects such as these may be small-scale, but they are a positive way to develop and increase food production that is sustainable into the future. Different names, such as sustainable, alternative, regenerative, biological and biodynamic farming, have been applied to various systems which

■ CASE STUDY - A SUCCESS STORY

A small-scale rural development project that has turned into a success story comes from the Dominican Republic in the Caribbean. Traditional systems of agriculture were collapsing and the people practised mainly slash-and-burn cultivation. A group of people with vision, a lot of determination and about two acres of waste land started a project in 1982. The land had been abandoned after growing groundnuts for 40 years and erosion was a major problem. Terraces were constructed and the earth walls become stabilised with vegetation; the land was triple dug and locally available manure was worked deeply into the soil, using different types of composted material in the different layers.

Within two years, the range of produce being harvested included corn, sweet potato and yams, chickens and eggs; carp and *Tilapia* were raised in fish ponds. Forage was cut from the banks to feed to pigs and other animals and their manure was returned to the soil. The yield from the small plot of land was remarkable, and was achieved by intercropping and multiple cropping. Gradually, the local villagers came by to watch, at first a little suspicious, later eager to become involved. The word spread, and 10 years later many 'students' from other villages had come to participate in programmes of instruction in what had become an active training centre.

These students have taken the ideas and methods back to their own plots of land. They in turn have helped others and a network of rehabilitated land with an improved variety of crops and higher yields is becoming established among the small-holders in the Dominican Republic. In the centre they use no chemicals; the methods are sustainable, based on soil conservation, contour cultivation and compost. Key factors leading to success are that the people from the local community are involved, working with and learning to understand the land, and are using tools that are appropriate, available and replaceable without the need for large inputs of money or energy. Families in many villages now grow vegetables in their gardens and eat vegetables as part of their diet. Almost certainly they are happier, healthier people. The same principles could be applied in many other locations.

recognise the need for agriculture to work in harmony with the environment. Their precise techniques may differ but the principles and practices that lie behind different systems are similar and are well summarised in the document describing the standards of the International Federation of Organic Agriculture Movements (IFOAM).

These are to:
• produce food of high nutritional quality in sufficient quantity;
• work with natural systems rather than seeking to dominate them;
• maintain and increase the long-term fertility of soils;
• use as far as possible renewable resources in locally organised agricultural systems;
• work as much as possible within a closed system, with regard to organic matter and nutrient elements;
• give all livestock conditions of life that allow them to perform all aspects of innate behaviour;
• avoid all forms of pollution that may result from agricultural techniques;
• maintain the genetic diversity of the agricultural system and its surrounding, including the protection of plant and wildlife habitats;
• allow agricultural producers an adequate return and satisfaction from their work including a safe working environment;
• consider the wider social and ecological impact of the farming system.

Q Use these points as a checklist. Go through each one in relation to conventional and organic methods of farming and consider the biology behind the statement. Work out how the job can be done, how it affects other things and the possible benefits or disadvantages. In particular, you might like to compare the merits of monoculture crop growing or intensive systems of animal husbandry with more traditional or organic systems in terms of long-term ecological stability. As a biologist, you must already realise that there are no simple answers, that one factor or event interacts with many others, that there are various unknowns and unpredictable consequences. Consider how far it is true to say that biodiversity is a key to maintaining a biological equilibrium between agriculture and the environment.

INDEX

A. mellifera '95
Aberdeen Angus 55, 107
absolute growth rate 12, 13
acclimatisation 93
acidification, of soil 11, 12
actin 107
additives 93, 114
adrenaline 61
Aegilops squarrosa 36
aggressiveness 73, 88
agriculture 34, 117, 118
agrochemicals 120
air cell 81
albumen 76, 77, 80
alevins 89
algal blooms 91
alimentary canal 64
allantois 80
amino acids 65, 108
ammonia 16, 65, 84, 86, 90, 91, 97
ammonium 9, 11, 12, 17, 18, 91
amnion 80
anaerobic 64, 103
ancestor 2, 41, 51, 54, 71
androgens 87
antibiotics 61, 65, 70, 115
antisense 106
aphids 30, 31, 117
apiculture 94, 99
Apis 94, 95
apple 27, 28, 34, 35, 43, 49, 50, 102, 112, 117
apricot 49
aquaculture 85
arable land 110
Aral Sea 119
artificial insemination 56, 60-2, 78, 97
artificial propagation 4
astaxanthin 92
automation 72, 112
autotrophic 6

β agonists 107
bacteria 61, 77
bananas 105
barley (*Hordeum vulgaris*) 4, 7, 12, 14, 22, 41, 42
battery (chickens) 72, 77, 83, 115
beans 17, 19, 23, 34, 49, 51, 52
beef 1, 54, 65, 66
bees 31, 96, 99
behaviour 63, 73, 88, 93, 115
beri-beri 40
biochemical oxygen demand (BOD) 91
biodiversity 117, 120, 122
biological control 27, 31, 32, 33, 117
black nightshade (*Solanum nigrum*) 23
blackberries 34, 99
blackcurrant 49
blastoderm 77
blastula 79
blood 65, 75, 79
bolting 47

bone 79, 106
Bos primigenius 54
botrytis 27, 28, 29, 49
bovine somatotrophin (BST) 107
brassicas 21, 27, 29, 34, 48
breeding 55, 85, 111
breeds 54, 71, 85, 106
broilers 71, 82, 84, 115
bromelin 108
brood nest 95
broody (hens) 74, 78
broodstock 89, 92
brucellosis 70
Brussels sprouts 48
bulls 55, 86
butter 53, 55

C3 plants 7, 8, 36
C4 plants 7, 8, 40, 42, 43
cabbages 23, 33, 34, 48
Cactoblastis larvae 32
cages 77, 92
calcium 12, 16, 75-7
calves 63-4
Calvin cycle 4, 7
calving 55, 62, 67
canthaxanthin 92, 93, 115
capillary water 11
carbohydrates 61, 64, 92, 114
carbon dioxide 6-8, 37, 39, 64, 79, 90, 102, 117
carbon monoxide 103
carcasses 55, 106
carnivores 1
carotenoid 78, 92
carrot 30, 34, 35, 46
carrying capacity 118, 119
caryopsis 35, 41
casein 67
castration 107
cattle 3, 5, 10, 18, 42, 43, 48, 53, 85, 94
cauliflowers 48
cellulose 64
cereals 34, 35, 41, 65, 84
cervical canal 57
charlock 25
Charolais 55, 107
cheese 53, 70
cherry 49
chickens 4, 5, 71, 78, 82, 94, 115, 120
chicks 82, 84
chickweed (*Stellaria media*) 22, 25
Chlorella 7
chlorophyll 6, 27, 103
chorion 80
citrus fruits 49
climacteric 103
climate 2, 34, 54, 83, 110, 117
clover 9, 17, 19, 52, 99
cock 73, 78
cockfighting 71
colostrum 63
colour 77, 92, 108, 114
common couch-grass (*Agropyron repens*) 22, 25

common poppy (*Papaver rhoeas*) 24
communication 73, 97
community 109
competition 111
Compositae 21
compost 17, 18, 19, 84, 118
concentrates 64, 65, 66
conservation 117, 121
consumer 83, 104, 112
consumption 109
controlled atmosphere (CA) 103
conventional agriculture 120
corn 41
corn marigold (*Chrysanthemum segetum*) 22
corpus luteum 57, 58, 59
couch-grass (*Agropyron repens*) 25
courtship 73, 87
crop loss 102
crop rotation 10, 27, 28, 46, 120
Cruciferae 23
cucumbers 19, 49
cultivation 15, 24, 25, 26, 27, 40, 43, 110, 120

dairy products 53
dairy cows 56, 66
damping-off disease 28, 38
dandelion (*Taraxacum officinale*) 25
daylength 35, 75, 87, 88
day-degrees 89
deadly nightshade 45
decay 101
decomposers 9, 11
deforestation 117
deoxygenation 108
desertification 118
deterioration 86, 93, 101, 102, 107, 118
detritivores 11
developed countries 34, 40, 109, 110
developing countries 34, 40, 73, 99, 109, 110
diet 1, 2, 63, 92, 115
digestion 64, 79
direct drilling 16, 19
disease 38, 76, 84, 99, 117
disease-resistant varieties 5, 27, 38, 40, 45, 111, 117
disposal of wastes 118
diversification 112
domestication 3, 4, 53, 71, 85, 94, 117
dormancy 40
downy mildews 28, 49
drones 94, 95, 96
drying-off 67

earthworms 11
ecological equilibrium 119, 120
ecological stability 122
economic damage threshold 30, 33
economically competitive 64
ecosystems 116
ectoderm 79
efficiency 55, 83
egg 61, 71, 73, 78, 83, 87, 88, 89, 95, 112

egg laying 74
egg tooth 81
einkorn (*Triticum monococcum*) 36
electricity 118
embryo 34, 51, 57, 61, 62, 77, 80
embryo transfer 56
embryology 57, 79
embryonic stages 57
emmer 36, 37
endoderm 79
energy 1, 64, 66, 86, 92, 112, 114
enforced dormancy 24
environment 56, 82, 112
enzyme 42, 54, 70, 98, 105, 108
ephemerals 23
erosion 118
Erysiphe graminis 38
ethical concerns 115, 119
ethylene 103, 105
eutrophication 18, 118
excretion 1, 65, 79, 86, 90
exploited 118
extender 61
extensive systems 120

Farm Animal Welfare Council 115
fat 53, 75, 114
fat hen (*Chenopodium album*) 22, 23, 25
feathers 82
feeding 54, 82, 92
feeds 42, 65, 84, 92
fermentation 64
fertilisation 41, 57, 61, 77, 87, 88, 95
fertilisers 10, 12, 13, 16, 17, 18, 36, 38, 40, 42, 65, 111
fetal stage 57
fibre 114
field bindweed (*Convolvulus arvensis*) 25
field capacity 11
fish 31, 85, 86, 92, 115, 116
fish farming 40, 85
fish kill 91
flame-weeders 26
flavour 51, 69, 93, 103, 114
follicle 57, 74
follicle stimulating hormone (FSH) 57, 59, 62, 75
follicular phase 57
food 53, 71, 101
food industry 101
food production 85, 109, 118-9
forage 48, 52, 65
fossil 54
fossil fuels 117
free-range 72, 73, 82
freedom 63, 83, 115
Friesians 55
fruit 27, 30, 49, 50, 51, 101
fry 89
fungicide 20, 28, 29, 32, 38, 45, 104
Fusarium 38

gas exchange 77, 80, 104

gastrulation 79
gene bank 56, 72, 117
gene technology 105
genetic change 85
genetic diversity 50, 55, 56, 72, 117
genetic improvements 111, 121
genetic pool 35, 72
geographical distribution 54
geographical range 118
germinal disc 77
germination 20, 24, 29, 34, 47
gestation 62
giant hogweed 25
gills 86, 91
glasshouses 112
global warming 118
glyceraldehyde-3-phosphate 7
glycogen 107
glycolysis 107
goats 3
gooseberry 49
Graafian follicle 57, 74
grading 83, 93
grafting 4, 50
Graminae 35, 36, 41, 43
grapes 27
grass 35, 65
gravitational water 11
grazing 36, 65, 117, 118
Green Revolution 120
green manures 10, 18, 19, 120
greenhouse effect 118
grey mould (Botrytis cinerea) 27, 28
ground elder (Aegopodium
    podagraria) 25
groundsel (Senecio vulgaris) 24
growing-on farms 89
growth 66, 82, 88, 90, 92, 93, 107
growth curve 12
growth performance 88
growth rate 13, 14, 66
growth rings 86
Guernsey 55, 68

haemoglobin 63, 108
harvest 36, 93, 102, 114
harvest index 4, 13, 38, 40
harvestable dry matter 13
harvestable protein 13
Hatch-Slack pathway 7
hatcheries 82, 89
hatching 73
hay 65, 66
health 116
heavy metals 91
heifers 59
hens (pullets) 82
herbicides 16, 26, 91, 111
herbivores 1, 2
herd 59
Hereford 55, 107
heterogametic 88
heterotrophic 1
high yielding varieties 111
hive 95, 96, 97, 99
Holstein 55
homing instinct 93
homogametic 88
honey 94, 96, 98, 99, 100
horticultural crops 112
hormonal control 68, 87

hormones 57, 65, 75, 87, 107, 115
horses 18
housing 66, 72, 112
hoverflies 32, 120
humidity 78, 104
humped 54
humus 10, 11, 16
hunger 110
hunter-gatherers 2
hydrophyte 10, 39
hydroponics 5, 112
hygiene 63, 69, 79
hypothalamus 59, 75, 87

IAA (indole acetic acid) 26
imports 110
income 110
incubation 73, 78, 89
induced dormancy 24
industrial effluents 91
infra-red absorption 70
infundibulum 76
inhibitors 104
innate dormancy 24
insecticides 27, 28, 31, 32, 91, 115
insemination 56, 60
integrated pest management 31, 33
intensification 63, 73
intensive systems 55, 66, 72, 85, 112
inter-specific competition 21, 22
intercropping 21, 27, 111
International Federation of Organic
    Agriculture Movements (IFOAM)
    122
intra-specific competition 21, 22
irrigation 19, 20, 23, 27, 28, 39, 110, 119
iron 9, 63
isthmus 76, 79
IVF 62

Jersey 55, 68
jungle fowl (Gallus gallus) 71

kales (Brassica oleracea) 48
killing-out percentage 106
knotgrass (Polygonum aviculare) 22,
    23

lactation 56, 66-9
lactic acid 65, 107
lactose 54, 67-9
lamella 103
layers 82
leaf area duration 14
leaf area index 14
lean meat 55
leghaemoglobin 10
legumes 2, 10, 12, 28, 34, 51, 52, 120
leguminous crop 111
lentils 52
lettuce (Lactuca sativa) 13, 19, 21, 27,
    34, 49
lime 12, 16
Limousin 55, 107
litter 74, 115
loams 10, 11, 15
Longhorn 54
loss of water 102
lucerne 12, 52
luteal phase 57
luteinising hormone (LH) 57, 75

maize (Zea mays) 4, 7, 12, 13, 22, 23,
    34, 36, 40, 41, 45, 52, 117
malate 7, 8
male sex hormone 75
malnutrition 110
Malus spp. 49
mammary glands 67
management 56, 72, 118
manure 10, 16, 17, 18, 53, 83, 119
marinading 108
marketing 93
marrows 34, 49
masculinised 88
mastitis 67, 70
mating 57, 60, 67, 78, 97
mature 88, 114
meat 54, 63, 71, 106, 115
membranes 76, 77
mesoderm 79
methane 64
methylene blue 70
microbial activity 104
microbial contaminants 114
microflora 64
microorganisms 64, 69, 86, 104
micropropagation 4, 27, 50
migration 93
milk 53, 68, 114
milking 56, 65, 68
millet (Setaria, Pennisetum,
    Panicum) 34, 42
milt 89
mineralisation 11
minerals 65, 92, 114
modified atmosphere (MA) 103
monocultures 5, 38, 116
moulting 82
mucus 76, 86
mulching 19, 27, 120
multiple cropping 111
muscles 63, 79, 106
mustard 19, 22
myoglobin 63, 108
myosin 107

nectar 96, 97, 98
nematocides 46
nematode 11, 46
net assimilation rate 14
nitrates 9, 10, 12, 16, 17, 20, 118
nitrification 12
nitrifying bacteria 9
nitrites 9
Nitrobacter 9
nitrogen 64, 83, 103
nitrogen fixation 9, 111
nitrogenous waste 86
Nitrosomonas 9
NPK 17
nutrient film technique 5
nutrients 91, 118
nutrition 107
nutritional value 114
nuts 49

oats (Avena spp.) 12, 34, 41, 43
oestrogen 57, 75, 87, 107
oestrous cycle 57-62
oestrus 57-60
oilseed rape 4, 19, 29, 48, 51, 99
omnivores 1, 2

onions 48
organic 112, 120
organic matter 91
organogeny 79
organoleptic qualities 114
osmoregulate 86
ova 57, 62, 74, 79
ovaries 57, 74, 87
oviduct 57, 75
oviposition 75
ovulation 57, 74, 76, 79, 87, 89
oxaloacetate 7
oxygen 79, 90, 102, 103
oxygenation 89, 92, 108
oxytocin 59, 61, 68, 75

packaging 105
packing 83, 104
papain 108, 115
Papilionaceae 51
parsnips 21
pasteurisation 69
peaches 30, 49
pears 49
peas 13, 23, 29, 34, 51, 52
pecking order 73
pectic substances 103
pellagra 41
performance 56
pesticides 27, 32, 40, 111
pest control 117
pH 11, 12, 16, 91, 98, 108
Phacelia 120
Phaseolus spp. 52
pheromones 33, 95
phosphatase test 70
phosphates 9, 11, 12, 18
phosphoenolpyruvate (PEP) 7
phosphorus 16, 17, 22
photoperiod 82, 87
photorespiration 7, 8, 36
photosynthesis 5, 6, 7, 8, 9, 14, 26, 30,
    36, 38, 43, 46, 48, 49
photosynthetic 118
Phytophthora infestans 28, 45, 46,
    117
pigs 3, 4, 18, 94, 107
Pisum sativum 52
pituitary gland 57, 75, 88
placenta 62
plant growth substance 103
plantains (Plantago spp.) 25
Plasmodiophora brassicae 23
ploughing 15, 16, 19, 20, 24, 25, 28
plums 49
poikilothermic (cold-blooded) 86
pollen 96, 97, 98, 99, 100
pollution 86, 91, 92, 118
polythene 112
ponds 91
population 109
postharvest 101, 102, 103, 112
potassium 16, 17, 22
potato blight 28, 45, 46
potatoes 11, 13, 14, 15, 27, 28, 29, 30,
    34, 35, 43, 44, 45, 46, 51, 117
poultry industry 71, 118
poverty 120
powdery mildews 29, 38
power stations 84
predators 83, 117

pregnancy 59, 67
prickly pear (*Opuntia*) 25, 27, 32
primary consumers 1
primary productivity 6
primitive streak 79
producers 1
production 54, 83, 85, 109
productivity 71, 72
progeny testing 56
progesterone 57, 67, 75
prolactin 57, 67, 78
propolis 96, 99
prostaglandin F2α 58
proteases 108
protectant fungicides 28
protein 65, 75, 92, 113, 114
Protoctista 64
puberty 60
Puccinia graminis 38
Puccinia striiformis 38

quality 35, 48, 56, 69, 90, 93, 112, 114
queen bee 94, 95, 96, 97, 99
quota 56, 112

radishes 21
ragwort (*Senecio jacobea*) 25
rainfall 118
rape 19, 48, 51, 99
rare breeds 55, 117
raspberry 34, 99
rearing 63, 74
recycling 65, 84, 119
red deadnettle (*Lamium prupureum*) 22
redd 87
regression 58
relative growth rate 13
religious 53, 71
reproductive system 57, 60, 74
residues 114
respiration 86, 102
Rhizobium 9, 10, 12, 17, 52
rhizosphere 11
ribulose bisphophate (RuBP) 7
ribulose bisphosphate carboxylase 7
rice (*Oryza sativa*) 4, 7, 34, 36, 39, 40, 45
rigor mortis 107
ripening 102, 112, 114
root crops 66
root nodules 9, 17, 19
rotation of crops 52
round dance 96, 97
royal jelly 96, 99
RuBP carboxylase 8

ruminant digestive system 64
rust fungus (*Puccinia*) 27, 38
rusts 27
rye (*Secale cereale*) 12, 41, 42

Saccharum spp. 43, 44
safety 93, 104, 115
salinity 118, 119
saliva 65
Salmo gairdneri 85
Salmo salar 85
salmon 85, 93
Salmonella 108, 115
salt-regulating mechanisms 93
salting 108
salts 86, 118, 119
saprotrophic 9, 11
scavenging chickens 73, 121
secondary consumers 1
seed dormancy 24
seed germination 6, 15, 20, 24, 29, 34, 37
seed viability 20
selection 38, 45, 54, 67, 71, 85
selective breeding 4, 35, 71, 97
selective herbicides 26
self-sufficient 109, 119
semen 56, 61-2, 78
senescence 102
set-aside 55, 112
sewage sludge 18
sex chromosomes 88
sex reversal 88
sex-linked 88
sheep 3, 5, 48
shelf-life 104, 112
shell 76
shell gland pouch 76
shellfish 85
shepherd's purse (*Capsella bursa-pastoris*) 24
shifting agriculture 110, 120
Shorthorn 54, 55
silage 13, 23, 25, 35, 41, 65
Simmental 107
slaughter 55, 63, 66, 84, 106, 107, 114
slurries 18, 66, 118
slurries 35, 36
smut fungus (*Tilletia caries*) 27, 29, 38
smuts 27, 29
soil 10-12, 15, 53, 110
Soil Association symbol 112, 114
soil porosity 11
soil-acting herbicides 26
Solanaceae 45, 51
Solanum tuberosum 44, 46
sorghum (*Sorghum vulgare*) 34, 42

soya beans 7, 9, 21
space 73, 82, 115
spawn 86, 87, 93
species 64, 116
sperm 56, 60-1, 76, 78, 87
spoilage 101, 107
sprouting 105
starvation 45, 110
sterilisation 69, 88
sterilising 68
steroid 107
stocking density 83, 90, 92
stomach 64
storage 103, 112
strawberries 27, 34, 49
stripping 89
subsidies 112
suckling 63, 67
sugar beet (*Beta vulgaris*) 14, 15, 47, 64, 94
sugar cane 7, 34, 43, 44, 47, 94
sugars 98-100, 114
sulphates 9, 11, 12, 16, 17
sunflower 51
supermarket 101, 112
superovulate 62
surpluses 110
sustainable systems 119, 121
swedes 48
sweet corn 21
symbiotic 9
systemic fungicides 29, 38

Taenia 108
tallow 53
tapeworm 108
taste 115
teats 56, 67-8, 70
technology 120
temperature 79, 86, 90, 103
tenderise 108, 115
territory 73
testes 60, 78, 87, 107
testing milk 70
tillage 15, 26, 32
tillering 21, 30
tillers 35, 36
tobacco 27
tomato (*Lycopersicon esculentum*) 8, 19, 34, 49, 51, 103, 105, 112, 117
toxins 91
trading 109
traditional crops 117
transgenic tomatoes 105
transpiration 6, 9, 104, 118
transport 63, 82, 88, 110
triploids 88

Triticale 42
Triticum spp. 36, 37
trout 85-93
tubular shell gland 76
turbidity test 70
turkeys 78
turnips (*Brassica compestris*) 34, 48

udder 56, 59, 67-8, 70
ultra heat treated (UHT) 69
undercropping 21
uniformity 48, 51, 112, 115, 117
unit leaf rate 14
urbanisation 110
urea 65
urine 60
uterus 57, 76

vaccination 121
vagina 57, 76
variation 56
varieties 71
Varroa jacobsoni 99
veal 54, 63
vegetables 32, 34, 47, 49, 51, 101, 111, 118, 121
vegetarian 115
vegetative cover 118
ventilation 79, 86
vernalisation 21, 48
vitamins 64, 75, 92, 114
volatile fatty acids (VFAs) 64
vulva 57

waggle dance 96, 97
water 8-10, 19, 20, 86, 90, 110
water hyacinth (*Eichornia crassipes*) 23
wax 96, 98, 100
weathering 10
weeds 16, 18, 19, 21-7, 111
welfare 63, 72, 73, 115
welfare regulations 63
wheat (*Triticum* spp.) 4, 7, 12, 13, 14, 17, 21, 28, 32, 34, 36, 37, 38, 40, 41, 42, 45
wild oat (*Avena fatua*) 22, 24
wilting 9, 30
worker bees 94, 95, 96, 97

yam (*Dioscorea* spp.) 34, 46
yeasts 64
yield 35, 40, 64, 78, 111
yoghurt 53, 70, 114
yolk sac 80, 89
yolks 74, 77-80

zebu 54